ELECTION ATLAS
OF
ANDHRA PRADESH AND TELANGANA

About the Authors

Prof. Kalpana Markandey has been teaching at Osmania University since 1979. She has published more than 20 books and about 40 research papers. She has also prepared two digital atlases. Prof. Markandey has guided 11 research projects and brought out 15 technical bulletins. She is former Head, Department of Geography, Osmania University, Hyderabad and also former Chairperson, Board of Studies of the same department. She has given lectures on about 35 topics for Educational Multimedia Country - Wide classroom of UGC as Subject Expert apart from being a resource person for various other programs. At present she is Coordinator, Centre for Advanced Study in Geography at Osmania University, Hyderabad, India.

Prof. Simhadri Somanaboina has been teaching at the Geography Department of Osmania University, Hyderabad, India for the past 30 years. He has been the Head of the Department and Chairman Board of Studies and during his Headship he introduced M.Sc Geoinformatics at Osmania University. He has published books and research papers on Telangana, Social Exclusion, and Development Studies. He is currently engaged in the OBCs India project.

ELECTION ATLAS OF ANDHRA PRADESH AND TELANGANA

Kalpana Markandey
Simhadri Somanaboina

CONCEPT PUBLISHING COMPANY PVT. LTD.
NEW DELHI-110059

© Authors

All rights reserved. No part of this work may be reproduced, stored, adapted, or transmitted in any form or by any means, electronic, mechanical, photocopying, micro-filming recording or otherwise, or translated in any language, without the prior written permission of the copyright owner and the publisher. The book is sold subject to the condition that it shall not, by way of trade or otherwise, be lent, resold, hired out, or otherwise circulated without the prior publisher's written consent in any form of binding or cover other than that in which it is published.

The views and opinions expressed in this book are author(s) own and the facts reported by him/her have been verified to the extent possible, and the publishers are not in anyway liable for the same.

ISBN-13: 978-93-5125-056-2

First Published 2014

Published and Printed by

Concept Since 1974

Concept Publishing Company Pvt. Ltd.
A/15-16, Commercial Block, Mohan Garden
New Delhi-110059 (India)
T: 25351460, 25351794, *F*: 091-11-25357109
E: publishing@conceptpub.com, W: www.conceptpub.com
Editorial Office: H-13, Bali Nagar, New Delhi-110 015, India.

Cataloging in Publication Data—*Courtesy:* D.K. Agencies (P) Ltd. <docinfo@dkagencies.com>

Markandey, Kalpana, 1956-
Election atlas of Andhra Pradesh / Kalpana Markandey, Simhadri Somanaboina.
p. cm.
Includes bibliographical references and index.
ISBN 9789351250562

1. Elections--India--Andhra Pradesh--Maps. I. Simhadri, S. (Somanaboina), 1955-, joint author. II. Title.

DDC 912.1324954 23

Preface

Electoral performance of political parties involves a complex process and a multifaceted and multivariate analysis is required to understand it. Votes cast are measures of attitudes, perceptions and bias. Voters select a party according to their own choice or views. Votes are related to income, ethnic status and other socio-economic characteristics. Geographers have concentrated on the studies of areal variations of voting pattern and their association with environmental, social and economic variables.

Income, type of employment, basic amenities, modern infrastructural activities, communication facilities, number of schools, colleges, institutions etc play an important role that causes variations in the attitudes of people which are ultimately manifested in voting. In the case of Andhra Pradesh socio-economic data for the Assembly and Lok Sabha constituencies is compiled from the data for lower level units through a process of aggregation. Primary data – both elections related and socio-economic for two districts is collected through structured questionnaires and analyzed. Election Data is collected from the Election Commission of India. This study has sought to interface the technological innovations with societal use.

Apart from providing a (Digital) Map Inventory of thematic information pertaining to Andhra Pradesh, the other tangible deliverables of this study have been a massive exercise carried out towards the correction of Mandal, Assembly and Village maps, which have been rectified at the boundaries, transformed and projected. They provide a spatial database for users in the future to map any type of data onto these units in a GIS environment. Also for the first time Constituency – wise Attribute Data has been generated and demographic compatibility with Parliamentary and Assembly Constituencies has been established. Thus the social base for understanding Elections is made available in an objective, statistical manner.

The Atlas was originally conceptualized and worked upon as 'Election Atlas of Andhra Pradesh', but subsequently when the Atlas was already printed and the Telangana Bill was passed in the Lok Sabha and Rajya Sabha in February 2014, for the creation of a separate state of Telangana from Andhra Pradesh, it has been rechristened as 'Election Atlas of Andhra Pradesh and Telangana'.

Kalpana Markandey
Simhadri Somanaboina

Acknowledgements

The Election Atlas of Andhra Pradesh is the outcome of a DST funded project 'GIS in Mapping Election Information System: Technology – Society Interface'. It was sanctioned to us in the Department of Geography, Osmania University, Hyderabad by the Department of Science and Technology (DST), Government of India in 2004 through the Andhra Pradesh State Council of Science and Technology (APCOST). We are grateful to Prof. J.M. Naidu, the then Member Secretary of APCOST for all the support and help he extended to us in the incipient stage of this project. We are thankful to all the officials of DST especially to Dr. Ritu Bhatnagar, Member Secretary, State S&T, DST, who has been ever so helpful at various stages of this work. We are also thankful to the officials of APCOST who have propelled our effort at various stages especially Mr. C.V. Ramakrishna, Mr. Shyam Sunder, Mr. Nagesh and Mr. Sailu. We are thankful to the Osmania University authorities for facilitating us in carrying out this project from the Department of Geography, Osmania University.

We are thankful to all the officials of various government departments who have directly or indirectly contributed to the success of this project. We thank officials of the State Election Commission, Survey of India, Census of India, Mandal Revenue Offices in various Mandals in Nalgonda and Guntur Districts, Municipal Corporation of Hyderabad, Guntur Municipality and Nalgonda Collectorate for all the help and support extended at the time of data collection.

This project would not have been completed but for the dedicated efforts of the staff members who were employed in this project. A special word of praise goes for the commitment, patience and devotion of Ms. V. Sri Usha and Ms. Ch. Latha Prasoona, Research Assistants who worked whole - heartedly for the success of this project. We are also grateful to Mr. John Samuel, Assistant Director, Census of India, who offered very valuable help and support on the mapping front. He had set an example of exactitude and perfection for the project staff. Our thanks are also due to Mr. Narsimha, Mr. Nagraj, Mr. Manohar, Mr. Srinivas and Mr. Krishna, Field Assistants who helped with primary data collection in Nalgonda and Guntur. We thank Mr. M. Mohan Babu and Ms. Kavita Singh who were very dedicated workers and gave their bit of time and talent for this project. We express our gratitude to Mr. B. Kiran

Kumar who had helped with the initial mapping process. We also thank Mr. V. Satish Kumar and Ms. J. Lavanya who helped with the end stage of this work.

October 2013

Kalpana Markandey
Simhadri Somanaboina

Contents

List of Figures

List of Coloured Maps

List of Tables

I
Introduction

The election atlas of Andhra Pradesh has been conceived as a thematic atlas of the state of Andhra Pradesh in India. It was conceptualized on the eve of the elections to the parliamentary and assembly constituencies in April 2004. It is for the first time that an Election Atlas is being brought out for a state of India. Earlier instances of Election Atlas pertain to U.S.A, Canada and U.K. The Election Atlas broadly deals with two categories of attribute data; the election data and the collateral demographic data as both of them are perceived to co-vary in space and time and at times the former is dependent on the latter. The time spans over which the maps are prepared extend back to 1978 in the case of Assembly Constituencies for election to the Legislative Assembly of the state of Andhra Pradesh and 1977 for election to the Lower House (Lok Sabha) of the Indian Parliament.

By having a glance at these maps the geographical patterns can be discerned. These can also help to visualize how phenomena relate in space and how different places are related to one another. The 'where' and the 'when' of the phenomena can also help in gleaning the 'why' and the 'how'. Thus the variables can be used dynamically to explain variations in time and space.

Electoral spaces can be viewed from the geographical, political, social, cultural, economic and psychological perspectives besides others. Each of these outlooks imbues the electoral scenario with a distinct identity. The sum total of these, which has manifestations ranging from the micro to the macro, comprises the multi – digitated electoral space.

A fusion of place into space in the micro web of electoral spaces is not a daunting task in the 21st century where technology has facilitated viewing social phenomena at varying levels in the cascading scale of continuous referencing with abundant ease and flair. Geographical factors influence a large number of social factors including elections. Some of these factors may be conducive for the electoral processes and outcomes, while others may not be so. These factors may be of significance for the bureaucrats, academicians, the contesting candidates and the contesting parties besides others. The carving out and analysis of Electoral spaces helps policy makers with ready information at the grassroots level and these can form a backdrop of their decisions most of which are made in the milieu of the electoral constituencies.

The outcome of elections, however, is influenced by several factors, the prominent among them being the levels of development in a region, the social structure and the psychological make-up of its people, the demographic forces operating in an area, the levels of political awareness of the people and the political mechanizations of the state machinery.

Heretofore, maps have been depicting physical, social, cultural, political, ecological and various other types of spaces. A later day addition has been Electoral Space and the evolving digital technology has made this electronically possible, where GIS captures, stores, analyzes, manipulates, and portrays data that is linked to specific location. In the context of Elections, Attribute (generally tabular) data can be linked to spatial data in a wide variety of ways. It could be linked to point or node locations, as for instance the facilities in a polling booth, perception of security in a polling booth, number of rooms in a polling booth, location of tension prone villages etc. Attribute data like distance and route chosen to a polling booth can be linked to the line or arc type of spatial data. Details like the total electorate in a particular constituency or even other administrative units, besides voter turnout, margin of votes secured by the winning party etc. can be mapped in their respective polygons or unit areas. Thus GIS facilitates acquiring and linking of the electoral data to all types of Spatial (graphic) data. This can be done at the micro as well as the macro levels in the administrative hierarchy.

Many iterative possibilities allow users to present the thematic data and the election results on the maps according to their needs. For example, the classification methods can be made to suit the thematic maps, constituency – wise located graphs can be prepared, alternatively data can be depicted in the form of dots or hatching patterns within a polygon. Besides those intending to correlate the demographic with the electoral data and results can also do so with ease, by preparing map overlays.

The atlas has been prepared keeping in mind the need for updating the maps that have been prepared herein. The GIS format of the maps allows easy redrawing of the boundaries every time the official delimitation of constituencies takes place. Also every time there is a General Election or a Bye Election the results can be plotted and analyzed. Elections being a repetitive phenomenon from the time perspective, these GIS maps come in handy so far as updation is concerned.

The technology of Geoinformatics and GIS in particular, have revolutionized and dramatized the way in which electoral studies are done. They have become more analytical and predictive studies have come to the fore in a big way. A progression from pure description of electoral outcomes in the 1980's to analysis and then to prediction in a short span of time has telescoped the way in which geographical studies in general have progressed, albeit over a much longer time frame. Thus there is a two-fold advantage in going in for the Geoinformatic tools like GIS in analyzing politico-social phenomena:

(i) The results are made available in a spatial perspective and these can be visually inter-correlated to sieve out the factors that explain the major variations.
(ii) Future predictions can be made in a spatial context, by viewing the past trends and also the changing spatial profile of an area onto which the election results regress.

These digital maps help in understanding the Electoral Geography of Andhra Pradesh or by extension any other state or country and making the elected representatives, party workers and the common man more spatially enabled. They are aimed towards making the students of Geography and Political Science, besides those engaging in various social discourses, more enlightened and equipped to understand the nitty-gritty of the correlations and co-variations that associate with the electoral outcomes. These include variables pertaining to population, size of household, literacy, sex ratio, employment etc. and if these can be spatially correlated with the election maps a lot of variations in the electoral outcomes can be explained. The geographical patterns can be used to compare and contrast the various regions and sub regions of the state apart from the urban and rural pockets, where the developmental criteria can be related to the election outcomes. These maps are also updateable when data for the elections in the future comes in. GIS can also help in monitoring the security arrangements in the elections. GIS and Election Information System (EIS) can help with the Delimitation policy of Electoral Constituencies. This study can also help with electoral reforms by helping to generate Street Address based Geocoded files of voters. The study can also be replicated in the case of other problem solving situations.

GIS as a tool has traditionally been used in a multiplicity of fields as a 'product-based decision support system'. Subsequently it has come to occupy a role where it is a 'services-based decision support system' and a location based service (LBS) which can even conveniently be used in a mobile environment. Among the manifold applications in this emergent field is that of GIS in 'Elections'.

In a country like India which has a multi-party system and varied and multi - layered levels of allegiance of the electorate, predicting elections becomes a rather dicey affair. It is here that GIS on one hand provides a technological prop to analyse and predict the outcomes of elections for the researchers as well as the common man and on the other, provides the essential decision support system to the administrator, so far as the location of amenities and facilities for the election are concerned.

Election results are influenced by several factors like the levels of development in a region, the social composition of its population, the demography of the area, the psychological bent of mind of its people, their levels of political consciousness and the political manoeuvrings of the state machinery. Hence, if elections results have to be predicted, they have to be viewed against this framework of the myriad causative factors. Descriptions, supported by tables and graphs or charts have always been the hallmark of election studies. However, the technology of GIS has altered the way in which electoral studies are carried out. They are now viewed against the backdrop of a spatial perspective which makes for a visual correlation of factors that explain variations in election data. This has brought predictive studies to the forefront in a big way.

Thus, while on the one hand, this study addresses a phenomenon which is the concern of all the citizens in a democracy, on the other, it utilizes the present day research tools like GIS to **measure scrutinize, forecast and depict** this phenomenon. This technology can also be used to make this **depiction dynamic and interactive** by customizing the maps to enable **interactive query-based retrieval and analysis.** While this is not a part of this study, it has been done elsewhere. These customized maps can be hosted on the web to cater to a wider viewer ship.

The main objective of this study has been to understand the processes and patterns of elections in the state of Andhra Pradesh in India.

DATABASE AND METHODOLOGY

The maps are prepared using GIS software. Basic spatial data, which is the digitized maps of the Assembly constituency Boundary, the Mandal Boundary of Andhra Pradesh and District Boundary and the State boundary of India were obtained from the Survey of India.

(i) Data is collected at the national level for the parliamentary constituencies. The attribute data pertains to demographic and election variables and the spatial data is generated by digitizing, geo-referencing and projecting the parliamentary constituency map available on the Election Commission of India website.

(ii) The Mandal boundary map of Andhra Pradesh obtained from the Survey of India was rectified wherever there were deviations from the Census of India maps. This was done to facilitate data linking. For instance, in the south eastern part of the state, the forested areas were shown as a separate entity in the Survey of India maps. These forested areas were merged in their respective mandals as they fall into them for administrative purposes. Similarly some of the water bodies were merged into their respective mandals. Thus the mandal level maps of Andhra Pradesh were ready and their boundaries were synchronized with the assembly constitutncy maps which were ready for attribute data linkage. These together with the district level maps were utilized for mapping the census demographic variations.

(iii) Census demographic variables were also mapped within the assembly constituency polygons, by aggregating individual village level demographic data as well as the urban ward level data within the assembly units. Several times problems were encountered in aggregating administrative unit data (that is village or urban ward) within the confines of the assembly constituency. This was because the units specified in the Election Commission of India records bore the names that were prevalent at the 1981 census as the previous constituency delimitation had taken place in 1976. However, in the subsequent census records, these unit names were changed, sometimes the units were split and ward numbers assigned to the sub-parts or they were merged with larger units and were again given numeric identities. In such cases a number of supporting maps from the respective Municipalities and

Urban development Authorities pertaining to block level data or lists of individual household addresses were utilized to solve the spatial imbroglio.

(iv) The assembly constituency units were merged within the parliamentary constituencies of which they were the constituent units, in order to map the demographic data within the parliamentary constituencies.

(v) As mentioned earlier, the attribute data is collected from the Census of India for the demographic variables and for election related variables at the macro and meso levels, it is collected from the Election Commission of India website and publications. This data has been collected from 1951 onwards, however, it has been mapped only from 1977 onwards as prior to that the constituency boundaries were different and these could not be reconstructed spatially due to paucity of requisite information.

(vi) To know the operational and other aspects of elections, a sample survey of two districts in Andhra Pradesh, namely, Nalgonda in the less developed Telangana region and Guntur in the more developed Coastal Andhra region and both incidentally adjacent to one another was carried out. Sample villages were randomly selected from every assembly constituency in each of the districts – there being 12 constituencies in Nalgonda and 19 in Guntur district. A 10 per cent sample of households based on the caste-wise stratification was chosen in each village for collecting primary data. Field data was thus collected in 27 sample villages in Nalgonda covering 812 households and 22 sample villages in Guntur covering 945 households. The data of each household was collected with the help of a structured questionnaire encompassing the socio-economic aspects of the respondents, their social and economic mobility, perception of the election processes and electoral behavior including various aspects of elections like geographical aspects, behavioural aspects, voter participation, detailed voter profile, awareness and use of Electronic voting machines, infrastructural aspects, role of government officials, conflicts and tensions associated with elections, criminalization, methods used to influence voters, role of Civil Societal groups, public awareness about elections and about leadership besides others. The respondents did give information, but with some misgivings. These results are plotted in the form of maps or located diagrams and portray the micro electoral spaces of Guntur and Nalgonda. The stage of work are outline in Fig. 1.1.

The Election Atlas of Andhra Pradesh (A.P.) is a Thematic Atlas of the state of Andhra Pradesh which portrays the state spatially through the lens of the election scenario. A spatial regression of this on the demographic and social and physical space of the state can also be glimpsed. The Election scenario of A.P. is also viewed against the general national election scenario of India. Thus a nesting of smaller spaces that are ensconced within larger spaces can also be looked at. The cascading scale thus encapsulates election, demographic, social and physical maps pertaining to Andhra Pradesh and micro level maps pertaining to case studies of two districts of Andhra Pradesh as the emphasis well nigh is on Andhra Pradesh.

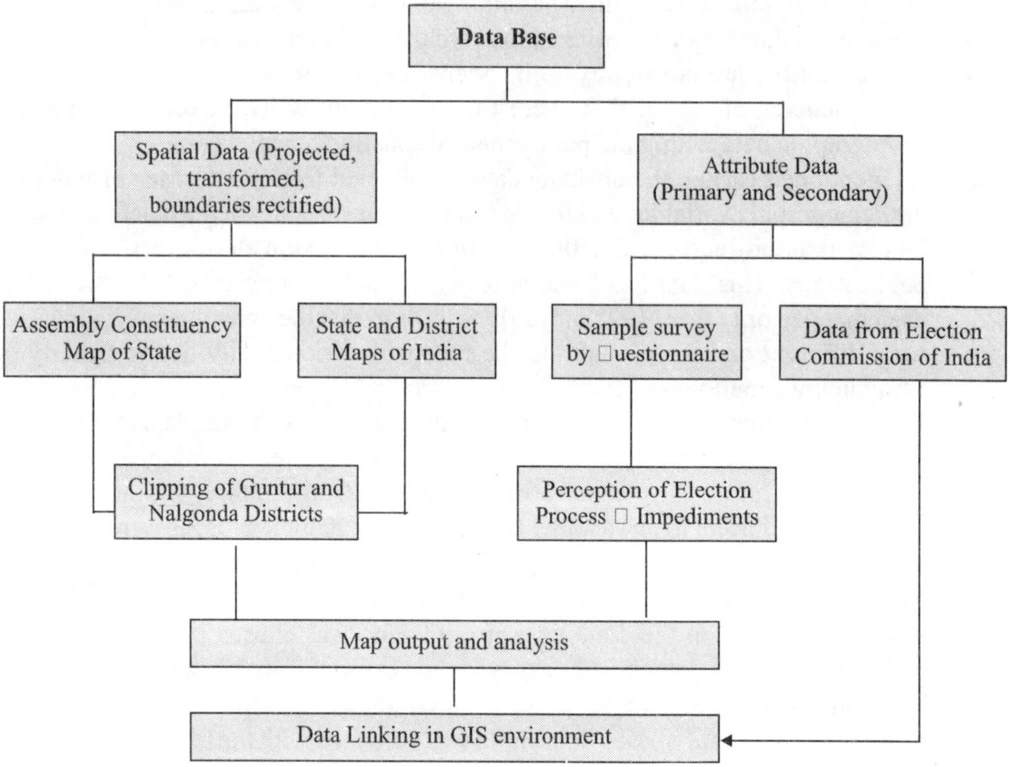

Fig. 1.1: Methodology

LOCATION AND DIVISIONS OF ANDHRA PRADESH

Andhra Pradesh State is situated between 12°38′ and 19°55′ North latitudes and 76° 45′ and 84° 45′ East longitudes. It has the Bay of Bengal on the east, Maharashtra on the north, Odisha and Chhattisgarh on the north east, Karnataka by and large on the west and Tamil Nadu on its south. Andhra Pradesh is located at the confluence of north and south India and exhibits convergent cultures in several places. It has an area of 275,068 sq.kms, and a population of 8.46 crore (2011). It takes up 8.37 per cent of the total area of the country and accounts for 7.41 per cent of its population.

The state is divided into 23 districts and these are further divided into 1125 mandals for administrative purposes (Map.1.1). The state consists of three distinguishable regions (Map 1.2) – with distinctive socio- cultural, economic, demographic and historical profiles. These are (a) Coastal Andhra, which comprises the nine coastal districts. It is also otherwise known as Costa and is bounded by Odisha on the north, Tamil Nadu on the south, the Eastern Ghats on the west and the Bay of Bengal on the east. It has areas of high fertility in East Godavari, West Godavari, Krishna and Guntur Districts which have the deltas of rivers Godavari and Krishna in them. The other districts in this region are Srikakulam,

Vizianagaram, Visakhapatnam, Prakasam and Nellore. (b) Telangana, which was a part of the Nizam's dominion and is relatively less developed compared to Coastal Andhra, has the now dynamic city of Hyderabad in it. It consists of ten districts: Mahbubnagar, Rangareddi, Hyderabad, Medak, Nizamabad, Adilabad, Karimnagar, Warangal, Khammam and Nalgonda. It is situated on the Deccan plateau with the Eastern Ghats to its east and, the states of Maharashtra and Karnataka to its west and Maharashtra and Chhattisgarh state to its north. (c) Rayalaseema which is a backward and drought prone region, consists of the four districts of Chittoor, Y.S.R. Kadapa (formerly Cuddapah), Anantapur and Kurnool. The state of Andhra Pradesh has 42 Parliamentary (Lok Sabha Constituencies) (Map 1.3) and 294 State Assembly Constituencies (Map 1.4).

DEMOGRAPHIC PROFILE OF ANDHRA PRADESH

The demographic profile of an area is reflective of centuries of impact of the physical environmental and the social and cultural forces as they condition the population composition and shape the population structure. This conditioning reflects itself in the form of pockets of high and low density of population, varying growth rates reflecting varying rates of birth, death and migration, families of varying size, variation in the proportion of working population linked as it is with the dependency ratios, preponderance of one or the other type of occupation, differing levels of literacy, varying sex ratio, child population, child sex ratio etc. All these factors, combined in varying measures constitute the demographic backdrop of an area. The complex mesh of these factors as they are juxtaposed vis-à-vis each other in every single region has a bearing on the economy and the polity of that area.

In this study some of the demographic variables pertaining to Andhra Pradesh for the year 2001 are analyzed. The database is taken from the Census of India and hence, is secondary in nature. The level at which the data was available was district, mandal and village. While the district level demographic data is plotted as it is, the village level data is aggregated at the level of the assembly constituency and parliamentary constituency and mapped at the level of these constituencies. This type of thematic mapping of demographic data for constituencies has been done for the first time and allows one to do away with conjecturing the demographic profiles of constituencies from district on taluk maps. The 2011 census data at the micro level was not available at the time of this study and and even at the level of the districts the figures were only of a provisional nature, hence the situation is dealt with, with the help of 2001 data.

The density of population of the state is found to be high in north Coastal Andhra and in Rangareddy and Hyderabad districts (Map 1.5). However, the population growth picture (1991-2001) is different. While Rangareddy and Hyderabad districts registered a high growth of population, the Telangana districts in the northern part of the state, in general have a high growth compared to Coastal Andhra region in the eastern part and the Rayalaseema Region in the South western part of the state. Incidentally, Visakhapatnam district in Coastal Andhra and Kurnool in Rayalaseema have registered high growth as they house the regional urban centers bearing the same names within them and these urban nodes obviously are drawing large streams of immigrants.

A perusal of Map 1.6 pertaining to size of family mapped within different micro- spatial units, indicates that the size of family is high in the western part of the state and tapers off to the east. The largest size is witnessed in Hyderabad. The range of family size varies from 6 or 7 in the west to 4 in the east. While the family size tapers off from the west to the east, the proportion of literate population tapers off from the east to the west (Map 1.7). There is thus, a perceptible inverse spatial correlation between family size and the level of literacy in a region. The only exception is in and around the vicinity of Hyderabad where family size as well as literacy are high. This can be explained by the tradition bound, though literate population of this pocket. The pattern of total literacy is replicated so far as the pockets of high and low male and female literacy are concerned (Map 1.8 and 1.9), though the proportions are less so far as the female population is concerned, yet the pattern is impressionable.

A perusal of Map 1.10 shows that Sex Ratio is high in the North Western, the north eastern part and the South eastern part of the state. While the figures which depict values at a higher level of aggregation (Parliamentary Constituency and District level) obscure the finer details, the figure at the Assembly Constituency level specifies large pockets in Nizamabad, Karimnagar and parts of North Coastal Andhra besides smaller pockets scattered all over the state as having a high Sex ratio. Some of these as in Nizamabad and Mahabubnagar are perceptibly areas of out migration of population owing to the strong push factors operating there apart from the lure of metros and the Middle East which the inhabitants cannot resist. A high Sex ratio as in such cases renders the female population back home, vulnerable to persuasion by the contesting candidates. In the absence of a psychological support base at home they fall prey to the canvassing tactics and promises and hence predictability of elections in such zones is a matter of great circumstantial detail.

A glance at Map 1.11 shows that child sex ratio, is higher in the north eastern part of the state. Some of the pockets where the proportion of female children to the male is high are also the tribal pockets of the state as is evident by comparing Map 1.11 pertaining to the child sex ratio in the different Assembly constituencies in Andhra Pradesh with Map 1.13 which relates to the proportion of Scheduled Tribe population in the state in the various assembly constituencies.

The distribution pattern of the Scheduled Tribe population in the state (Map 1.13) exhibits preponderance in Telangana, North Coastal Andhra and the Southern tip of Coastal Andhra. The distribution of the Scheduled Caste population (Map 1.12) shows that especially at the disaggregate level the areas of high proportion of Scheduled Caste population are also those of low proportion of Scheduled Tribe population (Map 1.13).

A glance a Map 1.14 pertaining to main workers that is workers who are employed for more than 183 days per year, shows that there is a concentration of these workers in West Godavari, Krishna, Guntur, Kurnool, Karimnagar, Ranga Reddy and Hyderabad districts in a broad sense and in select pockets in close vicinity of these districts at a disaggregate (assembly constituency) level. It reveals that the proportion of these workers is high in north central parts of the state, the central part as well as the north western part. The proportion of workers is inversely proportionate to the level of dependency. Thus it can be inferred that the proportion of working population is low and hence dependency is high in large pockets in north Coastal Andhra as also in Rayalaseema and northeastern Telangana. Some of these are incidentally areas that have a higher proportion of literate population as observed earlier and also the relatively prosperous areas.

The pattern of distribution of marginal workers (Map 1.15) is just the opposite of that of the distribution of main workers. Marginal workers are those who are employed for less than 180 days per year. In other words, they are the part time or seasonal workers. Thus it is north Coastal Andhra and Northeastern Telangana apart from pockets in Rayalaseema which have a higher proportion of Marginal workers.

Map 1.16 indicates that agricultural labourers are concentrated in the delta districts and parts of Kurnool district in Rayalaseema and pockets in Khammam, Prakasam and Nellore districts. This pattern is replicated for the female agricultural labourers, though the expanse of the highs on this count over area is much more extensive (though with a relatively lower magnitude) (Map 1.17). The distribution pattern of cultivators (Map 1.18) is the inverse of that displayed by agricultural laborers. Areas of high on one count are low on the other and vice versa. Thus the highs for cultivators are concentrated in Telangana and especially in its northern part as also in north coastal Andhra and Southern part of Rayalaseema. Lows characterize the Delta districts and pockets in south coastal Andhra, Kurnool and in and around Hyderabad this pattern finds a near mirror image in that of distribution of the female cultivators (Map 1.19).

The pattern of distribution of household industry workers (Map 1.20) shows a preponderance of these among workers in the Telengana part of the state and a very spotty occurrence in coastal Andhra and Rayalaseema. Females engaged in house hold industry also reflect a similar pattern (Map 1.21). While these areas are low on literacy they engage in these household industries in keeping with their inherent skills and hereditary crafts.

Other workers (Map 1.22) who are perceptibly tertiary sector employees are concentrated in the vicinity of urban areas in Hyderabad, Visakapatnam, Vijayawada, Guntur, Nellore and Tirupathi besides others. A near mirror image of this tendency is found for the female 'other workers' (Map 1.23) where they too exhibit a tendency to cluster close to larger urban centres.

II

Parliament (Lok Sabha) Election Results of India with Special Reference to Andhra Pradesh

The Indian Parliament consists of the President, the Lok Sabha (Lower House or House of the People) and the Rajya Sabha (Upper House or Council of States). The President is the head of state, and she/he appoints the Prime Minister- who is the Head of the government- according to the composition of the Lok Sabha. Though the Prime Minister heads the government, the Cabinet is the central decision making body of the government. In case a single party does not have an absolute majority in the Parliament, members of more than one party can make an alliance for the purpose of governance so long as they enjoy the confidence of the majority of the Members of the Lok Sabha. The Lok Sabha along with the Rajya Sabha is the main legislative body in India. The Prime Minister is supported by his/her Cabinet of Ministers in the decision making process.

The members of the Rajya Sabha are elected indirectly, not by the citizens directly. Rajya Sabha members are elected by each State Assembly/Vidhan Sabha using the single transferable vote system. The number of members returned by each state is more or less in proportion to their population. At present there are 233 members of the Rajya Sabha elected by the Vidhan Sabhas, and there are also twelve members nominated by the President as representatives of literature, science, art and social services. Rajya Sabha members can serve for six years, and elections are staggered, with one third of the assembly being elected every 2 years.

Districts and Parliament (Lok Sabha) Constituencies

According to the Constitution the upper limit on the size of the Lok Sabha in India is 550 elected members, apart from two members who can be nominated by the President to represent the Anglo-Indian community. There are also provisions to ensure the representation of scheduled castes and scheduled tribes, with reserved constituencies where only candidates from these communities can stand for election.

The Indian Parliament comprises 543 Lok Sabha (Lower House) constituencies (Map 2.1). They range in size from those with a large areal extent in the relatively thinly populated areas to those which are of a smaller size in states and regions having a dense packing of population. A glance at Table 2.1 reveals that Ladakh in Jammu and Kashmir is the largest Constituency in terms of area, followed by Barmer in Rajasthan, Kutchh in Gujarat, Arunachal East, Arunachal West, Mandi, Bikaner, Bastar, Jodhpur and Mizoram in that order (Table 2.1).

Table 2.1: Largest Parliamentary Constituencies (Area Wise)

Sl. No.	*Name of P C*	*State / UT*	*Area (Sq Mtrs)*
1.	Ladakh	Jammu & Kashmir	172374108504
2.	Barmer	Rajasthan	55074347377
3.	Kachchh (SC)	Gujarat	41414347585
4.	Arunachal East	Arunachal Pradesh	39703819946
5.	Arunachal West	Arunachal Pradesh	39613001158
6.	Mandi	Himachal Pradesh	32016685177
7.	Bikaner (SC)	Rajasthan	31400851943
8.	Bastar (ST)	Chhattishgarh	28613698301
9.	Jodhpur	Rajasthan	24257745589
10.	Mizoram (ST)	Mizoram	20267859342

Source: http://www.odishatoday.com/India/election.html

The smallest constituency is Lakshadweep followed by Mumbai South, Kolkata Uttar, Mumbai North Central, Mumbai South Central, Chennai Central, Hyderabad, Mumbai North East, Mumbai North west and Chandni Chowk in that order (Table 2.2).

Table 2.2: Smallest Parliamentary Constituencies (Areawise)

Sl. No.	*Name of P C*	*State / UT*	*Area (Sq Mtrs)*
1.	Lakshadweep	Lakshadweep	30292967
2.	Mumbai South	Maharashtra	39387943
3.	Kolkata Uttar	West Bengal	44312447
4.	Mumbai North Central	Maharashtra	45418289
5.	Mumbai South Central	Maharashtra	49054389
6.	Chennai Central	Tamil Nadu	62584855
7.	Hyderabad	Andhra Pradesh	66040709
8.	Mumbai North East	Maharashtra	68555700
9.	Mumbai North West	Maharashtra	72721974
10.	Chandni Chowk	Delhi	77504890

Source: http://www.odishatoday.com/India/election.html

The Delimitation of Parliamentary and Assembly Constituencies is supposed to be carried out every ten years so as to accommodate changes in population size accounted for by population growth. However, after the delimitation of constituencies in 1976, a Constitutional amendment was brought about which suspended further delimitation till 2001. This made for wide discrepancies in the population size of the constituencies, the range in the size of the electorate varying from as large a figure as 25,00,000 to as small a figure as 50,000 electors.

> *'The word "Delimitation" literally means the act or process of fixing limits or boundaries of territorial Constituencies in a country or a province having a legislative body. The job of delimitation is assigned to a high power body. Such a body is known as Delimitation Commission or a Boundary Commission. In India, such Delimitation Commission have been constituted four times, in 1952 under the Delimitation Commission Act, 1952, in 1963 under the Delimitation Commission Act 1962, in 1973 under the Delimitation Commission Act, 1972 and in 2002 under the Delimitation Commission Act, 2002. The main purpose of undertaking the delimitation exercise is to rationalize the structure and composition of the electoral constituencies, on the principle of "One vote and one value". The Delimitation Commission, set up under the Delimitation Act, 2002, was entrusted with the task of readjusting all parliamentary and assembly constituencies in the country in all the states of India, except the state of Jammu and Kashmir, on the basis of population ascertained in 2001 Census.*
>
> *On 14th January, 2008, the Government of India promulgated an Ordinance amending the Delimitation Act, 2002....it nullifies the Final Order of the Delimitation Commission for the state of Jharkhand. Later on, the Government have passed four separate Orders under Sec 10 A of the Delimitation Act, 2002, deferring the delimitation exercise in the four North Eastern states of Assam, Arunachal Pradesh, Manipur and Nagaland.'*
>
> *(http://www.eci.gov.in)*

Thus the boundaries of parliamentary or assembly constituencies are redrawn to ensure that the constituencies are more or less uniform in size so far as the population is concerned. The boundaries are intended to be examined after every population census to mirror changes in population. For this a Delimitation Commission is established. However, under a constitutional amendment of 1976, delimitation was suspended until after the census of 2001, apparently so that states' family-planning programmes do not impinge on their political representation in the Lok Sabha and Vidhan Sabhas. This has led to wide discrepancies in the size of constituencies, with the largest having over 25,00,000 electors, and the smallest less than 50,000.

Analysis of Indian Parliamentary Election Results

A glance at Tables 2.3 and 2.4 and Fig. 2.1 reveals that National parties have been on the forefront of the election scene, sharing about 70 per cent of the Lok Sabha seats. The state parties account for about 26 per cent of the total, followed by a miniscule proportion of

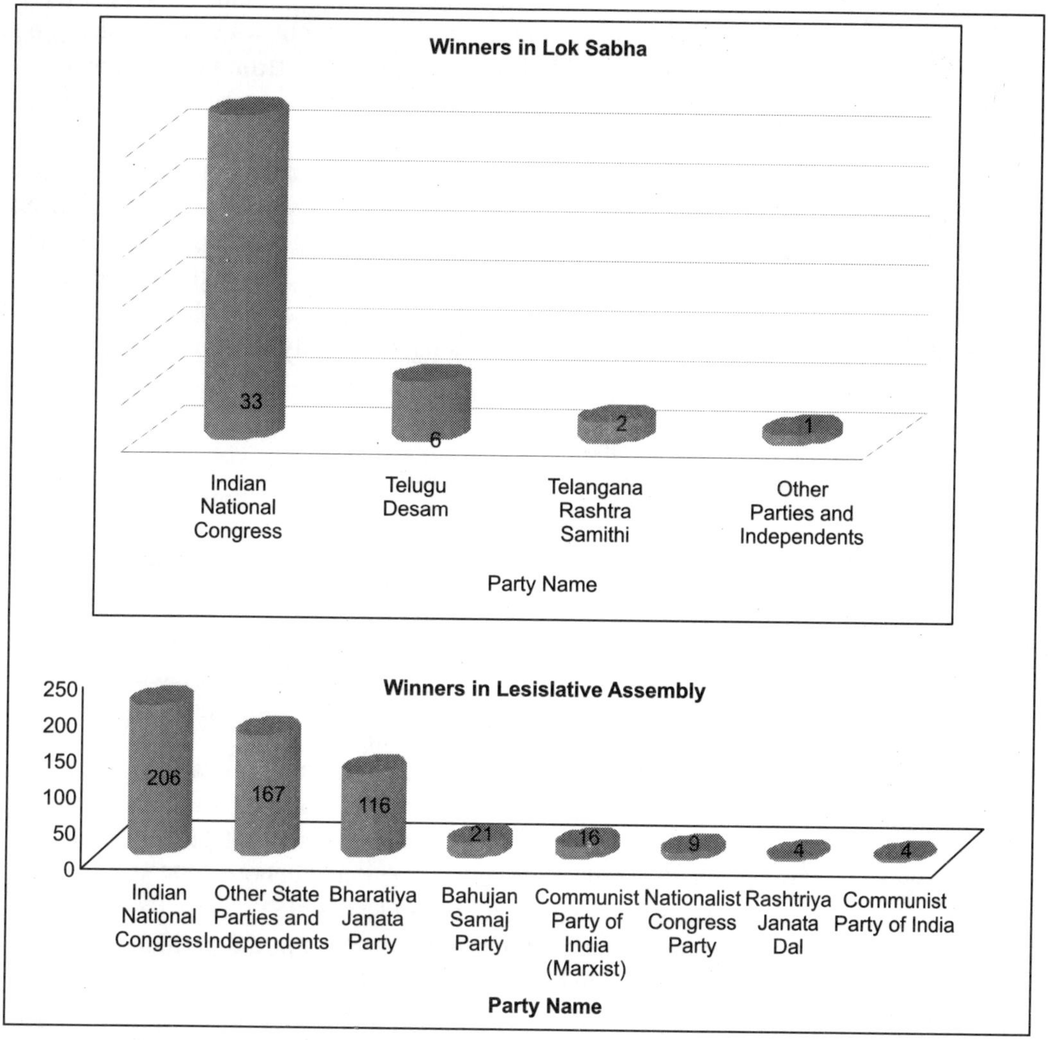

Fig. 2.1: Lok Sabha Election: Winner Parties 2009
Source: Election Commission of India, 2009

unrecognized parties and independents. This has been so both in 2004 and 2009. Fig 2.1 pertaining to 2009 further sheds light on the fact that, the Indian National Congress, which has been the first – past – the – post party in both the cases has outpaced the others in a disproportionate measure.

The Indian National Congress had a sway in almost all the states of the country in the 2009 elections. This has specially been so in Andhra Pradesh which has been the traditional stronghold of the Congress as also in certain other parts where it has made new inroads. These include Rajasthan, large parts of the north eastern part of the country like entire Arunachal Pradesh, Manipur and Mizoram, also parts of Madhya Pradesh, Uttar Pradesh,

Odisha and Kerala besides others. The region of influence of the Bharatiya Janata Party has shrunk even in its traditional bastions like Rajasthan in a big way, Karnataka and Gujarat to some extent and large parts of Madhya Pradesh. The saffron belt (comprising BJP and also its allies otherwise) straddling central India in 2004 has become inter-digitated with other hues, predominantly that of the Indian National Congress.

However, some of the states marked by the presence of the other national parties in 2004 like Bihar with Rashtriya Janata Dal and West Bengal and Kerala with a predominance of the Communist Party Marxist have witnessed an intermingling with other parties and the routing of their erstwhile dominant party in some instances. Regional Parties like Dravidra Munnetra Kazhagam in Tamil Nadu, Biju Janata Dal in Odisha, Nationalist Congress Party in Maharashtra and to some extent Samajwadi Party in Uttar Pradesh have however, held their own.

Table 2.3: India: Lok Sabha Elections: Winner Parties: 2009

Affiliations/Party Type	*2009*		*2004*	
	No.	%	No.	%
National Party	376	69.25	364	67.03
State Party	146	26.89	159	29.28
Unrecognized Party	12	2.2	15	2.76
Independents	9	1.66	5	0.92

Source: Election Commission of India, 2009

An interesting feature of the Indian election scenario has been that a miniscule proportion of women have contested elections, whether one looks at the situation in the context of the Lok sabha elections or the Legislative assembly elections in the state of Andhra Pradesh.

The proportion of women to the total contestants is 7 per cent in both 2004 and 2009 in the Lok Sabha Elections and 8 per cent in the Andhra Pradesh State Legislative Assembly elections (Fig. 2.2). Notwithstanding the fact that their numbers in the parliament or the state assemblies are dismally low, women have a better chance of winning in case they are fielded. Fig. 2.3 brings this out where the women among the winners are slightly high when compared to those among the contestants. They constitute 8 per cent and 11 per cent among the elected Members of Parliament (Lok Sabha) in 2004 and 2009 respectively and 9 per cent and 11 per cent among those elected for the Andhra Pradesh legislative assembly in 2004 and 2009 respectively (Fig. 2.3).

This shows that though a gender divide is very much evident as also is the lack of gender inclusivity so far as elected representatives to the various bodies are concerned, yet the people seem to repose more trust in the women candidates in case they are fielded for the elections. Their winnability is definitely high in case they are exposed to the electoral playing field (Fig. 2.3).

Fig. 2.4 and 2.5 convey the fact that voter turnout for elections has by and large been in the range of 60 per cent to 70 per cent both in the context of voting for the Lok Sabha elections within Andhra Pradesh as well as those to the Legislative Assembly of Andhra

Table 2.4: India: Lok Sabha Elections: Winner Parties: 2009

Sl. No.	*Party*	*Winners/ No of Seats*	*Party Type*	*Party Type Totals*
1.	Bahujan Samaj Party	21	National	
2.	Bharatiya Janata Party	116	National	
3.	Communist Party of India	4	National	National Parties 376
4.	Communist Party of India (Marxist)	16	National	69.25%
5.	Indian National Congress	206	National	
6.	Nationalist Congress Party	9	National	
7.	Rashtriya Janata Dal	4	National	
8.	All India Anna Dravida Munnetra Kazhagam	9	State	
9.	All India Forward Bloc	2	State	
10.	All India Trinamool Congress	19	State	
11.	Asom Gana Parishad	1	State	
12.	Assam United Democratic Front	1	State	
13.	Biju Janata Dal	14	State	
14.	Dravida Munnetra Kazhagam	18	State	
15.	Jammu & Kashmir National Conference	3	State	
16.	Janata Dal (Secular)	3	State	
17.	Janata Dal (United)	20	State	
18.	Jharkhand Mukti Morcha	2	State	State Parties 146
19.	Kerala Congress (M)	1	State	26.89%
20.	Marumalarchi Dravida Munnetra Kazhagam	1	State	
21.	Muslim League Kerala State Committee	2	State	
22.	Nagaland Peoples Front	1	State	
23.	Revolutionary Socialist Party	2	State	
24.	Samajwadi Party	23	State	
25.	Shiromani Akali Dal	4	State	
26.	Shivsena	11	State	
27.	Sikkim Democratic Front	1	State	
28.	Telangana Rashtra Samithi	2	State	
29.	Telugu Desam	6	State	
30.	All India Majlis-E-Ittehadul Muslimeen	1	Unrecognized	
31.	Bahujan Vikas Aaghadi	1	Unrecognized	
32.	Bodaland Peoples Front	1	Unrecognized	
33.	Haryana Janhit Congress (BL)	1	Unrecognized	Unrecognized parties 12
34.	Jharkhand Vikas Morcha (Prajatantrik)	1	Unrecognized	2.2%
35.	Rashtriya Lok Dal	5	Unrecognized	
36.	Swabhimani Paksha	1	Unrecognized	
37.	Viduthalai Chiruthaigal Katch	1	Unrecognized	
38.	Independent	9	Independents	Independents 9
				1.66%

Pradesh. The latest election ie. that in 2009, had the maximum turnout of voters, which was 72.45 per cent in both the cases. Though there have been ebbs in the proportion of voter turnout, a surge in their numbers has been a peculiar feature whenever there have been trilateral contests or whenever a new party appeared on the horizon. The fact that there has been a gradual upsurge so far as voter turnout at the elections for the Parliamentary and well as the Assembly Elections in AP cannot be ruled out. The proportion of people voting has breached the 70 per cent mark at the 2009 elections. This also shows, among other factors, the higher consciousness of the voters especially the younger lot to cast their votes.

Andhra Pradesh, which is the state under study, displays a relatively small variation so

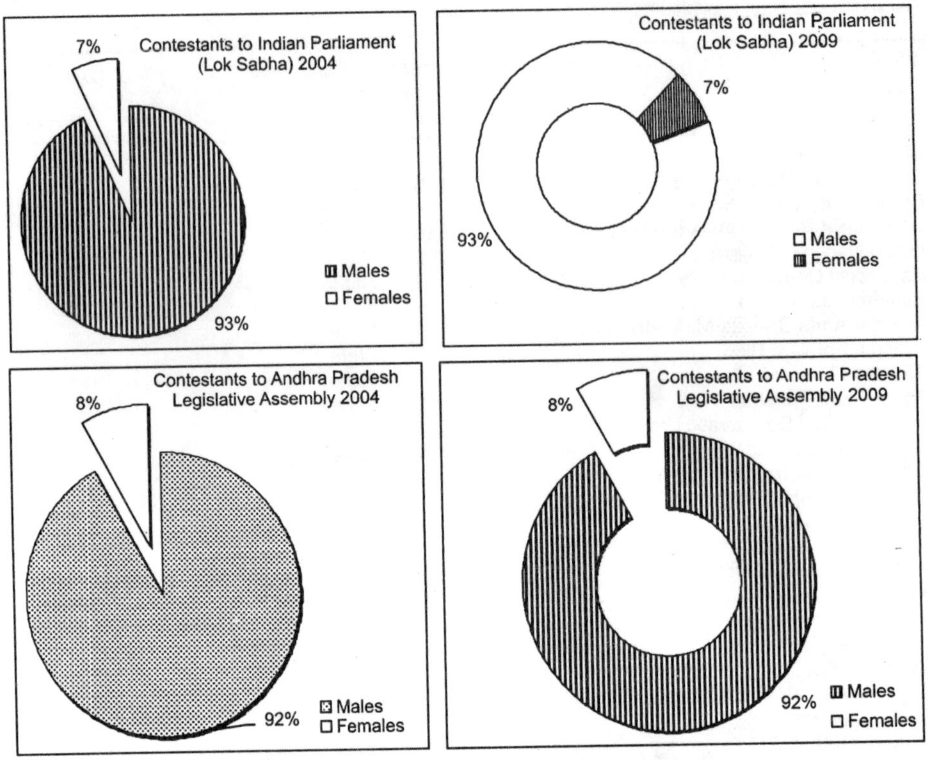

Fig. 2.2: Contestants to Indian Parliament (Lok Sabha) 2004

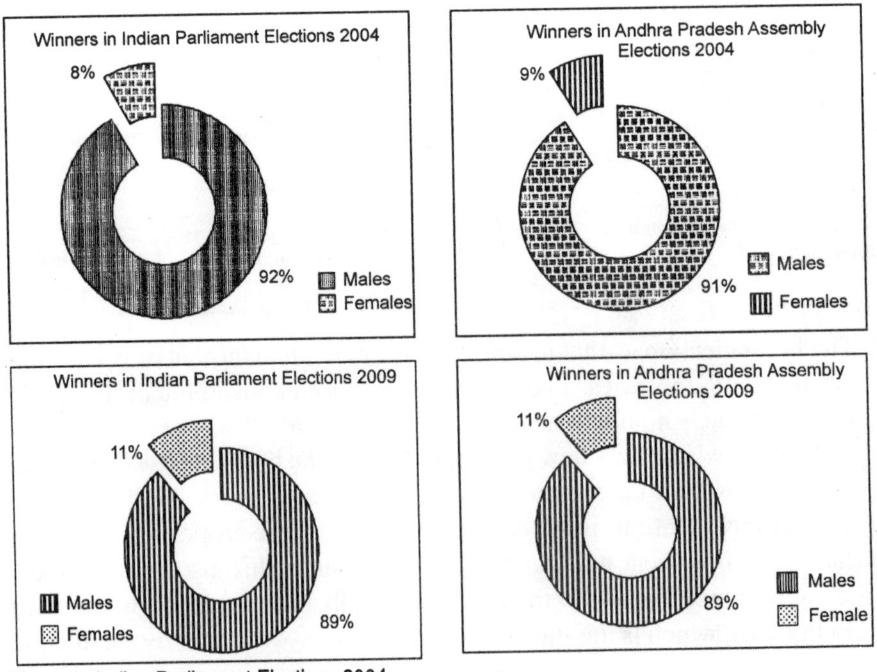

Fig. 2.3: Winner in Indian Parliament Elections 2004

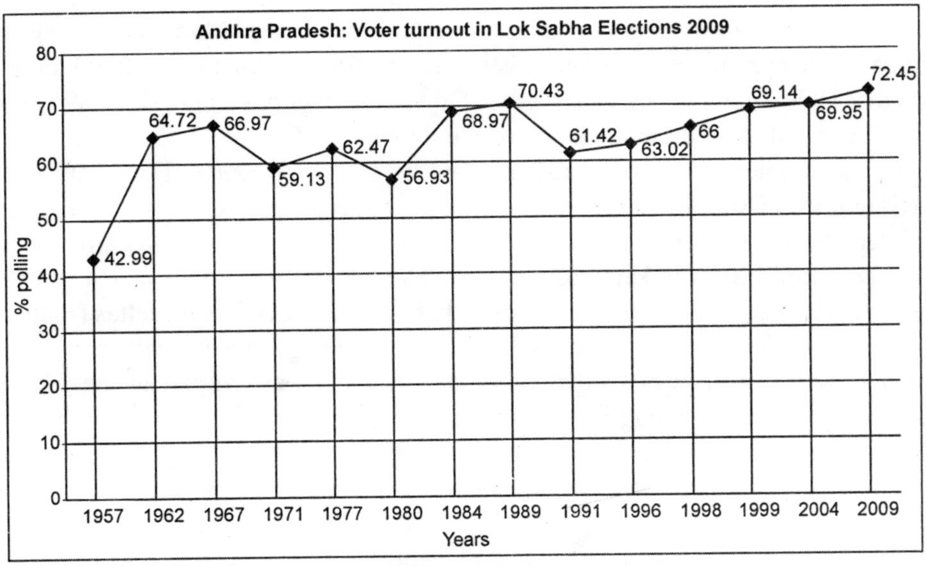

Fig. 2.4: Andhra Pradesh: Voter turnout in Lok Sabha Elections, 2009
Source: EENADU 25.4.2009

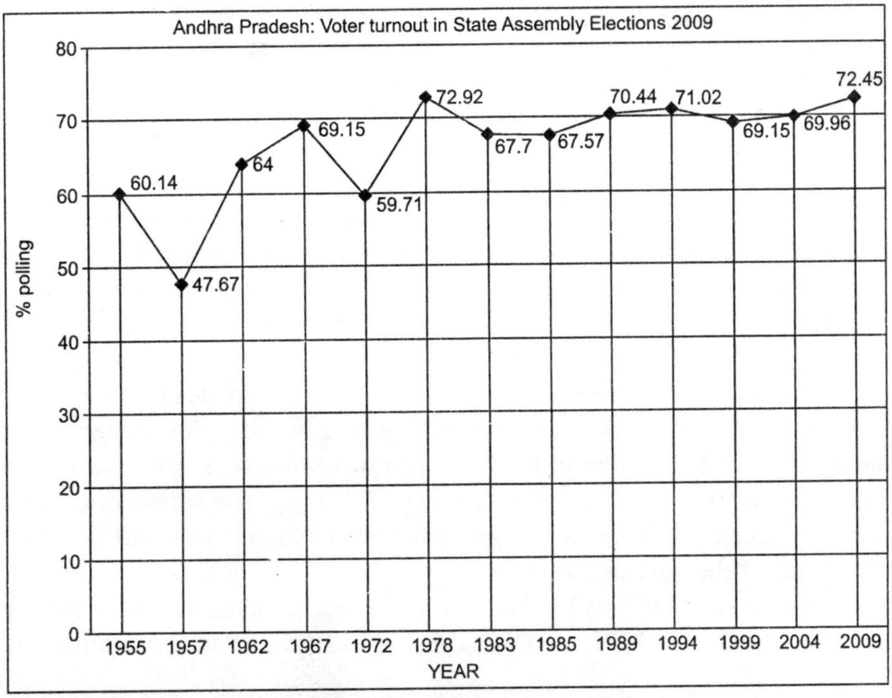

Fig. 2.5: Andhra Pradesh: Voter turnout in State Assembly Elections, 2009
Source: EENADU 25.4.2009

far as the areal extent of the Parliamentary Constituencies is concerned (Map 1.3). This is also so in relation to the number of voters, where the newly formed Malkajgiri Parliamentary constituency has the highest number of voters (21,90,361 on January 22, 2009) compared to Adilabad (ST) Constituency which has the lowest number of voters (11,16,895)*. A look at Map 1.3 reveals that the boundaries of the districts and Parliamentary Constituencies crisscross each other and on an average one district has two or parts of two Parliamentary Constituencies. Only East Godavari district covers parts of four Parliamentary Constituencies. The size of the constituencies decreases from the western towards the eastern part of the state. This is in keeping with the densities of population, which peak in the eastern quarter, especially in the vicinity of the Krishna and Godavari deltas (Map 1.5).

The pattern with regard to the Assembly (state legislature) Constituencies is no different. The size of these constituencies also decreases from the western part of the state to the east, the only exception being Hyderabad district in the western part which has a large number of small constituencies to cater to the needs of its huge population (Map 1.4). Otherwise it is the coastal stretch, especially the twin delta zone that seems to have a dense spatial mushrooming of Assembly Constituencies. This factor (of smaller polygons portraying Assembly and to a certain extent Parliamentary Constituencies in Coastal Andhra vis a vis larger polygons in Telangana and Rayalaseema) has to be taken cognizance of while viewing the maps portraying patterns, whether electoral or demographic or socio cultural. The seeming aberration of large area coverage of features or characteristics in Telangana and Rayalaseema has to be rationally rescinded by reference to the fact that they display large, relatively sparsely settled polygons, whether they refer to assembly constituencies or any other administrative divisions.

Analysis of Parliamentary Election Results

A perusal of Map 2.2 to 2.10 pertaining to the parliamentary elections from 1977 to 2009 drives home certain facts very clearly and unequivocally. The number of parties contesting elections have increased from a simple 'three' in 1977 to 'eight' in 1991 and 1998. Thus while the election space and the electoral scenario was simple in the earlier periods in time, it has become more complex and plural at a later period in time. This multiplicity is more evident in the northern part of the state especially in relation to the electoral outcomes; the vulnerability of the population of this area is largely reflected in this. A diagonal stretch of parliamentary constituencies from Mahbubnagar to Bhadrachalam extending along south western-north eastern axis brings out this tendency for change and variety in a large measure, apart from the scenario of general change witnessed in relation to the attitudes, perceptions and overt voting behaviour of the people.

While the general tendency has been from a change from a monolithic party structure dominated by the INC in 1977 and INC (I) in1980 to the TDP as the dominant party in a

* http://pibhyd.ap.nic.in/er20030901.pdf.

conglomerate of parties in 1984, INC in 1991, 1996, 1998 and the TDP in1999 and INC in 2004 and 2009.

It has also been noticed that the runner-up parties in such of those situations where the victory margins are small emerge as the victorious party in the subsequent election. This has been the case of the CPI and CPM from 1980 to 1984, (Map 2.3 and 2.4) where they were the runners at the earlier point in time and winners at a later point. So has also been the case of TDP from 1991 to 1996, (Map 2.5 and 2.6), in several constituencies in north, central and southern Andhra Pradesh and in parts of Coastal Andhra and Rayalaseema between 1998 and1999 (Map 2.7 and 2.8).

The specificities of the election scenario flow out from the generalities. While the plurality of parties contesting and winning has been witnessed from 1984 onwards, the proliferation of state level and subsequently, regional parties are also a very perceptible feature. This is a reflection of discontent with the prevailing policies of national parties in control and at times an expression of allegiance to the linguistic, sub-state regional or even caste or glamour quotient of the contestants. In fact, Andhra Pradesh has been the second state in the country where glamour has generated a lot of hype at the time of the elections and has been responsible for creating election history. Other states and constituencies have subsequently taken a cue from the overwhelming and sweeping wave of TDP in the early 1980s, which edged out its opponents by appealing to the linguistic and glamour fantasies of the electorate. Subsequently, the TRS has taken a slice of the electoral cake in extreme northern AP by winning five parliamentary constituencies. This was also done by pandering the regional sentiments of the relatively less literate population of these areas. This area also has an outstanding proportion of workers in household industries; a relatively high growth of population in 1991-2001, an above average sex ratio in general and a low proportion of female literates reflecting the vulnerability of the population who fall prey to the election propaganda process.

In tandem with the linguistic and regional parties, communal parties have also made their presence felt on the electoral horizon from1984 onwards. While the BJP made its presence felt in 1984, the MIM emerged from the shadow in 1991. The multifarious electoral scenario with its multispectral tints is now only too obvious and showcases the complexity of the social, demographic, psychological and economic elements which balance each other in a process of action, reaction and interaction in the state.

III
Mapping Elections for Legislative Assembly of Andhra Pradesh

ANALYSIS OF ASSEMBLY ELECTION RESULTS

An analysis of the Assembly Election results from 1977 to 2009, including eight election years has been done with the help of the following variables; Number of Voters in Assembly Elections, Voter turnout, Winning party, Votes Secured by Winners, Runner-up party and Votes secured by runner-up. While the election data had been collected even for the period preceding this and extending back up to the first election held in post-independence India, it could not be spatially portrayed in the form of maps owing to the non availability of compatible spatial data. Even a reconstruction of the then constituencies could not be done as the names and identities of several constituent units of the constituencies had changed and this data could not be traced and put together.

A glance at Map 3.1 to 3.7 pertaining to the number of voters in Assembly Election shows that there has been a general increase in the absolute number of voters in all the assembly constituencies across the state. However, while earlier pockets in the Eastern part along the Godavari and Krishna basin and delta as well as those in the southern part as well as in the vicinity of Hyderabad and Rangareddy had a high number of voters at successive points in time there has been a fair dissemination of large number of voters in all pockets extending across the state. The only peaks in an otherwise well spread out pattern are in the vicinity of Hyderabad and in Visakhapatnam.This however, is a relatively static variable, a function of the adult proportion of the total population and prone to change as the conditioning factor changes.

Voter turnout at elections (Map 3.1 to 3.7) however, is a relatively dynamic variable and is reflective of the intrinsic characteristics of the electorate as well as extraneous factors like campaigning etc.which have a bearing on it. Voter turnout in general has been high in the Godavari and Krishna river basin and delta areas which are relatively better off from an economic perspective. It is also high in some of the politically conscious pockets of an otherwise less developed Rayalaseema region. In fact at the 2004 election, the entire coastal Andhra region has shown a high voter turnout, a reflection of higher levels of consciousness and expectation. The gaps in the chain of the highs in coastal Andhra seemed to be almost bridged at the 2004 election with an overall high and highest ever voter turnout.

A perusal of the maps pertaining to the winning party in Assembly Elections (Maps 3.8 to 3.15) indicates that parts of northern Andhra Pradesh gave a varied mix of parties that have won elections at all points in time. The southern part has also exhibited a slight penchant for variety at different points in time. This is in contrast to the observation made earlier with regard to the winning party in the parliamentary elections; where it was observed that the northern part of the state displayed a plurality so far as the winning party is concerned and the southern part exhibited a kind of uniformity. Map 3.8 for the Assembly results of 1978 shows that the Janata Party had made inroads into the erstwhile bastions of the Congress party which had swept the southern part of the state in the parliamentary elections of 1977 (Map 2.2). There was a sway towards those who contested as independent candidates at the assembly elections of 1983 but were otherwise members of the unregistered TDP at the assembly elections of 1983 (Map 3.9). It was a kind of overt expression of disgruntlement over non-delivery of political parties, as also an expression of the awakening of the linguistic consciousness of the people. The sweeps of the TDP was witnessed in many of these very quarters in the Assembly elections of 1985 a reflection of the preceding parliamentary election results as depicted in Fig. 2.4 earlier. The alternation between the Congress party and the TDP taking a larger slice of the election outcomes has been a characteristic feature of the state elections.

Thus amidst all the tussles, a tendency for experimentation in the northern part of the state, specially parts of Telangana, the niches that the left parties have carved out for themselves in Telangana and also the emergence of communal parties in certain pockets of the state, the bi-party competition between the TDP and the Congress seems to have come to stay in the state. This tendency is very much manifest in Rayalaseema, compared to the other regions of the state. However, the multi cornered contest in 2009 accentuated by the formation of PRP (Praja Rajyam Party) made for a clean sweep for the INC. This is notwithstanding the fact that a large number of youth - including first time voters - voted in the elections in 2009 and with a large majority of them being from the quaternary and quinary sector of the economy, their option was quite predictable.

Maps 3.8 to 3.15 which also show the runner-up party in Assembly elections demonstrate that while the number of runner-up parties have increased from 1978 onwards, the spatial mix displaying the extent of variety was more in the earlier period in time and has become relatively less heterogeneous as time has passed further reinforcing what has been said above with regard to the setting in of a bi-partisan trend in the state.

Maps 3.16 to 3.22 pertain to the votes secured by winners in Assembly elections and it is very much evident that the constituencies where the winners secure a small per cent of votes are the ones which go in for a change at the next election. Therefore, those who are interested in going in for a prediction of the election scenario can keep a close watch on such constituencies which have a small margin of the winning vote.

Map 3.16 to 3.22 also display the votes secured by runners-up in the Assembly elections from 1978 onwards. These bear no correlation, whatsoever, to the votes secured by winners. However, a tendency towards a higher vote secured by the runner-up in Rayalaseema and Coastal Andhra is very much evident right from 1978 and found its maximum culmination in 1994, Telangana, on the other hand, has shown a relatively lesser proportion of votes secured by the runner-up party speaking of split loyalties of the electorate. The switch in loyalty from that to a single party to the surfacing of a multiplicity of parties is all too evident and is in keeping with the national trend for regional, communal and other splinter groups to surface.

IV
Micro Political Spaces

To get an in depth picture of the Election scenario, micro spaces in Guntur and Nalgonda districts (Map 4.1) of Coastal Andhra and Telangana respectively, are generated by carrying out a field survey in Sample Villages in all the Assembly constituencies in these two districts (27 villages in Nalgonda covering 812 households and 22 villages in Guntur covering 945 households). Guntur is located in the relatively prosperous Coastal Andhra region and Nalgonda in the less developed region of Telangana. The perception of the people was studied through a structured questionnaire and the results mapped after due processing.

The results pertaining to some of the variables are presented here. In relation to distance to the polling booth (Table 4.1 and Maps 4.2 and 4.3), people of both the districts differ in their satisfaction levels. Guntur shows high levels of satisfaction whereas in Nalgonda district the percentage of people 'not satisfied' is quite significant. It could be because of the fact that a certain section of people particularly tribals living in hamlets invariably are cut off from the mainstream villages thereby they suffer for want of collective infrastructure and are forced to travel for long distances to cast their vote. Naturally the rate of dissatisfaction in such circumstances is high.

Therefore, a mechanism has to be worked out either in terms of organizing mobile booths or some other method by which people could participate in voting without much complaint. For this a spatial picture portraying the belts of relative dissatisfaction comes in handy and this could be understood from Maps 4.2 and 4.3. It is found from these Maps that dissatisfaction level on this count is high all along the central part of Nalgonda district, specially the constituency in the central western part – Miryalguda. Dissatisfaction levels are also high in Nakrekal and Nalgonda constituencies. Steps could be taken to improve infrastructure and connectivity in these constituencies to make for higher levels of satisfaction among the people.

Table 4.1: Guntur and Nalgonda Districts: Booth Satisfaction in relation to Distance : 2005

S. No	*Booth satisfaction*	*Percent*	
		Guntur	*Nalgonda*
1	Satisfactory	91	70
2	Not satisfactory	4	21
3	No response	5	9

Source: Field survey, 2005

Another variable that is presented here is 'criminalization of politics'. Of late criminalization of politics has become a serious issue as certain criminal acts are authored and executed by the politicians and they are also influencing the elections. The media has given publicity to this issue in a big way before and especially during elections. When people were posed with this question, the cause of criminalization of politics is attributed to a large extent to the process of giving tickets to the moneyed. Thus, it proves the fact that though the moneyed sections do not give the impression, but it is money and greed for more money that is making moneyed people 'camouflaged criminals'. However in Guntur district, a large section of people also attributed criminalization to giving tickets to musclemen and criminals per se and this partially substantiates the dominant view (Table 4.2 and Maps 4.4 and 4.5). The role of violence and criminals during the elections is a relatively autonomous activity because the winning of an election and entry to the legislatures through the use of bullying brings unlimited dividends to the victorious person or a group of individuals. The relationship between power and space has to be given due credence.

Table 4.2 : Guntur and Nalgonda Districts: Criminalization of Politics: 2005

S. No	*Factors responsible*	*Per cent*	
		Guntur	*Nalgonda*
1	Giving tickets to moneyed people	57	90
2	Giving tickets to musclemen	24	4
3	Giving tickets to criminals	19	6

Source: Field survey, 2005

A check on the background of contestants underpins the oft held opinion that criminals have made inroads into the corridors of power. Fig. 4.1, which is based on affidavits filed by candidates with the Election Commission of India up to 2007 amply reinforces this point. It is found that even women parliamentarians figure prominently in the list of defaulters on the law and order front in the 14th Lok Sabha. It seems to be a problem that is circular and also cumulative in nature, where the people in power circles do not hesitate at committing crimes and once having committed ensure their perpetual stay in those circles so as to douse the future flames of blame. Guntur and Nalgonda, being a representative microcosm

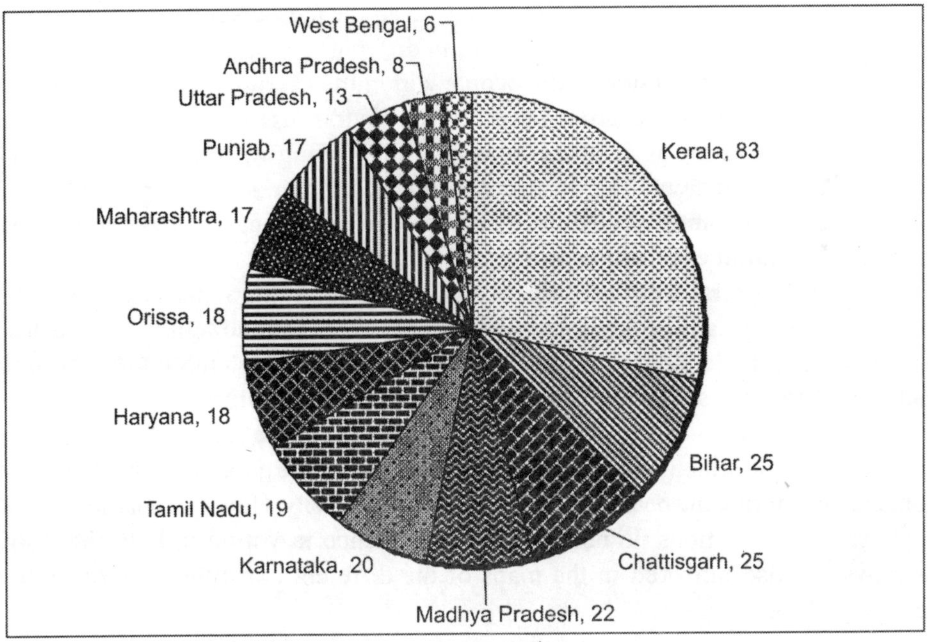

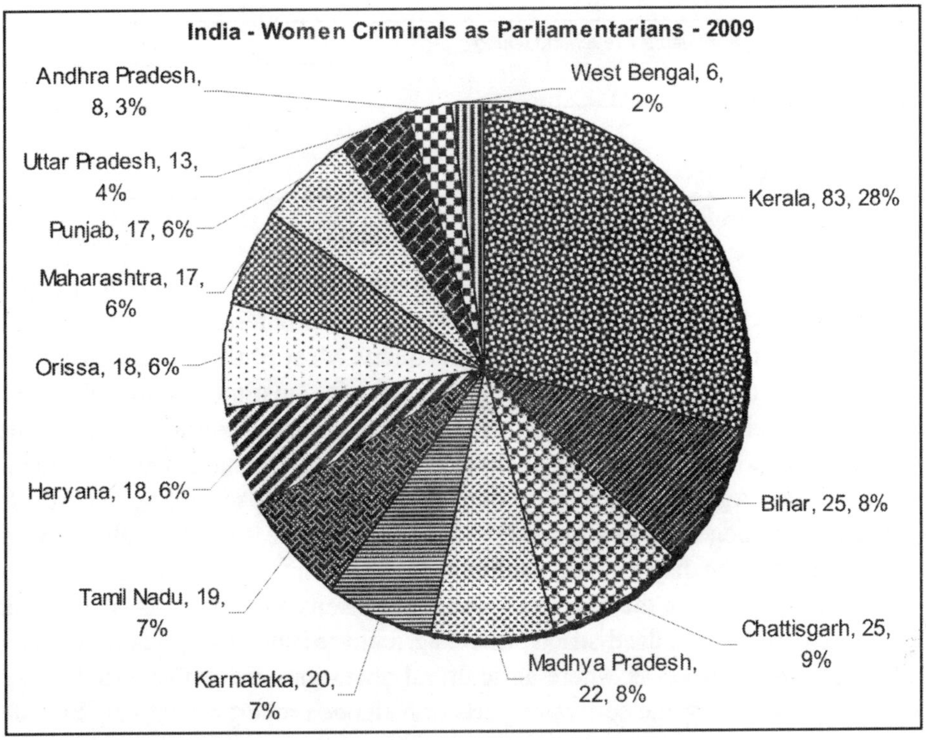

Fig. 4.1: India—Women Criminals as Parliamentarians, 2009

of this election scenario, symbolize this notoriety in ample measure, albeit at the contesting ticket allotment stage and at varying measures in different pockets.

An analysis of the perception of the people within the assembly constituencies of the study area has been done with regard to the perceived hindrances to voting. These hindrances have been identified as the agricultural activity itself – along with its various stages and phases, anomalous situations like drought, cultural commitments like festivals besides migration. The persons interviewed have also been asked about the ideal voting season keeping the agricultural cycle in view.

As people in the rural areas are largely engaged in agricultural activity which almost keeps them busy for the whole day, taking off from the work routine sometimes creates non seriousness among the less politicized sections towards elections. Table 4.3 substantiates the fact that there is a substantial section of people who expressed inconvenience to participate in the elections during the agricultural season. In the case of Nalgonda it is 32 per cent of the people which is twice that of Guntur. They have expressed inconvenience if elections are held during the peak season of agricultural activity. However a large percentage of people said that elections do not cause inconvenience in voting in both the districts. These views are also mirrored in the maps of the different constituencies of these two districts (Map 4.6).

Table 4.3 : Guntur and Nalgonda Districts: Agricultural Activity as a hindrance to Voting

S. No	*Agriculture Preventing voting*	*Percent*	
		Guntur	*Nalgonda*
1	Yes	16	32
2	No	80	65
3	No response	4	3

Source: Field survey, 2005

It is found from an analysis of Map 4.6, that, most of the people in both the districts under consideration feel that the agricultural activity is not a deterrent to voting. This is not withstanding certain 'Yeses' with regard to this query. Most of these are concentrated in Nalgonda district and in certain cases like the Nalgonda constituency and Bhongir their proportion reaches almost 50 per cent. Only in the relatively arid Devarakonda constituency, in the southern part of this district, agriculture is not reported to have a marked impact on the voting activity. Agricultural activity does not seem to impact voting according to a large number of respondents in Guntur District. This is more so in the relatively high – lying western part of the district compared to the eastern part. The response and the raison de etre for the same in both the districts show comparisons and contrasts. The physically disadvantaged parts of both the districts, where agriculture is not a major activity to reckon with, show a similar response, where agricultural operations are not reported to hamper elections. On the contrary, the cultivated parts of Nalgonda report a relatively high degree of interference of agriculture in voting.

The present study probed in to the impact of drought on voters so far as casting vote during elections is concerned (Table 4.4 and Map 4.6). Here drought has to be understood from the point of view of collapse of economic systems and its bearing on declining food security and large scale unemployment and therefore migration. Such devastating drought has vulnerable groups like landless, marginal and small farmers sometimes even middle level farmers who are also affected as the land is less productive in the absence of rain fall and water availability but the farmers have the immovable assets to make use of in times of drought. A significant proportion of respondents from the drought prone district of Nalgonda and upland areas of Guntur express that drought has an impact during elections. It is these sections that become vulnerable because of insecurity of life and likelihood of becoming a prey to various manipulations.

Table 4.4 : Guntur and Nalgonda Districts: Drought Impact in Casting Vote

S. No	*Drought impact*	*Per cent*	
		Guntur	*Nalgonda*
1	Yes	7	20
2	No	90	78
3	No response	3	2

Source: Field survey, 2005

The positive response on this score in a micro spatial context (Map 4.6) is witnessed in Nalgonda, Alair, Rammanapet and Bhongir Assembly Constituencies. These are the drought prone areas of this region. The reported impact of drought in casting vote is felt more in a larger number of constituencies of Nalgonda district compared to Guntur. A very negligible proportion in Guntur district report that drought has an adverse impact on voting. This being a coastal and an agriculturally prosperous district – especially the eastern part – it has reported the non occurance of the drought as an issue of consequence in voting.

Though a small segment of people expressed reservations about holding elections during festival time, 77 per cent in Guntur and 75 per cent in Nalgonda, had no problem with festival coinciding with the election date (Table 4.5 and Map 4.6).

Table 4.5 : Guntur and Nalgonda Districts: Festivals as a Hindrance in Voting

S. No	*Festivals as hindrance*	*Per cent*	
		Guntur	*Nalgonda*
1	Yes	13	19
2	No	77	75
3	No response	10	6

Source: Field survey, 2005

As expected, migration becomes a hindrance in participating in voting (Table 4.6 and Map 4.7). This is more the case in Guntur rather than Nalgonda. A migrant is often deterred by distance and may not show interest in casting vote. Gurzala, Mangalagiri, Bapatla and Narsaraopet constituencies in Guntur stand out in this regard where much more than 50 per cent of the respondents reported that migration definitely influences voting. It is the distance factor which has a negative impact in this context.

Table 4.6: Guntur and Nalgonda Districts : Migration as Hindrance in Voting

S. No	Migration-hindrance	Per cent	
		Guntur	Nalgonda
1	Yes	52	34
2	No	45	64
3	No response	3	2

Source: Field survey, 2005

So far as the ideal season for conducting elections is concerned, there was near unanimity for conducting elections during summer (Table 4.7 and Map 4.7).This is reflected in the case of Nalgonda with 90 per cent of the respondents approving of summer as the ideal season for holding elections and in Guntur with 87 per cent vouching for summer as the ideal season for voting. The spatial portrayal of this variable (Map 4.7) also finds a near conformity with the findings of the table and the near unanimity with regard to the choice of summer as the ideal voting season is further corroborated.

Table 4.7: Guntur and Nalgonda Districts: Ideal Voting Season

S. No	Ideal Season	Per cent	
		Guntur	Nalgonda
1	Summer	87	90
2	Rainy season	0.5	4
3	Winter	4	4
4	Summer and winter	6	0
5	No response	2.5	2

Source: Field survey, 2005

Elections demand Political Parties to articulate social tensions, economic aspirations, development visions and political philosophies and these should be meticulously intertwined in election agendas in order to appeal to the masses. It is more so in the context of the presence of competitive politics. Therefore parties come with agendas that would appease various social segments while retaining the dominance and continuation of hegemony over the society. There are two processes that drive the electoral agendas: one in terms of hidden agendas that camouflage the real intentions of political class by way of ideological persuasions—Right, Center and Left. The other is political appeasement by way of populist agendas that attract voters. The first approach sustains the political party in terms of political paradigm and the second approach influences vulnerable sections and strife ridden people temporarily. Though both the approaches enlist the support of various groups, this is not adequate for parties in winning elections. Therefore the political class deploys voter influencing methods and techniques and it largely depends on the resourcefulness of the parties and the social forces that support political infrastructure.

In a democracy numbers matter and this is determined by the voter. As stated above there are various ways of approaching a voter with a particular ideology on which the political parties are built; promises that parties make during elections; and the methods and techniques used in influencing voters. Besides this, how strong the civil society is in shaping the nation also influences the election process. All this put together determines the mandate in the elections and the inheritance of the power that governs people and determines the transformative course of the nation.

Parties operate on Ideological lines and essentially emanate from the Right, Center and Left leanings. There are various shades within them representing national, regional and sub-regional parties and articulating universal and particular political discourses giving rise to numerous formations. In the context of Andhra Pradesh the mainstream parties that are tested electorally are: Congress, TDP, BJP, CPI, CPI-M, TRS, BSP etc. and they root in the ideological discourse of nationalism, Telugu pride, Hindutva, Class, Region and Caste respectively. The slogans they resort to are Congress - '*Aam Aadmi*', TDP-'*Swarna*-Andhra Pradesh', BJP-'India Shining', TRS-'Separate Telangana' etc. However all parties speak about development but development of different visions and slants. Because of the strong socio-cultural roots the parties have and the ideological persuasions they resort to, each one of them clings to their own 'political constituencies'.

The other influencing methods and techniques used in mobilizing social constituencies assume significance during elections as large groups of people live beyond ideological radar and they have to be brought under their fold by all means to win elections. This necessitates the political parties to deploy political technologies that often defy election norms.

In the light of the above an analysis of the voter influencing methods and techniques and the consequent political arrangement in terms of parties and social forces is made in the context of AP. Political parties have been resorting to various forms in influencing voters. Some of them belong to legally permissible forms and others are statutorily prohibited and are illegal in nature. It is very difficult for the Election Commission to catch the people on the wrong side of the law and punish them. If we see the very expenditure in elections it is found that the Election Commission permits the contestants to spend 10 lakhs rupees for legislative assembly and 25 lakhs rupees for Lok Sabha. The reality suggests something different. It is learnt from the conversations across the political circles and also the reports that appear in the news papers and it is confirmed in the survey that in order to get a ticket of a political party a candidate needs to show the capacity to spend a couple of crores of rupees at legislative assembly level and in manifolds for the Lok Sabha seat. All norms are being flouted by the public representatives and democracy has become a farce as almost every person without money to spend is virtually eliminated from the elections for want of huge money. It is to the dismay of everyone that the money that has accrued due to globalization is being circulated in the political and business circles in the name of development and it is really making a mockery of democracy.

Elections engage the nation in a war of nerves making the stake holders to be a party to it. Political parties and individual contestants come up with political technologies that make them victorious, as winning matters in the entire exercise. In pursuit of influencing the voter, contestants try to score over the political rivals. As part of such exercise, parties have been engaging in using traditional and well tested methods and at times innovations in campaigning. Some such voter influencing methods identified are ideological campaign methods, propaganda forms, group influencing methods, bribing the voter etc.

INSTITUTIONAL AND IDEOLOGICAL INFLUENCE

Political Party and the force of its inherited socio-political capital along with its contestants determine the electoral influence over the voters. The ideological base and its political appeal make certain sections of people as their electoral base. In view of this the party is becoming an important force in vote catching. The survey results (Table 4.8 and Map 4.8) show that people largely identified themselves with party. 54 per cent of the respondents in Nalgonda district and 40 per cent in Guntur district confirm the same. Contestants emerge as the second important category in influencing voters and this is demonstrated by 35 per cent respondents in Guntur and 34 per cent in Nalgonda district. While looking in to the other factors, development does matter in influencing election and it is followed by ideology and propaganda in that order, the latter two being more prominent in most parts of Guntur, rather than Nalgonda. The outstanding nature of the impact of 'Party' vis a vis 'Person' or 'Leader' in influencing the outcome of elections is predominantly marked in the eastern, central and southern part of Nalgonda – in the constituencies of Tungaturthi, Suryapet, Miryalguda, Kodad and to some extent in Devarakonda, Munugode, Nalgonda and Chalakurthi. In other words, barring the northern constituencies of Alair, Ramannapet and Bhongir, where ideology is given greater importance, this tendency is widespread in all the other constituencies of Nalgonda. In Guntur district this tendency of attaching greater importance to 'Party' *vis a vis* other considerations is more rampant in the western constituencies of Macherla (U), Vinukonda (U), Gurazala and Narasaraopeta (R). It is also witnessed in Peddakurapadu, Mangalagiri (U), Tadikonda, Pothur, Ponnur Town (U), Bapatla (E) and Repalle Town (U) to some extent. It is generally witnessed that a multiplicity of factors influence elections in the urban areas which are more in Guntur and among the less developed areas it is just allegiance to the party which works. The less developed areas thus have a uni-dimensionality or at the most bi-dimensionality in influencing the outcome of elections, whereas in the more developed areas the trend is towards multi – dimensionality, where a wide variety of factors are instrumental in swinging the outcome of elections. The combined effect of all this speaks in terms of the electoral outcome.

Table 4.8 :Guntur and Nalgonda Districts: Institutional and Ideological Influences on Voters

S.No	Methods	Per cent	
		Guntur	Nalgonda
1	Person	35	34
2	Party	40	54
3	Ideology	7	3
4	Propaganda	4	0
5	Development	12	6
6	Others	0	1
7	No response	2	2

Source: Field survey, 2005.

INFLUENCE OF PROPAGANDA METHODS

With the advent of the electronic technology political parties are increasingly resorting to the modern means of communications besides the continuation of older forms of voter mobilization. The explosion of electronic media and its reach across the illiterate and semi-literate besides literate also have a significant influence over the voter. However the survey results (Map 4.9/Table 4.9) show that the traditional forms of public meetings and rallies continue to play a major role in influencing the elections. It is amply demonstrated by the survey results that about 65 per cent respondents in Nalgonda and 44 per cent in Guntur concurred in favour of meetings and rallies influencing voters in elections. The E-media constitute the second biggest influence over the voter and it is confirmed by 30 per cent respondents in Guntur and 7 per cent in Nalgonda. The other significant influence comes from posters and cassettes with 13 in Guntur and 7 per cent which is on the lower side as far as Nalgonda district is concerned. While the relatively less developed Nalgonda district has shown a greater reliance on traditional propaganda methods like 'Meetings and Rallies' the more affluent Guntur district shows a dependence on relatively modern forms of propaganda like 'E Media' and 'Posters' in addition to it. Guntur District also has nine urban constituencies amongst the total nineteen that it has and hence the hiked awareness on the electronic front and also resort to a diversity of methods of propaganda. The picture presented by the different constituencies of Nalgonda is more monotonous by contrast (Map 4.9). Flags and wall writings also make the parties' presence felt in both the districts. It is clearly evident from the above that contrasting trends have emerged in line with development and backwardness. Guntur district which happens to be part of the developed Andhra region experienced the high impact of modern technology in influencing the voter. On the contrary, Nalgonda district happens to be part of backward Telangana region and the traditional forms of rallies and meetings continue to dominate in influencing voters. The impact of the modern technology plays a lesser role because of the electronic divide that exists between two districts and by extension the regions.

GROUP INFLUENCING METHODS

As time passes by and also because of high money involved in the elections, contestants

Table 4.9: Guntur and Nalgonda Districts—Propaganda Methods Influencing Voters

S. No	Methods	Per cent	
		Guntur	Nalgonda
1	Posters	13	3
2	E-media	30	7
3	Cassettes	7	1
4	Flags	3	1
5	Meetings & Rallies	44	65
6	Any other	1	21
7	No response	2	2

Source: Field survey, 2005.

are venturing into the fray with new ideas and initiatives. In order to influence the group behaviour, community oriented methods (Map 4.9 and Table 4.10) are deployed. Digging bore wells, distribution of cricket kits and renovation of religious places have assumed a lot of significance in the elections. About 32 per cent of the people in Nalgonda and 29 per cent in Guntur have positively responded in confirming the influence of such measures in the elections. Equally big appeal is seen in terms of the distribution of cricket kits as this game is increasingly becoming popular among the youth. About 29 per cent in Nalgonda and 24 per cent in Guntur have said 'yes' to this factor in influencing the voter. Renovation of religious places and function infrastructure like tents, cooking vessels etc. played a significant role in influencing the groups, castes and communities. However, quite interestingly, certain factors which are prominent for one district are not so in others. Linking social and interest groups to political party is part of the political strategy and party networking and thus influence elections.

Table 4.10: Guntur and Nalgonda Districts—Group-Influencing Methods used in Elections

S. No	Methods	Per cent	
		Guntur	Nalgonda
1	Distribution of cricket kits	24	29
2	Function infrastructure	4	0
3	Renovation of religious places	15	2
4	Digging bore wells for drinking water	29	32
5	Any others	21	18
6	No response	7	19

Source: Field survey, 2005

BRIBING THE VOTER

The importance of money is going up manifold from election to election. Supply of liquor is another traditional method of influencing voter is also seen rampantly across the board. However the change is noticed in terms of quality of liquor- from native *gudumba* to IMFL, which is supplied during elections. It is established from the Table 4.11 that Liquor and money are the two popular forms of bribing the voter. Located graphs (Map 4.9) and Table 4.11 show that 37 per cent of the sample surveyed from Guntur district and 44 per cent from Nalgonda district confirmed the supply of liquor as the method of bribing the voter. Similarly 42 per cent of the respondents from Guntur and 15 per cent from Nalgonda confirmed the money distribution in the elections. While liquor ranks first in all the constituencies of Nalgonda, money ranks first in 14 out of the 19 assembly constituencies in Guntur, liquor ranks first in four of them as a form of inducement during elections. Other material forms used in the elections in influencing the voters are distribution of Saris, T shirts and TV sets. Money and T-shirt distribution is high in Guntur district and liquor and sari distribution is comparatively high in Nalgonda district. In fact all these methods are vitiating elections and thereby subverting democracy. There is every likelihood that large sections of voters feel obligated when the contestants extend favours to them.

Table 4.11: Guntur and Nalgonda Districts—Bribing the Voter

S. no	*Methods*	*Per cent*	
		Guntur	*Nalgonda*
1	Saris	3.5	7
2	T-shirts	5	2
3	Liquor	37	44
4	Money	42	15
5	Feast	1	0
6	TV-sets	0.2	0
7	Others	9.3	15
8	No response	2	17

Source: Field survey, 2005.

OFFICIAL INFLUENCE AND EVM MANIPULATION

Officials' influence in voting is also reported in the press. About 53 per cent respondents in Guntur and 35 per cent in Nalgonda said 'yes' when asked whether officials influence voters (Map 4.10 and Table 4.12). However the remaining also said 'no' to the same question. The maximum number of 'yeses' were reported from Gurazala, Tadikonda, Sattenapalle and Vinukonda (U) constituencies. While looking in to the manipulation of Electronic Voting Machine a small segment of people nurse the feeling that it can be manipulated and turned against the electorate (Map 4.10 and Table 4.13). However 87 to 89 per cent of the respondents approved the effectiveness of EVM.

Table 4.12: Guntur and Nalgonda Districts— Polling Officials Influence on Voting

S. No	*Officials Influence*	*Per cent*	
		Guntur	*Nalgonda*
1	Yes	53	35
2	No	42	61
3	No response	5	4

Source: Field survey, 2005.

Table 4.13: Guntur and Nalgonda Districts— EVM Manipulation

S. No	Manipulation	Per cent	
		Guntur	Nalgonda
1	Yes	3	5
2	No	89	87
3	No response	8	8

Source: Field survey, 2005.

It is amply demonstrated from the above that illegal forms of influencing the voter take over elections in a big way and tilt the scales against the electorate and subvert the very constitutional ideal of holding free and fair elections.

It is true that the illiterate masses and also the educated, expect the assistance in different ways at the polling booth. Table 4.14 and Map 4.10 conforms the fact and in both the districts the percentage figure is almost the same. In Nalgonda a substantial percentage of people i.e. 20 per cent did not show any interest for assistance. The reason for such response needs to be explored by going in to the social base of such respondents.

Table 4.14: Guntur and Nalgonda Districts—Need for Assistance at Polling Booth

S. No	Need	Per cent	
		Guntur	Nalgonda
1	Yes	71	75
2	No	9	20
3	No response	20	5

Source: Field survey, 2005.

The above analysis proves the fact that the social base of electoral politics is truncated making the social exclusion as the norm of democracy. It is aggravated further with the intensive use of political technology involving extra legal forms in influencing the elections. The realization of the ideal of constitutional democracy is getting withered away. It is amply supplemented with the socially inclusive democratic aspirations and assertions surfacing in the articulations of identities of regional, gender and social groups. Every time they are pushed under the carpet, they resurface as issues needed to be addressed by the political system.

Table 4.15: Guntur and Nalgonda Districts—Need for Mapping Elections

S. No	Need	Per cent	
		Guntur	Nalgonda
1	Yes	93	70
2	No	1	26
3	No response	6	4

Source: Field survey, 2005.

Surprisingly a large section of people showed interest in mapping elections. 90 per cent people in Guntur and 70 per cent people in Nalgonda have positively responded for mapping elections (Table 4.15 and Map 4.11 and 4.12). This amply demonstrates the validity of taking up such exercises to empower people with maps and related information. It also speaks of the diminishing 'Digital Divide' in the country.

SUMMARY AND CONCLUSION

It could be said in summarizing this section, that people in general are happy with the arrangements for elections by the government, the distance to the polling booth, the infrastructure present there etc. This is notwithstanding, complaints of the involvement of big money in getting tickets to contest, the role of musclemen and the criminalization of elections in general. These are the things that can be paid heed to by the authorities to nip emerging problems in the bud.

The two districts under consideration have distinct micro spaces, both from the economic and cultural perception point of view as also from that of electoral outcomes – the two extremes being linked by causal chains. For one, both the districts show a distinct parity of perception with the underlying physical factors – an open-minded view being exhibited by the people in better endowed habitats and a more circumspect view being the rule in the less endowed ones. The dry pockets of Nalgonda and the upland areas of Guntur show a similar kind of perception, so far as the attitude of the people towards agricultural activity as a hindrance to voting is concerned. So is also the case when it comes to the situation with regard to the drought influencing the voting behavior. Migration as a deterrent to voting is more prevalent in Guntur rather than in Nalgonda. Also a near unanimity of the people with regard to festivals as not being a deterrent for voting is evident. Thus, while for some variables, which are of a general nature, the districts show a pattern that is homogeneous, for others, which are more area specific in nature, there are pockets of variation.

This is likewise reflected in the election outcomes, where areas that are more vulnerable to the vicissitudes to the natural or physical factors are more prone to experiment with change, so far as the party they vote for is concerned. Conversely, those areas which are less vulnerable, show a steadfast or unwavering pattern over the years, when it comes to voting behavior. Here a distinct difference between Nalgonda and Guntur on one hand and between the arid areas of the former and upland areas of the latter vis a vis the coastal areas of the latter district is very much evident. Thus strains of determinism guiding the voting patterns are very much evident.

The above analysis also proves the fact that the social base of electoral politics is truncated making the social exclusion as the norm of democracy. It is aggravated further with the intensive use of political technology involving extra legal forms in influencing the elections. The realization of the ideal of constitutional democracy is getting withered away. It is amply supplemented with the socially inclusive democratic aspirations and assertions surfacing in the articulations of identities of regional, gender and social groups. Every time they are pushed under the carpet, they resurface as issues needed to be addressed by the political system.

V
Caste and Power

INTRODUCTION

Election Atlas of Andhra Pradesh (A.P.) is primarily an exercise in mapping elections. The aim of making an atlas is to put electoral data of the different elections starting from 1952 to 2009. The data pertains to elected representatives of AP to the State Legislative Assembly and Loksabha. The data available through Election Commission and other published sources have been used and they largely relate to the electoral categories like party, winner, runner, voters etc. Mapping of elections could be possible from 1978 onwards. The earlier maps showing electoral boundaries for Assembly and Loksabha could not be procured as the officials of State Election Commission expressed inability in locating them. A few more categories have been added in mapping and these are population, social profiles of the representatives and the deeper analysis of electoral practices and the voter response.

Generation of tables and mapping of elections have produced spatial and temporal patterns of data representing changing socio-political processes. The presence or absence of party/parties or the demise or birth of parties or alignments and political configurations of parties or gender and social democratic assertions in the political plane demand an explanation from the analysts and the answers could be obtained from the study of geo-economic-socio-political-cultural frameworks. Therefore a brief survey of AP is presented here to put the data and mapping elections in perspective.

The data pertaining to elections goes with the time period 1952 to 2009 and the site for analysis is the state of AP. However AP state came in to existence in 1956 after prolonged campaigns and counter campaigns for Telugu speaking people after the merger of the Andhra state and Telangana region of earstwhile Hyderabad state.

The present chapter examines various aspects of caste and power. The chapter begins its analysis introducing its scope and a few facets like geographic space, social landscape and indices of social forwardness etc. In the second section, the study attempts at mapping 'power' where the temporal aspects of elections for Assembly and Loksabha right from first general elections, 1952, to the latest 2009. A few other aspects like swings and majorities have also been discussed. The third section deals with electoral and political processes. The dimensions covered are ticket/B Forms distribution, voting by caste, gender and caste, status of winners by party, region, women and caste and also straight/tri-corner contests within and across social groups. The last section deals with development and democracy.

GEOGRAPHICAL SPACE

Geo-spatially, on a generalized macro scale, AP can be divided in to three regions- Telangana, Coastal Andhra and Rayalaseema. Some times, Northern Andhra is also talked about as having separate geo-cultural identity. Physiographically, the state is encompassed with hilly areas, plateau, river valley, delta, coastal plain etc.

Sub humid and semi arid climatic conditions dominate the terrain of AP and drought is central to south Telangana and Rayalaseema. These two geographical spaces constitute coarse – grained red soils and receive scanty rain fall ranging from 45 to 80 cm and it is inadequate to support plant life and agriculture in the absence of irrigation supplementing the water needs. Two major perennial rivers—Krishna and Godavari and also Penna pass through AP. Irrigation development took place for the advantage of the fairly good rainfall zones. In fact, the coastal plains and the lands associated with river delta need not depend on surface water irrigation. The uneven distribution of river waters and large wastage of Godavari waters in to the sea have produced the conflict between regions. Therefore the regional movement is demanding for judicious use of river waters depending on agro-climatic needs.

SOCIAL LANDSCAPE

As given in table 5.1, the distribution of social groups is diverse by state and heterogeneous by regional pattern. At the state level, SCs constitute 16.2 per cent, STs 6.6 per cent, Muslims 9.2 per cent, other minorities 1.7 per cent, OBCs 44.5 per cent and upper castes 22 per cent of the population. Regional distribution of social groups vary as Telangana constitutes a high proportion of STs-8.9 per cent, Muslims-12.4 per cent and OBCs-50.7 per cent and Coastal Andhra has relatively low presence of STs, OBCs and Muslims. Rayalaseema has the lowest presence of STs. In the case of SCs there is almost an equal distribution across all regions adhering to the state average. However, the presence of intra social group may vary regionally. OBCs in Rayalaseema constitute 43 per cent and coastal Andhra 39 per cent of the population. Upper caste presence is high in coastal Andhra with 32 per cent, followed by Rayalaseema- 24.2 per cent and it is the lowest in Telangana-10.7 per cent. Telangana excluding Hyderabad contains high concentration of OBCs-53 per cent and STs-10 per cent. Muslim population is largely concentrated in Hyderabad with 41.2 per cent and other minorities are also relatively largely found here (CCSA 2010).

Table 5.1: Distribution of Social Groups-AP-2001

Sl. No	*Reg*	*SCs*	*STs*	*Muslims*	*Other Minorities*	*OBCs*	*Upper Castes*
1	AP	16.2	6.6	9.2	1.7	44.5	22.0
2	Telangana including Hyderabad	15.8	8.9	12.4	1.5	50.7	10.7
3	Telangana excluding Hyderabad	16.9	10.0	8.4	1.2	53	10.5
4	Hyderabad	8.0	0.9	41.2	3.2	35	11.8
5	RayalaSeema	16.7	2.9	12.5	0.9	43	24.2
6	Costal Andhra	16.3	6.0	4.5	2.2	39	32

Source: Census 2001 and NSSO 64th Round, Sri Krishna Committee Report-2010

Social heterogeneity is characteristic of geographical diversity having climatic/ topographic variations such as semiarid and sub-humid areas with the territories having hilly, plateau, plain, forest and coastal distribution. Most of the social groups which associate with traditional occupations are geographically determined. STs are categorized as two groups being determined by hilly and plain conditions. So is the case with cattle and sheep rearing communities whose occupation is determined by grazing lands which are largely associated with semi arid conditions. Fishermen are of two types determined by access to sea and inland tanks. Muslims have become by and large an urban community associating with erstwhile princely state of Hyderabad ruled by Qutubshahis and Asafjahis. Social segments influenced by modernization have gravitated to urban locations. The concentration of peasant communities in irrigated pockets, delta, and coastal plains go with the settled agricultural territories. The peasants have stepped in to the spaces vacated by urbanizing social groups. Every village is an abode for high concentrations of artisan, service and pastoral castes without whom it is difficult to imagine the village life. We find no village without having substantial presence of SCs. The presence of denotified/seminomadic/ nomadic tribes is also very high in AP. Social landscapes built on the platform of occupation-cum-caste conform to the geo-climatic spaces and also urban areas.

Regional analysis of social structure may portray spatial variability of castes and numerical presence or absence of their distribution. As there is a geographical variability of occupational groups there also happens to be a variation in caste distribution. In fact, occupation and caste are traditionally interrelated. Most of the service castes such as Chakalis (washerman), Mangalis (Barbers), Viawabrahmins and Kummari (Potters) are found all over the state. However a large proportion of Madigas, Muslims, Yadavs (Golla-Kurumas) and Gouds (todding tappers) are found all over the state but their distribution is very high in Telangana and Rayalaseema. Kapus (Reddys) mostly inhabit Telangana and Rayalaseema including south coastal Andhra which was earlier a part of Rayalaseema. Malas are also distributed all over the state but their presence is very high in coastal Andhra. Telangana has significant populations of Mudiraju, Munnurkapu, Padmasalis, Lambadas, Gonds, Koyas etc. Rayalaseema has significant concentrations of Boyas and Balijas. Kapus are found all over coastal Andhra but predominantly found in Godavari delta. Settibalijas are significantly located in the Godavari delta. Kammas are largely concentrated in Krishna delta and they are also spread into other regions as migratory streams in select nitches. Northern Andhra demonstrates differently with a large presence of numerous backward castes like Turpu kapus, Koppula velama, Polinati Velama, Kalinga etc. Rajus are found in these tracts in few pockets. Jatapu tribe is seen predominantly in these areas. Christians are significantly found in coastal Andhra besides their concentration in urban areas of other regions. Several other numerically miniscule castes spreading across the state also constitute the social spaces.

INDEX OF FORWARDNESS

Index of Forwardness was constructed by Hannurav at the instance of Backward Class Commission, Government of Andhra Pradesh. The present study considered the indices in relation to caste, power and forwardness. In fact, the composite index of forwardness is constructed based on the survey of 18.60 lakh sample households which by any standard is the largest multi stage sample. The study constructed composite index of forwardness based on four indices that have been constructed for social, educational, economic and political aspects. 172 castes that have come under the radar of the study in AP have been identified and the levels of backwardness/forwardness of their population assessed. The present study, based on I(F), compiled (Table 5. 2) for the castes that have minimum of one per cent population in the state. 25 castes have figured out of 172 castes across the state. The Index of Forwardness, I(F), of these castes and their ranks have been prepared and they are as follows.

Table 5.2: Andhra Pradesh: Forwardness/Backwardness of Castes

Sl. No	*Caste*	*% population*	*Index of Forwardness I(F)*	*Forwardness Rank*
1.	Brahmin	1.84	9999	1
2.	Kamma	3.69	8922	3
3.	Unclassified Reddy	3.68	7924	7
4.	Velama	0.44	7507	10
5.	Vaisya	2.92	7332	12
6.	Converted Christian	1.25	5103	34
7.	Kapu(C)	3.68	4903	39
8.	Munnurukapu	1.52	4848	42
9.	Padma Saali	2.57	4607	53
10.	Telaga(C)	1.17	4593	54
11.	Viswa Brahmin	2.33	4166	64
12.	Shia Muslim	3.61	4082	68
13.	Ediga	4.71	3581	81
14.	Golla	5.92	3389	87
15.	Mangali	1.21	3136	94
16.	Kummari	1.04	3101	95
17.	Besta	2.14	2879	101
18.	Rajaka	3.13	2758	103
19.	Mudiraj	3.66	2718	106
20.	Maala	7.58	2680	107
21.	Thorpu Kapu	2.34	2546	113
22.	Lambadi	2.02	2361	125
23.	Boya	1.89	2336	128
24.	Madiga	8.12	1985	137
25.	Waddar	1.71	1907	140

Source: Socio-Educational-Economic Survey Castes & Communities of Andhra Pradesh, 1998.

The list of castes based on ranks appeared much closer to popular perception of the people. Brahmins topped the list followed by Kamma, Reddy, Velama, Vaisya, Converted Christian and Kapu in the rank order based on composite index of forwardness. They all form part of the forward castes. The rank order as stated showed Munnuru Kaapu, Padma Saali, Telaga, Viswa Brahmin, Muslim, Ediga (Goud), Golla (Yadav), Mangali, Kummari, Besta, Rajaka, and Mudiraj as middle and lower middle castes and in fact they have been categorized as OBCs by the government. The remaining castes in that rank order appeared as part of the fourth quarter of the present list are Maala, Thoorpu Kaapu, Lambadi, Boya, Maadiga and Waddar. Except Thoorpu Kaapu, Boya and Waddar who have been categorized as the most backward classes, the remaining that appeared in the last quartile belong to SC/ST.

By any standard the Index of Forwardness reflects the political reality in relation to Kamma, Reddy, Velama and Kapu. Brahmins are relegated to insignificant position in relation to political institutions in AP and the study has amply proved the fact. So is the case with OBCs and lower OBCs as they faced political exclusion and it is truly reflected in the analysis of caste and power. Muslims also figured among the OBCs reflecting the status of OBCs in terms of forwardness/backwardness. In terms of backwardness SCs and STs are relegated to the last position in the rank order of 25 castes. However, they got representation proportionate to their population in the legislative bodies but stand far away from exercising power because of their historically inherited social relations and undemocratic value system prevalent among the castes and communities. It is quite a disturbing fact that six decades of 'functioning democracy' could not eliminate the culture of inequality and systemic discrimination.

THE TWO SPACES

The state of Andhra Pradesh came into existence in 1956 with the merger of Telangana part of Hyderabad state and Andhra state having two different histories, cultures and social-political-developmental consciousness. Telangana was under feudal rule for a very long time whereas Andhra areas under the direct rule of the British having the culture of modernization. Geographically, Telangana and Andhra differ from one another.

Developmentally speaking, before independence the spaces of Telangana and Andhra had undergone feudal and colonial economic practices respectively. Independent India brought both the entities under the same development mode of welfare lead modernization. The state of Andhra Pradesh has been pursuing globalization since 1995. Thus the people and their economy have become the products of these three developmental modes.

Andhra Pradesh, having two cultures and consciousness, gave rise to two different levels of advantages to its people. The early exposure to colonial modernization gave an advantage to Andhra society to further gain from independent India's modernization. They had already undergone the experience of colonial modernization and it had shaped their thinking and attitude to equip with and participate in the development processes and programs. This is not so in the case of Telangana as the region and its communities had the experience of feudal relations, economy and culture. The differential advantages of modernization under the Andhra leadership made the two regions to continue to produce two different levels of cultures and consciousness. The statehood movement is the product of historical wrongs committed against Telangana and socio-cultural consciousness of its people.

MAPPING POWER

AP Legislative Assembly 1952-2009

Prior to the formation of the state of Andhra Pradesh in 1956, the two constituents—Telangana and Andhra (including Rayalaseema) existed as two independent political entities forming part of Hyderabad state and Madras state respectively. Andhra which was constituent of Madras Presidency later got separated and formed Andhra state in 1953. However, Telangana continued to remain the constituent part of Hyderabad state till 1956. Therefore Table 5.3 showing election data from 1952 to 2009 has to be examined based on the spatial changes taken place over the years.

During the first general elections in 1952, Telangana and Andhra (including Rayalaseema) had the strong presence of Congress and Communist parties. Communist party in Telangana contested as PDF and in Andhra as CPI. PDF won in 30 MLA constituencies, Congress in 35 and there were about 19 independents/others. The Communists had a strong base among people as they were leading an armed struggle against feudal landlords during the 1940s and early fifties. In Andhra, CPI won 21 seats and Congress 19 seats and independents and others 47 seats. In Rayalaseema the Congress could win 16 and CPI five and Independents and others 14 MLA constituencies.

After the formation of Andhra Pradesh state, the first government headed by Prakasam was pulled down and it led to midterm polls in 1955. In Andhra region Congress won 74 seats and CPI six and independents and others 59. In Rayalaseema Congress could win 44, CPI 10 and independents/others 14.

In fact until 1950 Brahmins dominated Andhra politics because of landedness, education and their participation in freedom movement. The factionalism and intra-party rivalry between two leaders, Prakasam and Pattabhi Sitaramaiah coming from Brahmin caste led Reddys to take advantage of it and they have dominated Andhra politics after 1950. In fact Reddys were patronized by Pattabhi himself.

During the second general elections in 1957 Andhra and Rayalaseema have not gone to polls but allowed to continue their MLAs from 1955 to 1962. Only Telangana part of AP was to go to elections in 1957 and there was a big victory for Congress with 67 seats and the strength of PDF had come down to 22. At one point of time communists were expected to form the government in AP (Andhra Pradesh). For the first time in 1962 all the constituents of AP had gone to polls together and the electoral outcome favored Congress once again. Congress won 65 seats in Telangana, 89 in Andhra and 23 in Rayalaseema. The main opposition headed by communists won 18 assembly seats in Telangana, 16 in Andhra and

Table 5.3: Andhra Pradesh: Legislative Assembly Elections (MLA) – Winners: 1952-2009

Region	*Party*	*1952*	*1957*	*1962*	*1967*	*1972*	*1978*	*1983*	*1985*	*1989*	*1994*	*1999*	*2004*	*2009*
Telangana	INC	35	67	65	64	79	12	42	16	50	5	41	45	51
	INC(I)						62							
	CPI			18	4	3	3	4	5	8	12		4	4
	CPM				4	1	5	5	2	4	8	2	6	1
	JP						12	1		1			2	
	PDF	30	22											
	SWT			3										
	SWP												1	
	BJS				1									
	BJP							2	3	5	2	9	1	2
	RPI				1									
	TDP							46**	50	21	65	54	10	39
	TRS												26	10
	PRP													2
	IND/Others	19	15	19	26	18	5		2	8	5	1		
	DMC*	18	19											
	MIM													7
	Muslimeen									1	1	4	4	
	TDP Rebal													1
	Loksatha													1
	PRP Rebal													1
Coastal Andhra	INC	19	74	89	72	107	15	11	21	93	11	29	100	74
	INC(I)						78							
	CPI	21	6	16	6	5	3		4		6		2	
	CPM				1		3		6	2	6		2	
	JP						35							
	SWT			7	18	1								
	BJS				2									
	BJP							1	3			2	1	
	BSP												1	
	RPI				1									
	TDP							125**	88	40	107	91	25	36
	TRS													0
	PRP													13
	IND/Others	47	59	28	30	21	5		6	4	7	4	7	
	DMC*	18	30											
Rayalaseema	INC	16	44	23	30	40	3	8	11	37	10	21	39	32
	INC(I)						36							
	JP						12		3					
	CPI	5	10	5	2		0		2		1			
	CPM				1		0		4	1	2		1	
	SWT			8	10	1								
	BJP								2			1		
	TDP							46**	30	13	43	35	17	17
	TRS													0
	PRP													3
	IND/Others	14	11	19	11	11	3		1	3	0		0	
	ICJ							1						

Source: Compiled from 'Andhra Pradesh at 50', Data News Features, Hyderabad. * Double Member Constituency **Includes independents

Note: 1. During 1952 elections Telangana formed part of Hyderabad State and Coastal Andhra and Rayalaseema were in Madras State.

2. Andhra State (consisting of CA & RS) came into existence in 1953. During 1955 the government was defeated and elections were conducted in 1955.
3. Andhra Pradesh (consisting of Telangana, CA & RS) came in to existence in 1956.
4. Assembly Elections were held in 1957 for Telangana but for Coastal Andhra and Rayalaseema the term of elected MLAs of 1955 had been extended up to 1962.
5. The system of Double Member Constituency was existent in 1952 and 1957.
6. The data related to 1978 – 2009 is shown in the maps.

five in Rayalaseema. Swatantra party made a dent in to AP politics winning three seats in Telangana, seven in Andhra and eight in Rayalaseema.

More parties entered assembly during 1967 elections. Because of the split of CPI in 1964, Congress got the advantage of capturing power in the fourth general elections. Communists came to the house as CPI and CPI (M). This time two more new parties, RPI and BJS, entered the Assembly. Swatantra continued to show its presence in the elections. In Telangana Congress won 64 seats, four each were of two communist parties and one each of RPI and BJS. In Andhra Congress won 72 constituencies, CPI-six, CPM-one, Swatantra 18, BJS-two and RPI-one. Congress continued to do well in Rayalaseema with 30, Swatanthra with 10, CPI with two and CPM with one. The Congress got split for the first time in 1969 at the national level. However it got victorious in the 1972 Assemby elections. The small parties disappeared in the elections with the Congress retaining the strong hold on state politics and communists fared in a marginal way.

The 1978 elections to state assembly were held in a different atmosphere. For the first time, the Congress was out of power at the center because of post- emergency political developments. Many parties had come together under JP movement and formed Janata Party and become victorious in 1977 general elections at the national level. Secondly, Congress got split for a second time and fought elections in 1978. Congress (I) became victorious and formed government on its own. The splintered groups in the form of Congress, Janata party along with communists entered the Assembly. Janata party won 12 seats in Telangana, 35 in Coastal Andhra and 12 in Rayalaseema. Subsequent to the elections all the groups got merged with Congress and the new identities disappeared.

Congress ruled the state for three decades continuously since the first general elections. The Congress rule in AP was essentially a Reddy rule with occasional exceptions. The Kammas under the leadership of NG Ranga were a force to reckon with in politics till the emergence of AP in 1956. They lost to combined strength of Reddys of Telangana and Rayalaseema in the state of Andhra Pradesh and got adjusted as secondary partners in the power arrangement. For the first time, the Reddy monopoly in AP politics was broken with the entry of TDP in 1983 under the leadership of NT Rama Rao, a cinema actor. Though he appeared to have come to power with 'Telugu Pride' as his catch phrase but it was essentially an assertion of Kammas and their long cherished aspiration to rule the state. Weaker sections have also rallied around him because of the resentment against the long rule of Reddys. TDP triumphed with large majority and the elected members were shown as independents by the election commission because of non recognition of party and also refusal of party symbol in the elections. TDP won 46 seats in Telangana, 125 in Coastal Andhra and 46 in Rayalaseema. We also see a few belonging to others in this category. Congress for the first time in the history of AP politics lost the election. Congress got 42 seats in Telangana, 11 in Coastal Andhra and eight in Rayalaseema. In fact OBCs got a small opportunity during the 1972 elections where in spite of opposition from Channa Reddy, the Brahmin leadership tried to push OBCs by giving more tickets.

There was a revolt within TDP, engineered by Nadendla Bhaskar Rao who became CM for a brief while. Once again NT Rama Rao (NTR) got reinstated in power. However NTR opted for dissolution of the house and went for polls. NTR came back to power once again with huge mandate in the 1985 elections. TDP won 50 MLAs in Telangana, 88 in Andhra and 30 in Rayalaseema. Communists got 23 in all three regions put together and it happened because of their alliance with TDP. BJP also got eight MLAs in alliance with TDP. Congress got 16 in Telangana, 21 in Andhra and 11 in Rayalaseema. TDP lost elections in 1989 to Congress. TDP won 21 in Telangana, 40 in Andhra and 13 in Rayalaseema. Where as Congress won 50 in Telangana, 93 in Andhra and 37 in Rayalaseema. Communists could secure 15 MLAs in AP Assembly.

Once again in the 1994 elections TDP won with a thumping majority: 65 in Telangana, 107 in Andhra and 43 in Rayalaseema. Congress could remain satisfied with five in Telangana, 11 in Andhra and 10 in Rayalaseema and all put together 26 and it is the lowest in the history of the Congress in AP. TDP could come back to power in 1999 elections under the leadership of N Chandrababu Naidu. The family feud made NTR to be out of power in 1995 and it was engineered by Naidu (his son-in-law) himself. NTR passed away much before the 1999 elections. This time TDP got 54 seats in Telangana, 91 in Andhra and 35 in Rayalaseema. Congress improved its position to 91 in the state assembly.

N Chandrababu Naidu pushed the agenda of globalization aggressively and the economic reforms he pursued alienated people from TDP and the party lost heavily to Congress alliance in the 2004 elections. TDP could get 10 seats in Telangana, 25 in Andhra and 17 in Rayalaseema. Naidu's globalization made communists to leave alliance with TDP. In 2004 elections communists entered in to an alliance with Congress. Congress also entered in to an alliance with TRS, working for statehood for Telangana. Communists won 15 seats and TRS 26 seats. Congress won 45 in Telangana, 100 in Andhra and 39 in Rayalaseema. Under the leadership of YS Rajasekhar Reddy, Congress pursued Globalisation/economic reforms in much more aggressive way compared to Naidu. The alliance partners, CPI, CPM, TRS left Congress and farmed a grand alliance with TDP and fought elections in 2009. However TDP and its allies (TDP+) lost the elections. The alliance partners also lost heavily. CPI got four seats, CPM one and TRS 10. TDP improved its position by cornering 91 MLAs of which 39 are from Telangana, 36 from Andhra and 17 from Rayalaseema. PRP's role as the third political center failed to succeed electorally though it could split Congress and TDP vote equally and won 18 seats. Congress got 157 MLAs of which 51 are from Telangana, 74 from Andhra and 32 from Rayalaseema. Inspite of aggressive Economic reforms pursued by YSR, The Congress could come back to power as it had also taken up pro-poor welfare policies. Some of the policies of Congress headed UPA government were supported by the left and other democratic parties at the national level which softened the immediate adverse effects of Globalization.

LOKSABHA MEMBERS ANDHRA PRADESH: 1952-2009

So far from 1952 to 2009 fifteen general elections have been held as part of national elections. Several parties have participated in the Loksabha elections in AP. Some were present initially and a few disappeared from AP's political scenario. Later a few new parties cropped up.

Congress had significant presence all through the period but sometimes it was sweeping the whole space. Communists contested initially under two banners, in Andhra they contested under CPI and in Telangana as Progressive Democratic Front (PDF). In 1952 they performed well by winning 12 MPs and four in 1957. CPI got split in 1964 because of which they did not recover much afterwards except making their presence felt in a couple of constituencies that too because of being alliance partners. Socialists, KMPP and SCF made their mark in 1952 and after the emergence of AP they disappeared from the electoral scenario. For a brief while, Telangana Praja Samithi swept the polls by winning 10 out of 14 seats in Telangana and it had happened because of a separate Telangana movement. Afterwards TPS got merged with Congress and disappeared from Telangana. The emergence of Telugu Desam Party in 1982 stalled the Congress monopoly of AP politics. TDP continued as a dominant regional party resisting Congress till 1999. From 2004 onwards TDP got marginalized and Congress reestablished their dominance. Telangana Rastra Samithi was established in 2001 and as an alliance partner of Congress in 2004 it won five MPs, later two in the company of TDP and others. For the last several general elections, MIM has been winning in Hyderabad constituency.

Table 5.4: Andhra Pradesh: Loksabha Members: 1952-2009

Sl. No	*Party*	*1952*	*1957*	*1962*	*1967*	*1971*	*1977*	*1980*	*1984*	*1989*	*1991*	*1996*	*1998*	*1999*	*2004*	*2009*
1.	INC	14	37	34	35	28	41	41	6	39	25	22	22	5	29	33
2.	BJP	–	0	0	0	0	1	–	1	0	1	0	4	7	–	–
3.	Janatha	–	–	1	3	0	–	–	–	0	0		1		–	–
4.	CPI	–	2	7	1	1	0	0	1	0	1	2	2	0	1	0
5.	CPM	–	–	–	0	1	0	0	1	0	1	1	0	0	1	0
6.	MIM/AIMIM	1	0	–	–	–	–	–	–	1	1	1	1	1	1	1
7.	TPF/PDF	7	2	–	–	10	–	–	–	–	–	0	0	0	–	–
8.	Socialis	1	0	0	0	–	–	–	–	–	–		0	0	–	–
9.	TDP	–	–	–	–	–	–	–	30	2	13	16	12	29	5	6
10.	TRS	–	–	–	–	–	–	–	–	–	–				5	2
11.	PRP	–	–	–	–	–	–	–	–	–	–	–	–	–	–	–
12.	IND	1	2	1	2	1	0	0	1	0	0	0	0	0	0	0
	Total	**24**	**43**	**43**	**41**	**41**	**42**	**41**	**40**	**42**	**42**	**42**	**42**	**42**	**42**	**42**

Source: Telugu Theerpu

PARTY MLAs BY DISTRICT-2009

District level analysis of the presence or absence of parties (Table 5.5) and their MLAs show that the main political parties, Congress and TDP, also suffered from marginalization in a couple of districts. Otherwise they used to be two important players in all the districts. Congress is reduced to be a marginal one in Adilabad and Nizamabad districts. TDP also suffered from the absence of its MLAs from Hyderabad and marginal presence in Medak, Srikakulam, Prakasam, Kadapa and Vizianagaram districts. Congress is very strong in several districts and they are—Guntur, Prakasam, Medak, Srikakulam, Vizianagaram, Kadapa, etc. TDP is stronger in Mahabubnagar and Krishna districts. Both of them demonstrate moderately in other districts. PRP is present only in 10 districts and they did not open their account in the remaining 13 districts. PRP does not exist in eight out of 10 districts of Telangana.

Table 5.5: Andhra Pradesh: District-wise Tally of Assembly Seats: 2009

Districts	*Cong*	*TDP*	*PRP*	*TRS*	*CPI (M)*	*CPI*	*BJP*	*Lok Satta*	*MIM*	*Others*
Adilabad	1	4	1	3	–	1	–	–	–	–
Karimnagar	3	5	–	4	–	–	–	–	–	1
Nizamabad	1	5	1	1	–	–	1	–	–	–
Medak	8	1	–	1	–	–	–	–	–	–
Hyderabad	7	–	–	–	–	–	1	–	7	–
Rangareddy	7	5	–	–	–	–	–	1	–	1
Mahabubnagar	4	9	–	–	–	–	–	–	–	1
Nalgonda	7	3	–	–	1	1	–	–	–	–
Warangal	7	4	–	1	–	–	–	–	–	–
Khammam	5	3	–	–	–	2	–	–	–	–
Srikakulam	9	1	–	–	–	–	–	–	–	–
Vizianagaram	7	2	–	–	–	–	–	–	–	–
Visakhapatnam	7	4	4	–	–	–	–	–	–	–
East Godavari	10	5	4	–	–	–	–	–	–	–
West Godavari	9	5	1	–	–	–	–	–	–	–
Krishna	6	8	2	–	–	–	–	–	–	–
Guntur	11	6	–	–	–	–	–	–	–	–
Prakasam	10	1	1	–	–	–	–	–	–	–
Nellore	4	5	1	–	–	–	–	–	–	–
Kurnool	8	4	2	–	–	–	–	–	–	–
Anantapur	8	6	–	–	–	–	–	–	–	–
Kadapa	9	1	–	–	–	–	–	–	–	–
Chittoor	7	6	1	–	–	–	–	–	–	–
Total	**157**	**91**	**18**	**10**	**1**	**4**	**2**	**1**	**7**	**3**

TRS, CPI, CPM, the alliance partners of TDP, also suffered for want of their presence in many districts. TRS is a party confined to Telangana and it is seen in five districs only and that too it has a low to very low presence. In the rest of the five districts of Telangana, it did not send MLAs to the legislative assembly. In fact, it is a very poor reflection on the party. Telangana movement in many districts is strong and people do not identify with TRS alone. Others also pretend that they are working for Telangana state. CPI won four of which one each was from Adilabad and Nalgonda and two were from Khammam district. CPM's lone MLA in the assembly is from Nalgonda district. Apart from them communists do not exist in any other district. Excepting three districts of Telangana they do not have a presence, MLA wise, in the other districts and it is the same with the two other regions—Andhra and Rayalaseema. BJP won one each from Hyderabad and Nizamabad districts. In Andhra and Rayalaseema they do not exist at all. MIM has seven members in the assembly and all of them come from Hyderabad only. The rest of Andhra Pradesh is devoid of its presence. Lok Satta has one member in the assembly and that too from Hyderabad only.

SWING IN ELECTIONS

Voter shifts in Assembly and Parliament elections for the years 2004-2009 have been analyzed based on the data generated by CSDS (Table 5.6). Vote loss is shown across all parties, ruling and opposition, because of the entry of PRP and Lok Satta during 2009 elections. The loss of vote of major political parties is registered in both assembly and parliament elections. The TDP's vote loss in assembly is very significant by 9.47 per cent and it is followed by TRS. The loss of TRS vote is 2.76 per cent. Congress' loss of vote is 1.97 per cent and CPI/CPM 0.86 per cent. BJP gained marginally and it is because they contested in large number of seats this time. PRP, the newly entered party in to the electoral fray could corner 16.12 per cent votes.

Table 5.6: Swing in Assembly Elections, Andhra Pradesh, 2004-2009

S. No.	*Party*	*2009*		*2004*		*Loss or gain*
		Vote share%	*Seats*	*Vote share%*	*Seats*	
1	Congress	36.53	157	38.50	185	–1.97 (–28)
2	TDP	28.03	91	37.50	47	–9.47 (–44)
3	TRS	3.99	10	6.75	26	–2.76 (–16)
4	CPI/CPM	2.52	5	3.38	15	–0.86 (10)
5	BJP	2.97	2	2.66	2	0.31 (0)
6	PRP	16.12	18	—	—	+16.12
7	Lok Satta	1.75	1	—	—	+1.75
8	Others	8.09	7	11.23	19	–3.14 (12)

Source: NES 2009/ The Hindu, May 26, 2009

Though there is a significant loss of vote for TDP but it registered a substantial gain in terms of seats. With the strength of 47 MLAs in 2004, TDP won 91 seats in 2009. In the case of the Congress, seat share has come down from 185 to 157 in the legislative assembly. TRS fared badly and in terms of change it has come down from 26 to 10. So is the case with CPI/CPM where they have been brought down from 15 to five. PRP's vote share is substantial but it did not reflect in the number of seats and it won 18 only. BJP's strength remained unchanged with two and it amounts to almost absence of its existence in AP politics. However, it makes noise disproportionate to its strength. MIM is much bigger compared to BJP by seven MLAs and Lok Satta could open its account in assembly with one member.

Congress' vote share is higher in Loksabha (Table 5.7) compared to assembly and it got 38.95 per cent. TDP's per cent vote share has come down compared to Assembly and it got 24.93. TRS got 6.14 per cent vote in Loksabha polls and it is a little lower compared to previous elections. In the case of CPI/CPM there is an increase in its per cent vote share from 2.38 to 2.85. BJP's vote share declined drastically from 8.40 to 3.75. The change in the vote share is explained because of change of alliance partners—TRS and CPI/CPM, from Congress to TDP. Earlier BJP was in alliance with TDP and it was dumped from its alliance in the 2009 elections.

Table 5.7: Swing in Loksabha Elections, Andhra Pradesh, 2004-2009

S. No.	Party	2009		2004		Loss or gain
		Vote share%	Seats	Vote share%	Seats	
1	Congress	38.95	33	36.53	29	–2.59 (+4)
2	TDP	24.93	6	33.11	5	–8.18 (–1)
3	TRS	6.14	2	6.83	5	–0.69 (–3)
4	CPI/CPM	2.85	0	2.38	2	+0.47 (_2)
5	BJP	3.75	0	8.40	0	–4.65 (0)
6	PRP	15.76	0	–	–	+15.76
7	Lok Satta	1.32	0	–	–	+1.32
8	Others	6.30	1	7.73	1	–1.43 (0)

Source: NES 2009 / The Hindu, May 26, 2009

The loss of vote for Congress is higher in Loksabha polls compared to Assembly but it gained seat wise and moved from 29 to 33. The TDP's vote loss is less in Loksabha polls compared to Assembly. But seats secured by TDP are six with difference of one from its previous performance. TRS moved down from five to two and CPI/CPM came out with a blank against their winning in two Loksabha constituencies previously. MIM retained its hold over its lone seat. PRP got a substantial vote in Loksabha but failed to open its account in Loksabha. As expected, BJP remained where they are having no member from AP in Loksabha.

The tri-cornered contest of 2009 elections as against straight fight of alliances in 2004 caused loss of power to TDP. With great hopes of coming to power by cinema actor headed party, the PRP had to end up by winding up its party in due course of time. The PRP's slogan of social justice remained a far cry. Perhaps future political initiatives have to articulate the agenda of social justice as it has not been attempted meaningfully by the organic leadership in mobilizing masses and tapping their simmering democratic aspirations.

WINNER BY MAJORITY

Table 5.8 shows the regional analysis of winners' majority of votes based on political parties. The majority votes obtained by the winners are divided in to various classes. There are 12 winners at the state level in the lowest category of less than 500 majority votes and it is followed by seven with a 500-1000 majority, 24 with a 1000-2000 majority, 23 with a 2000-3000 majority, 28 with a 3000-5000 majority, 75 with a 5000-10000 majority and 125 with more than 10000 majority. Any group or party that influences 2000 voters can change the status of a party whether it has to be in power or out of power. Almost one third of the elected members won with comfortable majority of 10000 and above. About 114 MLAs have won with less than 5000 votes. It is likely that a little shift in vote would bring in a sea change in power arrangement.

Table 5.8: Andhra Pradesh Elections 2009

		<500	*500-1000*	*1000-2000*	*2000-3000*	*3000-5000*	*5000-10000*	*>10000*
Telangana	INC	3		6	4	3	15	19
	TDP	1	1	1	4	2	9	21
	TRS	1		1			2	6
	AIMIM						2	5
	CPI				1	1	1	1
	PRP				1		1	
	IND				1		1	1
	CPM					1		
	BJP							2
	LSP							1
Coastal Andhra	INC	4	4	7	5	8	19	27
	TDP		2	2	3	5	10	14
	TRS							
	AIMIM							
	CPI							
	PRP	2		1	2	2	4	2
	IND							
Rayalaseema	INC			2	1	5	9	15
	TDP	2		3	1	1	2	8
	TRS							
	AIMIM							
	CPI							
	PRP			1				2
	IND							
Andhra Pradesh	INC	7	4	15	10	16	43	61
	TDP	3	3	6	8	8	21	42
	TRS	1		1			2	6
	AIMIM						2	5
	CPI				1	1	1	1
	PRP	2		2	3		5	6
	IND			1	1		1	1
	CPM					1		

Source: Compiled from a Telugu Daily

Regionally speaking there is a broad commonality of victory margins between Telangana and Andhra but Rayalaseema varied in relation to upper margins as the contestants have won with more majorities. 32 out of 119 won with less than 5000 majority in Telangana; 47 out of 123 won in the same class in Andhra and 16 out of 52 won in Rayalaseema. The remaining got elected in above 5000 vote category in all the three regions.

ELECTORAL/POLITICAL PROCESS

B Forms/Party Tickets and Caste

These days an aspirant in politics needs to have an access to capital accrued through globalization coupled with dominant caste identity and he/she will be qualified to be a big leader instantaneously. The party and its cadre accept him/her at the cost of its member/

leader coming from backward social group and working for people for long. The financial worth and the candidate's affordability of electoral expenditure becomes the basis of identifying contestants. Parties believe that caste base and money power determine the winnability of the contesting candidates. Distribution of B Forms/tickets by parties by and large forecloses the possibility of a social group entering in to the corridors of power. Democratic principle of equality is given a go by while choosing contestants and issuing B Forms during elections. Political inclusion and pluralizing social base remain a political rhetoric. The following explains how a few politically dominant castes matter in B Form/ticket distribution.

Table 5.9 : Party Tickets distributed to MLA Contestants Elections in Andhra Pradesh – Caste-wise-2009

Sl.No.	*Caste*	*Congress*	*Mahakutami (TDP+)*	*PRP*
1	Reddy	88	66	42
2	Kapu	14	8	37
3	Kamma	16	46	11
4	Vaisya	5	3	5
5	Velama	8	12	4
6	Ksathriya	5	9	2
7	Brahmin	4	1	1
8	Others	7	0	0
	Total	**147**	**145**	**102**
9	Madiga	23	21	19
10	Mala	25	28	31
	SC Total	**48**	**49**	**50**
11	Lambada	6	5	12
12	Koya	6	6	4
13	Others	7	6	7
	ST Total	19	17	23
14	Munnurukapu	9	8	13
15	Yadav	11	7	12
16	Gouda/Settibalija	10	14	13
17	Mudiraj	6	3	9
18	Padmasali	3	4	7
19	Koppula Velama	7	8	7
20	Turpukapu	7	3	6
21	Boya	2	1	5
22	Mthsyakarulu	3	4	2
23	Kalinga	2	2	2
24	**Other BCs**	**9**	**17**	**28**
	OBC Total	**69**	**71**	**104**
25	Minorities	11	12	15

Source: Eenadu 5.4.2009 & Vaartha 10.4.2009.
Note: MahaKutami (TDP+) is an alliance of TDP,TRS,CPI,CPM.

Table 5.9 shows distribution of B Forms to MLA contestants and their caste base during the 2009 elections. Congress party gave 88 B Forms and TDP 47 B Forms to Reddys. In fact 'Mahakutami' (Grand Alliance- TDP+) distributed 64 B Forms. If we go by proportion of Reddy population of six per cent they should get about 18 B Forms. Kamma's are expected to get 11 B Forms according to their population of 3.69 but got 41 from TDP (45 from Mahakutami) and 16 from Congress. When it comes to Kapus, which is another important political community, Congress issued 14, TDP 5 and PRP 37 against their proportion of 15. The distribution pattern of B Forms shows how partisan parties are in promoting their own caste and their leadership. It establishes the fact that the Reddys see congress as their party, Kammas, TDP and Kapus PRP. This amounts to obstructing democracy and doing away with the principle of equality.

Velama caste being a miniscule minority with 0.46 per cent population is expected to get about 1 B Form but got eight from Congress and 11 from Mahakutami. This shows how powerful the velama caste is. Brahmins were to have six B Forms but got four from Congress and none from Mahakutami. Vaisyas were to have about nine B Forms but received five from Congress and three from Mahakutami. Though Brahmins and Vaisyas belong to forward category they are neglected politically.

While examining the distribution of B Forms to OBCs it is found that according to their population they were expected to get about 150 B Forms but Congress gave 69 and TDP+ gave only 71. A gross neglect of OBCs is taking place in allocating B Forms. Muslims were expected to get 28 but Congress gave 11 and TDP+ 12. They are equally denied of opportunity of getting B Forms. It is a gross injustice committed against Muslims and other Minorities by all political parties. The legitimate share that is expected of by Brahmins, Vaisyas, OBCs and Muslims was cornered by Reddy, Kamma and Velama castes.

Among the OBCs, Yadavs constitute the largest population of 7.61 per cent and they were expected to get 23 B Forms but received 11 from Congress, nine from TDP+. Gouds (including Settibalija) occupy second place in OBCs with over five per cent population and they were expected to get about 15 B Forms but got 10 from Congress and four from TDP+. Mudhiraju constitutes about five per cent of population and they are third largest constituent of OBC population. They are expected to get 15 B Forms but received six from Congress and five from TDP+.

The other numerically significant constituents of OBCs are Rajaka 3.13 per cent, Padmasali 2.57 per cent, Viswabrahmin 2.41 per cent, Turpukapu 2.34 per cent, Matsyakar 2.14 per cent, Koppula Velama 1.62 per cent, Munnurukapu 1.52 per cent etc. Dozens of castes of OBCs have not been given B Forms so far by any of the political parties. SCs and STs, because of their social, economic and educational backwardness, have got constitutional reservation in politics and therefore they get B Forms proportion to their population. However, several small castes and tribes within SC/ST do not figure in B Form distribution. SC/ST get representation proportionate to their population in legislative bodies but they are denied of power because of parties being controlled by dominant castes.

Table 5.10 shows the distribution of tickets to contestants in Loksabha election during 2009. Out of 42 constituencies FCs got 20, OBCs10, Minority one and the remaining eight were for SC and three for ST from congress. The TDP+ gave FCs 16, OBCs 12, SC seven and ST three. Paradoxically enough Congress gave one general ticket to SC.

Table 5.10: Ticket Distribution to Loksabha Contestants in AP: 2009

Sl.No.	Caste	Congress	TDP/TRS/CPI/CPM	PRP
1	OBC	10	12	14
2	SC	8	7	7
3	ST	3	3	3
4	OC	20	16	12
5	Minority	1	4	6

Source: Eenadu 5.4.2009 and Vaartha 10.4.2009

TRI-CORNER/STRAIGHT CONTESTS AMONG/ACROSS CASTE

There are 63 constituencies in AP where same caste people contested from all the three dominant parties or alliances. In Coastal Andhra such constituencies are 29; in Telangana 20 and in Rayalaseema 14. Reddys contested in 18 constituencies, Malas in 10, Madigas in seven, Kammas in six, Lambada and Velama in five each, Kapu and Koya in three each, Jathapu is two and Bagatha, Kalinga, Kuruma/Yadav and Muslim in one each. Tri-cornered contests of Reddys are more i.e. ten in Rayalaseema. So is the case with Malas with eight and Kammas with six in Andhra region. In Telangana six such constituencies have been contested by Reddys, five by Lambadas and four by Madigas (Table 5.11).

Table 5.11: Andhra Pradesh: Caste primacy in Constituencies

Sl. No.	Same contesting caste from all parties	Telangana	Coastal Andhra	Rayalaseema	Andhra Pradesh
1.	Reddy[3]	6	2	10	18
2.	Mala[3]	1	8	1	10
3.	Madiga[3]	4	1	2	7
4.	Kamma[3]	–	6	–	6
5.	Lambada[3]	5	–	–	5
6.	Velama+[3]	1	4	–	5
7.	Kapu[3]	–	3	–	3
8.	Koya[3]	2	1	–	3
9.	Jathapu[3]	–	2	–	2
10.	Bagatha[3]	–	1	–	1
11.	Kalinga[3]	–	1	–	1
12.	Kuruma[3]	–	–	1	1
13.	Muslim[3]	1	–	–	1

Note: Caste [3] = same caste from 3 dominating parties (Congress, TDP + and PRP).
Velama+[3] = Velama, Koppula Velama and Polinati Velama.

Normally same caste people contest from three sides in areas where the presence of that particular caste is dominant and influence the electoral outcome. The absence of OBCs in such tri-corner contest is explained because of competition among unequals in the sense of commanding political resources.

In order to cover-up caste bias, the leadership argues that OBCs and Muslims cannot win elections against general constituencies. But the analysis of the facts mentioned in the table in relation to OBCs proves the argument wrong. It is found that the lie is perpetuated by the leadership to keep OBCs and Muslims away from political power. The details are mentioned as follows Table 5.12.

Table 5.12: Andhra Pradesh Assembly Elections: 2009

Sl. No	*Winner Caste/Community Versus Runner Caste/Community*		*Winners*			
	Winner	*Runner*	*Telangana*	*Coastal Andhra*	*Rayalaseema*	*Andhra Pradesh*
1.	Reddy	Reddy	23	8	17	48
2.	Kamma	Kamma	–	12	–	12
3.	Kapu	Kapu	–	3	–	3
4.	Velama	Velama	3	–	–	3
5.	OBC	OBC	7	16	2	25
6.	Reddy	OBC	10	3	5	18
7.	OBC	Reddy	7	3	2	12
8.	OBC	Kamma	2	5	1	8
9.	Kamma	OBC	2	3	–	5
10.	Reddy	Kamma	1	5	1	7
11.	Kamma	Reddy	–	1	6	7
12.	Kapu	OBC	–	6	–	6
13.	OBC	Kapu	–	2	–	2
14.	Velama	Reddy	4	–	–	4
15.	Reddy	Velama	1	–	–	1
16.	SC	SC	19	20	9	48
17.	ST	ST	12	7	–	19
18.	Muslim	Muslim	5	–	–	5

Compiled from Newspapers.

The contests held across the social groups show that OBCs won in 12 constituencies against Reddys; eight against Kammas and two against Kapus. Whereas Reddys won 18 against OBCs, Kammas won five seats, against OBCs and Kapus won six seats against OBCs. When the contests were held among dominant castes, Reddys won seven against Kammas and one against Velama. Kammas won seven against Reddys and Velamas four against Reddys. This adequately proves the fact that if B Forms are given to OBCs, they can win against Reddys, Kammas and Kapus. Therefore branding OBCs in general category as losers is baseless. In fact OBCs, Muslims and women fare well if they are given their due.

While examining the winner and runner categories of the contestants of same caste/community is found that the Reddys are both winners and runners in 48 constituencies of 233 and it is 12 among Kammas, three each in Kapus and Velamas, 25 in OBCs and five in Muslims. The under representation of OBCs and Muslims in legislative bodies is not because of their lack of winnability but because of political prejudice and non issue of B Forms. The process of political exclusion of women, OBC and Muslim happens before the electoral battle begins. The political exclusion is systemic and it is built in favor of the politically privileged.

VOTING BY CLASS, GENDER AND CASTE/COMMUNITY

We have seen how parties showed bias in ticket distribution and now we see how different social groups respond to parties and their contestants. Do we also find any pattern that we have seen in ticket distribution? It can be explained in the following analysis (Table 5.13). Here we have used the survey done by the CSRD, a research centre, and results appeared in Hindu, English news daily. The major categories identified in studying voting pattern are Class, Gender and Caste-community.

Very poor, poor, lower middle class and upper classes have shown uniformity in voting for the Congress Party and it is more or less uniform, though that for TDP+ is low except for the Middle and upper classes. In fact upper classes benefited most because of TDP's policies of globalization. However TDP could have had problems because of its alliance partners where two more agendas like anti-globalization approach of communists and statehood movement of TRS are concerned and these could not be taken kindly by the aggressive middle and upper classes. They have responded more positively towards Congress as Congress carried forward the globalization policies in a more aggressive way and benefits might have trickled more in favor of these classes. Secondly the statehood agenda is cleverly manipulated by Congress.

Table 5.13: Andhra Pradesh Elections: Voting Pattern–2009

Sl. No.	*Social background*	*Congress*	*TDP/CPI/CPM/TRS*	*PRP*
	Gender	*%*	*%*	*%*
1.	Male	44.9	33.3	11.5
2.	Female	41.3	37.2	13.5
Economic Class				
3	Very poor	45.5	41.2	8.6
4	Poor	42.9	39.6	12.6
5	Lower	43.6	38.1	12.3
6	Middle	42.2	33.2	14.0
7	Upper	43.0	27.8	10.9
Caste - community				
8	Upper castes	38.2	33.7	4.5
9	Reddys	65.9	20.1	3.4
10	Kammas	21.0	63.7	7.3
11	Kapus	30.8	16.2	53.1
12	Yadavs	35.0	45.9	10.8
13	Gouds	36.4	40.3	10.8
14	Other OBCs	38.3	37.7	15.5
15	Malas	51.0	28.8	13.5
16	Madigas	47.7	46.1	4.7
17	STs	54.3	33.3	7.2
18	Muslims	50.7	24.8	6.9

Source: NES 2009 / The Hindu May 26, 2009.

When it comes to Gender, male and female social groups have sided more with Congress. TDP+, received comparatively low response from male and female groups but females are slightly kind towards it.

The real contentious category of caste in power and politics comes in true colors in extending allegiance towards political parties. Among the upper castes, as survey has put it, Reddys in large percentage i.e., 65.9 have identified with the Congress in voting. If we recall ticket distribution the Congress Party gave highest number of seats to this social group and Reddy voters in large numbers identified with the party. This may conclude the fact that the Reddy voters are voting largely on caste lines as they think Congress is Reddy Party. Only 20 per cent voted for the TDP+. It could be because of Reddy contestents in the alliance apart from other factors.

While analyzing the voting pattern of Kammas, it is equally revealing that Kammas have voted TDP+ to the extent of 63.71 per cent and for Congress to the extent of 21 per cent. Kammas behaved exactly like the Reddys in voting for their caste leadership. TDP, CPI and CPM are headed by Kamma leaders in the state and the pursuers of caste and class found comfort in voting for their caste and their leadership.

The third social group aspiring for power is Kapu and 53.1 per cent of them have voted for PRP. Cinema actor, Chiranjeevi, coming from the same caste headed the party. Kapus, by and large, thought of realizing their long cherished dream of wresting power from the two political castes-Reddy and Kamma, as both have been sharing power alternatively in the state. Kapus have also voted for Congress as they think that they are better represented in it. It could also be because of Reddys being called as Kapus in rural areas and at the same time they have a resentment against Kammas.

OBCs by and large split equally between Congress and TDP+ with a little edge in favour of TDP+. They have also cast their vote in favour of PRP and it could be because of the party's slogan of social justice. However, PRP did not appear serious about the agenda. Muslims have favoured Congress in a big way and it could be because of the extention of rule of reservation to the community.

SCs and STs have voted for Congress in a big way. Madigas tilted in favour of TDP+. SC, ST, OBC, Muslim and others from economically backward sections felt that the Congress had done slightly better compared to TDP in terms of the welfare of these communities. The subtle articulation of globalization and welfare programmes helped Congress to come back to power in 2009 elections.

STATUS OF WINNER BY REGION AND CASTE

Tables 5.14, Map 5.1 a, b and c and Fig. 5.1 show the details of elected members of legislative assembly in AP during 2009. Ticket distribution involves selection, in the process many individuals and groups get filtered and excluded before entering in to actual electoral battle. Thereby many social groups get axed before entering the legislative Assembly. Therefore, who should enter Assembly and who should not is predetermined by political parties and their leadership. It is obvious that the castes that lead parties have a soft corner towards

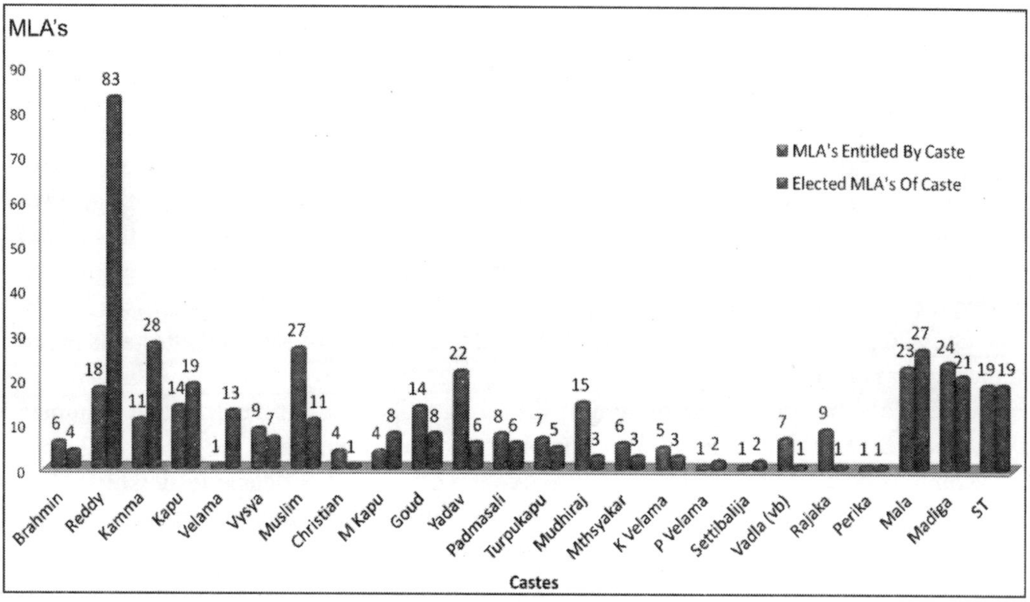

Fig. 5.1: AP Legislative Assembly Election—Relationship between Elected MLA's and Entitled by Caste, 2009

their kinship and castes and communities in decision making, besides others. Let us examine winners in relation to regions and castes as shown in the table and the details are given as follows.

Regional distribution of political power of castes shows that the dominant political caste, Reddy, cornered 83 MLAs of 294 Legislative Assembly members in AP during the 2009 elections. If we go by population share of the Reddys they are entitled to represent in about 18 constituencies. The results defy the democratic essence of equality of opportunity and it is open for individuals and social blocs to draw conclusions. Regionally speaking their presence is very strong in Rayalaseema by cornering 50 per cent of the constituencies i.e. 26 members of the regional total of 52 MLAs. The Reddys, continue to get a big share in Telangana with 40 out of 119 MLAs. They got 17 MLAs against the coastal Andhra total of 123 MLAs. This has happened because Reddys as population group is almost absent in seven to eight districts of total nine districts. The distribution of Reddy population is confined to adjoining tracts of Rayalaseema-Nellore, Prakasam and Guntur districts.

The Kammas won 28 seats and they constitute the second largest social group representing the state assembly. If we go by their share in population they needed to be represented in 11 constituencies. The regional spread shows that they have won 18 seats in coastal Andhra, four in Telangana and six in Rayalaseema. The large presence of Kamma legislators from Andhra can be explained, as population wise, they are largely located in Krishna, Guntur and Prakasam districts of Andhra region. They have a few migratory pockets in two other regions and therefore they are restricted to small tracts. The presence and visibility of Kammas in power has gone up manifold with the TDP coming to power in 1983.

Table 5.14: AP Legislative Assembly Elections (MLA)- Winners – Region/ Caste – 2009

Sl.No.	Caste	Telangana	Coastal Andhra	Rayalaseema	AP 2009
1	Brahmin	2	2	–	4
2	Reddy	40	17	26	83
3	Kamma	4	18	6	28
4	Kapu	–	18	1	19
5	Velama	11	2	–	13
6	Raju	–	7	–	7
7	Vysya	–	5	2	7
	Total	**57**	**69**	**35**	**161**
8	Muslim	7	1	3	11
9	Christian	1	–	–	1
	Total	**8**	**1**	**3**	**12**
10	M Kapu	8	–	–	8
11	Goud	5	1	2	8
12	Yadav	2	3	1	6
13	Padmasali	3	2	1	6
14	Turpukapu	–	5	–	5
15	Mudhiraj	3	–	–	3
16	Mthsyakar	–	3	–	3
17	K Velama	–	3	–	3
18	P Velama	–	2	–	2
19	Kalinga	–	3	–	3
20	Turpukapu				
21	Settibalija	–	2	–	2
22	Vadla	–	1	–	1
23	Rajaka	1	–	–	1
24	Perika	1	–	–	1
25	Gavara	–	1	–	1
	OBC Total	**23**	**26**	**5**	**54**
26	Mala	8	14	5	27
27	Madiga	11	6	4	21
	SC Total	**19**	**20**	**9**	**48**
28	Lambada	5	–	–	5
29	Koya	5	1	–	6
30	Gond	2	–	–	2
31	Kondadora	–	1	–	1
32	Bagatha	–	2	–	2
33	Jathapu	–	2	–	2
34	Kondareddy	–	1	–	1
	ST Total	**12**	**7**	**–**	**19**
	Total	**119**	**123**	**52**	**294**

Source: Compiled from Surya Telugu Daily, May 17, 2009.

Kapus have won in 19 constituencies in the state and they represent largely from the districts confining to the Godavari delta. 18 MLAs have been contributed to the kitty of Kapus from Andhra alone. Only one person got elected from Rayalaseema. The explanation for Kapus getting confined to small geographical tract goes with its population distribution. As per their population share they needed to represent in about 15 MLA constituencies.

Velamas constitute 0.46 per cent of state's population and accordingly they are entitled to have about one seat in the legislative assembly. The phenomenal presence of 13 MLAs in the state Assembly defies all explanations of social democratic principle. However some may argue that the election is through democratic method and one cannot find problem with it. This may amount to the justification of excessive presence of a social group denying democratic opportunity to the others. The inherent flaw of the system facilitating the strong and cornering a big share needs to be explained by the parties and their leadership. 11 of the 13 Velama MLAs have been contributed from Telangana region alone. There is a similar social group having common caste ties called Koppula Velama and Polinati Velama in Andhra and they are categorized as OBCs. Together they won five seats from Andhra besides 13 seats won by Velamas in general.

Once again Raju is numerically a small caste but they won in seven constituencies. Vaisyas have improved their position by winning seven seats against their share of nine and all of them got elected from Andhra only, though they are found all over AP. Brahmins have won four MLAs. Two each have been contributed by Telangana and Andhra regions. In fact, they should have had six MLAs according to their population.

Other social groups which had to contest from general seats are OBCs and Minorities. OBCs constitute about half of AP population and they are entitled for 150 seats. However, they got elected in 54 constituencies and it comes to about 18 per cent of the members of the state legislative assembly. There are about 142 castes categorized as OBCs by AP government of which a large number of castes do not even figure in the lists of MLAs. Many of these castes have not stepped in to the legislative assembly since its inception. This is a major aberration of practicing democracy.

There are only 15 castes out of 142 of OBC castes contributing MLAs to the state legislative assembly and none of these castes represent to the proportions of their population except Munnur Kapus. A dozen castes from OBC appear in assembly but their presence is highly skewed. To state a few, six Yadavs are elected to Assembly against their entitlement for 23 MLAs. So is the case with Gouds/Settibalijas who won 10 against the entitlement of 15; Mudhiraj three against 15; Rajaka one against nine; Viswabrahmin one against seven; Masthyakar three against six; Turpukapu five against seven etc. Mangalis have significant population in the state and it is distributed all over AP and they are totally left unrepresented. Political parties do not even think of accommodating aspirations of several such social groups while developing leadership and issuing tickets. They have been crippled because of numerous social, educational and development problems faced by these social groups. The nomadic, semi nomadic and denotified segments categorized as OBCs are in fact leading a subhuman life and they are all left unrepresented in the legislative bodies.

Muslims are the single largest social group in AP having 9.2 per cent of population. They have won 11 MLAs against their entitlement of 28. Seven of them have been contributed from Telangana that too from Hyderbad and three from Rayalaseema and one from Andhra. Hyderabad alone has 41.2 per cent Muslim population and Rayalaseema 12.5 per cent, Telangana 12.4 per cent and Andhra 4.5 per cent. This is another major social group that got denied of legitimate space in AP legislative assembly.

Because of constitutional reservation SCs and STs have their own share in legislative bodies. However there are numerous smaller groups within them that are left unrepresented in the assembly. Many of them have not even walked in the corridors of power since the inception of the Assembly.

There is a serious problem with current political dispensation as only moneyed and influential political families/castes could corner a major share of political power in the name of elections and parties. This also has corresponding influence in sharing developmental and institutional spaces and that has led to severe imbalances in the society. Democracy cannot afford to live with it as the presence of caste and casteisation of power negates the very meaning and purpose of democracy.

Mapping of MLAs belonging to different social groups/castes/communities for the elections of 2004 and 2009 in AP has been given. It in fact gives a spatial view of elected representatives belonging to different castes and communities. The change in the representation of MLAs from different social groups between 2004 and 2009 elections is given here (Map 5.1 a, b, c and d).

Reddys and Kammas are found predominantly in both the elections but Reddy MLAs have come down from 94 in 2004 to 83 in 2009 and Kamma legislatures from 36 to 28. The partial reduction of legislators in 2009 could be attributed to the sustained campaigns of the agenda of social justice and also the emergence of PRP as a third alternative in AP politics. Velamas improved phenomenally and TRS headed by a Velama also contributed towards this rise. Vysyas also improved from 3 to 7 and Brahmins remained where they are. Kapus have come down marginally from 21 to 19. However, they still exceed the entitled share of population.

There is a rise of Madiga MLAs from 14 to 23 and this could be attributed to sustained Madiga moblisation taking place around their share within SCs for the last decade and a half. Among the STs there is a marginal increase of legislative representation of Lambadas, Koyas and Gonds. Muslims remain far behind from their entitlement and improved their tally by one MLA. There is a perceptible increase of Munnur Kapus and it is above their entitlement. Gouds improved their position from 9 to 10 and Yadavs from 5 to 7 during 2004 and 2009. Vaddara belonging to the most backward community appeared in 2004 and subsequently they did not figure among the elected representatives. For the first time an MLA from Vadla community got elected to the Assembly.

Mapping of elected Loksabha members (MPs) during 2009 in AP is also done (Map 5.1e). 20 castes/communities have represented in the 2009 Loksabha. Reddys captured the large share of Loksabha space with 12, followed by Kammas. About half a dozen OBC MPs have been elected to parliament. There is a an SC- Madiga elected to Loksabha from general constituency in 2009.

STATUS OF WOMEN BY REGION, PARTY AND CASTE

Here status of women by region, party and caste is examined from the table compiled below (Table 5.15). In 2009 elections women candidates have won in 31 constituencies contributing to about 10 per cent of the 294 Members of Legislative Assembly of the state. Regionally speaking Telangana contributed 14 MLAs to women against the regional total

Table 5.15: Andhra Pradesh Elections 2009 : Regional Pattern of Party/Caste background of Women MLAs

S. No	Caste	Telangana			Andhra			Rayalaseema			AP
		INC	TDP	PRP	INC	TDP	PRP	INC	TDP	PRP	
1	Reddy	4	1					1		1	7
2	Kamma							1	1		2
3	Kapu						1				1
4	Vysya				1						1
	OC TOTAL	**4**	**1**	**—**	**1**	**—**	**1**	**2**	**1**	**1**	**11**
5	Padmasali	1			1						2
6	K Velama					1					1
7	Kalinga				1						1
	BC TOTAL	**1**	**—**	**—**	**2**	**1**	**—**	**—**	**—**	**—**	**4**
8	Mala	1			3			1	1		6
9	Madiga				1	1		1			3
	SC TOTAL	**1**	**—**	**—**	**4**	**1**	**—**	**2**	**1**	**—**	**9**
10	Lambada	1	3								4
11	Koya	1	1								2
	ST TOTAL	**2**	**4**	**—**	**—**	**—**	**—**	**—**	**—**	**—**	**6**
12	Christian	1									1
	TOTAL	**9**	**5**	**—**	**7**	**2**	**1**	**4**	**2**	**1**	**31**

of 119, Andhra 10 against 123 and Rayalaseema seven against 52. Though they constitute about 50 per cent of the population, irrespective of region, their share is very low with less than 10 per cent. This amounts to making a mockery of democracy in the age of rising women assertion.

Status of women by party is explained by the fact that no party is good enough to call it as democratic and women sensitive. However, in all the three regions there is Congress that has an edge over TDP+. The bias is inbuilt in the party as women are considered hardly as equals in contesting for power. Often it happens that family member of a male leader is substituted with women contestants. Politics is still a male dominated zone.

Status of women by caste is explained by women belonging to politically significant social groups in general category and social groups having constitutional reservations as they are found in the assembly: Reddys won seven, Mala six, Lambada four, Madiga three, Kamma two, Padmasali two and Christian one. Large number of castes from general category belonging to Brahmin, Vaisya, OBC and Muslims are left unrepresented in the women category. Political class which is male dominated refuses to recognize that women from different categories would contribute greater wisdom in legislation and policy making.

THE LINE OF PROPORTIONATE REPRESENTATION

The Fig. 5.1a and 5.1b have been constructed based on social category/caste on X axis and the population proportion versus legislative representation on Y axis. The line graph developed explained largely three trends. The Zero line is Line of Equal Representation where population

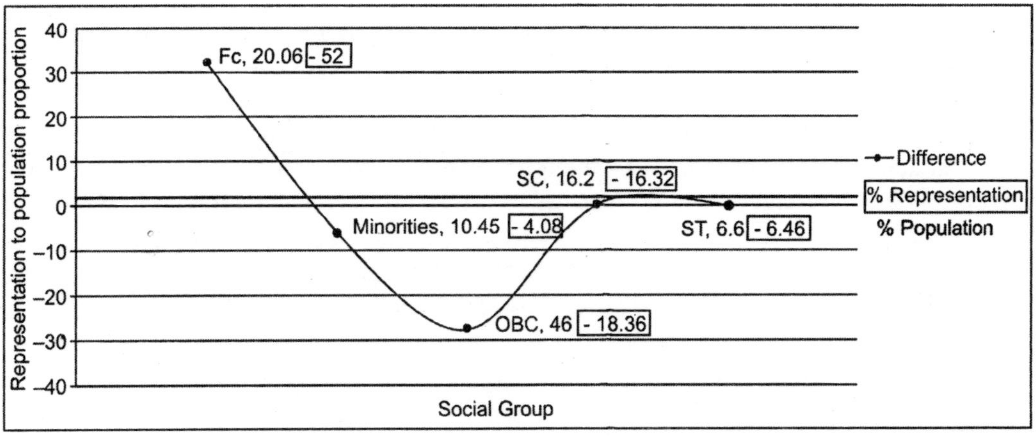

Fig. 5.1a: AP Legislative Assembly Election Difference between Proportion of Winners vis-a-vis the proportion of Social Group in the total population 2009

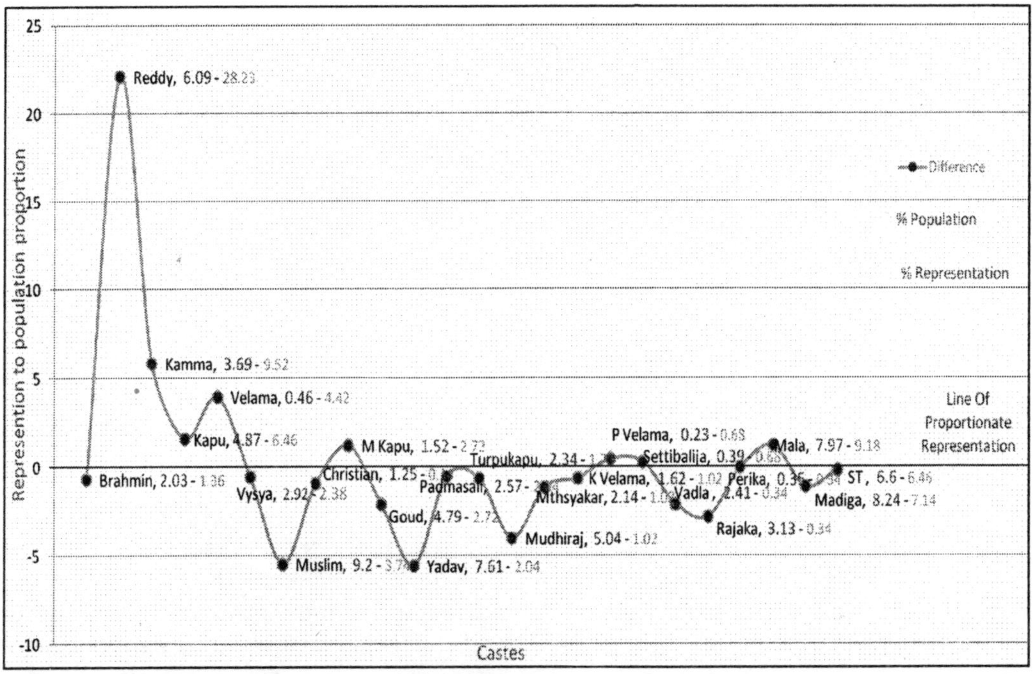

Fig. 5.1b: AP Legislative Assembly Election Difference between Proportion of Winners vis-a-vis the proportion of Caste in the total population 2009

proportion of social group and legislaters proportion of the same are equal to each other. The Positive Deviation from Zero Line/Line of Equal representation in the line graph is studied as the excessive legislative representation i.e. excessive to the entitlement of the given social group/caste. Likewise Negative Deviation to Zero Line/Line of Equal Representation is studied as under representation in legislative entitlement of social group/caste.

Disproportionate trends in relation to social categories have resulted and it may be viewed as deviations to democratic/equal representation. Reddys, Kammas, Velamas and Kapus have represented excessive to their legislative entitlement. SCs and STs have conformed almost with line of equal representation and it happened because of constitutional representation. Brahmin and Vysyas, though they belong to forward class, have figured as part of under representation in terms of legislative entitlement. Muslim and OBCs have fared very badly by occupying low to very low representation entitlement and it could be because of their contesting elections as part of the general stream. Straightening of the curve means participation of social groups in political process with self respect and dignity. Equal participation amounts to deepening democracy and therefore giving rise to the society overcoming from graded hierarchy.

DEVELOPMENT AND DEMOCRACY

Caste and Development

English education, urbanization, Freedom movement and Vishalandhra movement gave early leadership advantage to Brahmins in Andhra region. However the formation of Kamma, Reddy, Velama caste associations around 1910 and participation in Non- Brahmin movement led to the rise of caste power. Kisan movement (1930s) produced the leadership from dominant landed castes. The growth of left movement (1934-47) promoted the leadership of peasantry from Reddy and Kamma castes.

Abolition of Zamindari system (1948) accentuated the process of Brahmin migration and that led to land transfer to Kamma and Kapu castes. Hyderabad Tenancy and Agricultural Lands Act (1950) protected six lakh tenants largely belonging to landed castes. The introduction of the third tier of administration, Panchayati Raj, consolidated the landlord class and established effective control over rural communities. Rural Credit Cooperative Societies facilitated economic strength of the landed segments. Expansion of government employment promoted the early educated to emerge as middle class. Green Revolution led to soft loans and subsidized inputs in agriculture. The setting up of industrial and financial corporations and the contracts associated with irrigation, roads and buildings and excise and bore wells led the landed upper castes to diversify in to other profitable economic activities.

The nexus between landed, political, bureaucratic, contract and business classes promoted the dominance of Kamma, Reddy castes. The economic diversification of Kammas started with money lending, agro processing, construction and transport in 1930s. The presence of Kamma families of Devineni, Yarlagadda, Yalamanchali, Kavuri, Chalasani, Kakani, Surapaneni, Vallabhaneni, Gogineni etc. in PWD and Railways is a pointer towards occupational diversification and economic development. Further we see their participation in Tobacco export and to name a few families are Yarlagadda, Rayapati, Chebrolu, Devineni, Yemparla, etc. Kamma monopoly in cinema in terms of production, action, direction, distribution, studios, theatre contracts, multiplexes etc. is a classic case in caste enterprise.

Akkineni, Nandamuri, Daggubati, Gattamaneni, etc. are some of the Kamma families who dominate film industry in AP.

The rise of TDP further facilitated Kammas to enter in to construction of canals, highways, bridges, flyovers, etc. They also moved in a big way in to developing infrastructure companies, corporate education, star hospitals, Real estate, SEZ, IT, TV media, pharma, Malls under TDP led globalization. The known Kamma names in pharma are Nimmagadda, Divi, Nnnapaneni, Jasti, Vasireddy, etc. Kamma owned corporate hospitals are Kamineni, KIMS, Mullapudi, etc.

Reddys started as small time government contracters in canal, roads and buiding works, excise, borewells etc. Now we find them in hotels, alcohol, shipping, drugs and pharmaceuticals, manufacturing, power, infrastructure, real estate, dairy products, mining etc. and all this spiraled up during state facilitated globalization. To name a few Reddy families associated are: Gunapati, Tikkavarapu, Magunta, Kaallam, Bandi, Ergam, etc.

The Raju families who got in to modern economy include Pusapati, Gokaraju, Ramalingaraju, Sriniraju, Alluri, Manthena etc. Velama caste that got in to enterprise are: Raja of Bobbili, Pithapuram, Narsaraopet, Nuzivid, Venkatagiri, Mirzapuram etc. Pennar group and Yashoda hospitals also fall in this category. GMR and Sanghi are known names among Vaisyas participating manufacturing and service (Harish Damodaran).

HEGEMONISING DEVELOPMENT /MODERNIZATION/ GLOBALIZATION

As discussed above and to sum up Telangana, the constituent of Hyderabad state ruled by Nizam and Andhra (including Rayalaseema) was part of Madras presidency and it was under British colonial rule which gave rise to feudal and colonial cultures and consciousness respectively. The colonial modernization and English education made the Andhra region different from Telangana which had scanty Urdu education. The administrative merger of two spaces, colonial and feudal, gave uneven advantage of new space (AP) to Andhras, as the newly formed state embraced the Indianised (colonial) economic and cultural model and it is continuously integrating in to the global economic system. Therefore the continuation of two different experiences becomes the basis for the vertex of uneven development. The same is flowing into the cultures, consciousness, discourse and political practice around developmental hegemony.

The developmental processes produced divergences, dominance, monopoly and hegemony of classes in the structures of economy, politics, institutions, society, culture and the development discourse. The welfare centric development and modernization practiced by the native political system got transformed in to a market driven developmental globalization. The political class/party that built public sector ended up privatizing it for the benefit of its own social forces. Such a U turn of the political class further alienated the masses and communities from mainstreaming the nation.

The socio-political class, that dominates public space and monopolizes power, position and development, initiated its journey fighting against the dominance of a social class during the 19th century. The western educated elite coming from landed/peasant background started organizing around modernization in the expanding colonial economic space. However, while leading the public space, the then aspiring social groups retreated from the democratic spirit and promoted kinship, clannish and social centric articulations. The idea of fighting dominance is lost in dominating the public domain. It went on with the same spirit and emerged as a class capturing offices and opportunities. The regional political class acquired consciousness around social dominance and dominated the state and its institutions. Though it appeared as democratic and development oriented it essentially remained a social-centric, hierarchical and graded one.

With the demise of British colonialism, the landed political class headed governments and engaged in modernizing agriculture, irrigation, industry, power and other social infrastructure. Introducing land reforms, building public sector, promoting local self government, engaging in green revolution, nationalizing banks, developing infrastructure and perspectivising social justice have become the mile stones during the first four decades of Indian planning. The introduction of market-centric globalization during the 1990s has given a go by to welfare-centric modernization. In the name of growth rates and GDP the state resorted to privatizing economy and increased the role of private participation. In the process the difference between private and public is lost. The political class that benefited from modernization pushed its own kith and kin into the structures emanating from globalization. Government offices, public contracts, excise, transport, mining, licenses, distributory networks etc. have been cornered by the same social class. In fact any wealth that is promoted here is basically promoted by the state. Hardly we see assets being created outside the state domain. Therefore the capital-private or public, that is created is more state centric and it is willingly promoted by political class. The political class that acquired assets and wealth through state reinstated its hold over power and capital and engaged in hegemonising public space. The monopolistic aspirations of the same class and market forces pushed the nation in to the new paradigm of globalization and concomitant development.

The globalizing socio-economic classes and the market forces started aiming at national and international capital. Liberalisation, privatization and globalization offered huge opportunities to the regional classes. They started expanding in to national and international markets privatizing public enterprises, land, resources, mining, power, services, infrastructure etc. Therefore creation of SEZs, construction companies, corporate education, corporate health, star hotels, real estate, media, IT, ITES, telecommunications, six-lane roads, ports, airports, flyovers, metros, etc. have gone into the hands of the same social classes. Globalization in Andhra Pradesh has ended up in hegemonizing the public space on the basis of caste and class. Capital accumulation and control over power lead to monetizing democracy. Now the common man is alienated from himself and indoctrinated consciousness is volunteering to hand over power to the rich and the dominant. In the entire development discourse and budget-making, traditional occupations and dependent social groups have found no place. Therefore traditional producer is now seen as a laborer as he/she has lost historically endowed professional capital. The state is highly contented with reeling out growth rates, GDP, BPL and other statistics and it is elated whenever it is talked about India as emerging Asian power/global power.

POLITICAL CONSCIOUSNESS

AP's political space is dominated by two centers. One is headed by Reddy caste and whose numerical strength is about six per cent of the state population spreading across Telangana and Rayalaseema regions. Reddys have been a landed community and village leadership is held by them right from the pre independence times. The primacy of Reddy dominance in the state continued till date as the Congress came handy to their politics. Though a segment of Reddy leadership went with the national leadership heading occasional split in Congress at the center but it used to rejoin the Congress that got electoral success and continued to command power. Basically Reddys always tagged on to power and they learnt it so well that they could derive it through Congress and that led to Reddyisation of power and politics. SCs and Muslims have by and large associated with Congress/Reddys in the power game. In fact, they have always been dependant social groups and have not developed independant leadership of their own except Hyderabadi Muslims having a party of their own but still tags on always to a ruling party. Other peripheral backward social groups continued to go with Congress.

The other political center is headed by Kammas and whose population is about 3.7 per cent of state's population and they are largely concentrated in Krishna delta confining to south central Andhra encompassing Krishna, Guntur, Prakasham and adjoining parts of Khammam district. They are also seen in migratory pockets of Ananthpur, Nizamabad and Hyderabad districts. Kammas are basically a farming community but they have made use of early modernization and emerged as the most enterprising community expanding in to business, industry in the early part of the twentieth century. They were contesting Reddy power initially under the leadership of NG Ranga but they had to give up because of the formation of AP and the rise of Reddy consolidation. The Kammas got diversified in to business, contracts and industry. Under the leadership of Telugu cinema actor, NT Rama Rao, all Kammas have rallied behind him and floated a regional party called Telugu Desam Party (TDP). Kammas have defeated the Reddy headed Congress in 1983 and ruled for about sixteen years with an interregnum of five years from 1989 to 1994.

All those who got politically excluded from Reddy headed politics rallied around TDP and the main segments that got under the fold of TDP were OBCs and a few social groups here and there. Under Kamma leadership, N Chandrababu Naidu headed government aggressively pushed globalization and got benefited from the state-centered economic reforms. Though OBCs stood by TDP they did not get the benefits of globalization. Rather many social groups lost heavily because of globalization as they could not get the state support to rise to the level of managing globalizing economy. In fact, power that facilitates social development reduced OBCs to a vote bank but were never allowed them to capture political leadership. TDP rule remained a Kamma rule and it facilitated Kammaisation of development, power, institutions and culture.

Velama is a numerically small caste with 0.46 per cent population of the state. They are categorised as forward caste in Telangana. They are seen as scattered families in a few geographic tracts along the Godavari valley. They are basically a landed community dominating village life and capturing disproportionate power. Velamas though appear as a caste but function as kinship group leading the extended family living. Because of its primacy over socio-economic space and also being a cohesive social group, Velamas could rise to the level of Chief Ministership. Today they are heading a party centred around Telangana movement. Though they have emerged as a formidable political force but they have to be dependant on some social group or the other because of numerical vulnerability.

Kapus belong to a farming group concentrated in Godavari delta. Turpu Kapus are distributed across northern Andhra, Munnuru Kapus are spread over across Telangana and Balijas in Rayalaseema. Though the various Kapu groups assert identities at different levels they often come together to forge a grand bloc to influence power and political system. Together they constitute one of the largest social groups in the state. Kapus in fact form part of forward classes but the other three are categorized as OBCs.

Politically Kapus of Godavari delta are almost equal to those of the other political castes. However they have not held the office of Chief Minister and do not command the power as Reddys and Kammas do. After Reddys, Kammas and Velamas, it is Kapus who compete to claim the state leadership. In fact, Praja Rajyam party was floated with an aim of capturing state power under the leadership of a cinema actor, Chiranjeevi, during 2009. They got about 16 per cent vote winning 18 legislators. Later the party merged with the Congress.

OBCs constitute almost half of the state's population. They are largely concentrated in Telangana, Rayalaseema and Northern Andhra. They are distributed in coastal planes and delta regions. OBC is a conglomeration of castes having variation in political consciousness. Within OBCs a few castes are numerically dominant and they are: Yadav, Goud, Mudiraj, Padmasali, Chakali, Viswabrahmin, Mangali etc. There are several other castes within OBC with small populations and they are the most backward social groups.

Denotified, Nomadic and Semi nomadic Tribes also form part of OBC and their social backwardness is unthinkable. Often caste names are used as abuse and their social standing is subhuman in the eyes of main stream society. Almost all denotified tribes and many of the numerically small castes of OBC are yet to step into the corridors of power. No political party comes forward to give a ticket to these communities in the elections. They have been denied of representation in the state legislative assembly and parliament since the inception of the democratic institutions.

Goud, Yadav, Mudiraj and Padmasali etc. figure as members of legislative assembly and Parliament but none of these castes are represented in proportion to their population. There is a middle class emerging in these castes and asserting itself at the grass roots level. They are also seen as an aspiring class and an initiative is on in forging larger identity of OBC and at the same time dominant political groups are resorting to promoting division invoking most backwardness. In fact, OBCs can provide a social base for the formation of a separate party articulating identity and their aspiration. It is very likely that such a step is not too far in AP politics.

Muslims are the single largest social group in the state. They constitute about 9.2 per cent of the population and they are largely concentrated in Hyderabad, Telangana (minus Hyderabad) and Rayalaseema. They are also distributed significantly in Andhra. Though they were the ruling class before independence they are reduced to backwardness during the post independence times. Within Muslims several social groups are categorized as OBCs because of backwardness and underdevelopment. Muslims are largely confined to urban areas engaging in all kinds of activities for livelihood. There is a large segment of Muslim population participating in informal sectors having less pay and insecurity of life. Politically speaking they are highly underrepresented and their political share is cornered by Reddy, Kamma and Velama castes.

SCs are constituted by several sub castes with a population of 16.2 per cent. Malas and Madigas are the two largest social groups belonging to SCs. Though Malas and Madigas are spatially distributed across the state, Malas are densely populated in Andhra and Madigas in Telangana and Rayalaseema. They occupy the lowest rung of the socially graded hierarchy. The untouchability that is practiced by the mainstream society is the most inhuman and it is being experienced by the SCs since ages. In spite of its being declared as illegal by the Indian constitution it is still continued. They lead the life of landlessness, poverty and backwardness. Because of Constitutional reservation SCs are represented in democratic institutions in proportion to their population. However they do not find place in decision making. SCs are leading several socio cultural movements and the middle class of the community is engaged in ideological and political debates. Though there is a rise in social assertion, atrocities against them are still continued. Madiga social movement for the last two decades has created a lot of churning not only among madigas but also several other communities for the promotion of social mobilization and democratic inclusion.

STs constitute about seven per cent of the population and they are largely concentrated in the districts of northern AP stretching from Adilabad to Srikakulam. Gonds, Koyas, Chenchus, Konda Reddys, Jatapus, Erukalas, Lambadas/Sugalis etc. form part of tribal communities. Plain tribes are spread over Telangana and Rayalaseema. ST population is high in Telangana followed by Rayalaseema and Andhra. Lambadas are relatively assertive among plain tribes and participate better in education and employment. Constitutional reservation facilitates Adivasis in obtaining a better representation in politics, but the political consciousness among them is far behind compared to all other social groups. They suffer from poverty, malnutrition, backwardness and they are prone to repeated health hazards. Educational backwardness of hilly and forest tribe is extremely high and therefore they are left behind in modernizing communities. Female illiteracy is the highest and lack of social mobility is structural. STs form the lowest rung in human development Indices.

Others constitute socially advanced segments and they form small proportion of population. Brahmins constitute two per cent and Vysyas (Komatis) have about three per cent of population. By and large Brahmins are confined to urban areas participating in service and priestly sectors. Once they used to be landed groups and modernization made them to move in to urban areas. The political primacy of Brahmins in 1950s is lost out to farming castes and they are almost left unrepresented politically in AP. Vysyas are also under-represented politically.

Developmental modernization broke the back of caste based occupations as planning and budgetary allocations, ignored the traditional skills and productivity. Instead of modernizing occupations, the promotion of machine-driven production displaced the eco friendly production systems and labour intensive avenues. Policy makers did not think of providing alternatives to the displaced traditional talent. The globalization that got initiated during the 1990s is peripheralising the disempowered social groups further and thereby getting alienated from the electoral process and the consequent power. Modern development and democracy promoted political exclusion of large groups of castes.

INCLUSIVE DEMOCRACY

India is seen as the largest democracy in the world and it is said so because its political class claims and it is based on the elections held at the regular intervals and people participate as voters. Besides this the democracy is constructed based on the structures created around parliament, Executive and Judiciary.

Further the political parties and commentators belonging to different shades of life argue that democracy is getting strengthened because of modernizing society and adhering to secular values. Is this all about democracy or should we have to go deeper in seeing associated social relations and pluralizing democracy?

The regular conduct of elections, no doubt, contributed for the voter participation and election of people's representation to different houses. However, the point to be understood is did this process allow representation from different segments of the society? The answer is emphatically no. The mapping of elections in AP proved that only a few castes and communities-Reddy, Kamma, Velama and Kapu could represent legislative bodies disproportionate to their population. A few other social groups—SCs and STs, could make it to their proportion because of Constitutional reservation. Many other castes and communities could not make it to their population share. A large number of social groups could not get an entry in to the legislative bodies in the last six decades of elections. In the near future also there is no such scope for their inclusion in to the legislative system because of the limitations of political practice and also non availability of legislative measures. They belong to most vulnerable groups—denotified tribes, nomadic and semi-nomadic social groups. In the absence of legislative facilitation and also because of OBCs and Minorities contesting from general/unreserved seats fall short of the representation in proportion to their population and it is also the same with a few forward castes like Brahmins and Vaisyas. The representation of women is much worse and they do not figure anywhere near to their population which is in fact fifty per cent of population. There are no answers to these exclusions in the existing electoral practice.

The state embracing modernization and the development model adopted as part of it failed in facilitating all those social groups-women, Nomadic and Semi nomadic tribes, Minorities, OBCs and the poor, to enter into democratic space by way of elections. The proponents of modernization thought it would strengthen democracy and the whole analysis proved that it did not happen. The development pursued by the state has facilitated largely the landed social groups to get modernized and dominate the systems created by democracy. Globalisation, further strengthened the same social groups in making use of privatizing and liberalizing policies of the state and its economy. It is amply proved all over the world that globalization promoted the rich to become richer and furthered the gulf between the rich and the poor. In the context of market driven globalization, the social class that controlled the reins of power used its wealth and legislative power to further their interests and accrue the benefits to its own social class denying development space for others. Such a development would facilitate only the existing social power and therefore the reality in AP is seen by way of Reddyisation and Kammaisation of developmet, power and institutions. The hitherto domination of social class is turned out to be a hegemonic one leading to a limited democracy and failing to fulfill the very meaning of democracy.

The meaning and purpose of democracy is to transform social relations as it is founded on the principle of equality, justice and liberty. The society ridden with numerous inequalities such as economic, educational, gender, tribe, caste, religion, regional etc. would obstruct maturing democracy. There is a need to creatively articulate the assertions of various democratic aspirations and more so with strengthening civil society. In the existing democratic practice there is hardly any scope for inclusive democracy. Therefore there is a need to have a continuous mobilization of peripheralised groups. As no single group guarantees the other in the hierarchy ridden graded society it is for the civil society encompassing different social groups to pluralise democracy. Monoculturisation of political system has to be changed. The basic condition for democracy is to reduce inequalities-social and economic, and that would realize the true meaning of democracy.

REFERENCES

Harish Damodaran, (2008), *India's New Capitalists: Caste, Business, and Industry in a Modern Nation*, Permanent Black, Ranikhet.

Linga Murthy, V., (1982), Political Parties in Andhra Pradesh, in Prasanna Kumar *et al.*, Government and Politics in Andhra Pradesh, S. Chand and Company Ltd., New Delhi.

Prasanna Kumar, (1982), Caste and Leadership,in Prasanna Kumar *et al.*, Government and Politics in Andhra Pradesh, S. Chand and Company Ltd, New Delhi.

Carolyn M. Elliot, (1995), Caste and Faction among the Dominant Caste: The Reddis and Kammas of Andhra, in Rajni Kothari, *Caste in Indian Plitics*, Orient Longman, Hyderabad.

T.V. Hannurav, (1998), Socio-Educational-Economic Survey of Castes and Communities of Andhra Pradesh, Vol. I, *Methodology, Basic Indices and Index of Forwardness*, Report submitted to Justice (Retd) K.S. Puttaswamy, Chairman, B.C.Commission, Government of Andhra Pradesh, Hyderabad.

XLIV No. 39

Nicholas B.Dirks, (2002), *Castes of Mind: Colonialism and the Making of Modern India*, Permanent Black, Delhi.

Simhadri,S., (2009), Developmental Consequences of Globalisation: Andhra Pradesh Experience, in, Nandkumar Sawant, *et al.*, ed. *Globalisation: Issues and Challenges for India*, Institute of Indian Geographers, Pune.

Simhadri, S., (2008), Kulam Needalo Abhivruddi Rajakeeyalu, (Caste and Development Politics) in Telugu, FEWS, Hyderabad.

VI
Summary and Conclusions

The present study is an effort towards bringing out an Election Atlas for a State in India that is Andhra Pradesh, by using the latest Technology of Geoinformatics and GIS. Though the major thrust is in explaining the variations in the socio - economic, demographic and political profile of the state of Andhra Pradesh; the macro space, that is the State scenario and the micro space, that is select villages within the state of Andhra Pradesh, have also been woven into the study to make the picture more holistic in nature. The maps are thematic in nature and span the entire spectrum of the Election Scenario encompassing within their ambit maps pertaining to the behaviour of the electorate, the election outcomes, the demographic and socio economic variables on which they regress, the scheme of things into which they fit, the larger picture of which they are a part and even the micro details of micro spaces to a large extent. These maps which provide a '(Digital) map inventory' have been prepared in the form of traditional static maps as well as user friendly customized query-based dynamic interactive digital maps which can be hosted on the web for wider viewing and usage. These constitute the Election Information System (EIS) at varying levels of scale. Both the types have been prepared by using the GIS Technology and highlight the way in which something which is of interest to the common man can be brought to his door step on the platform provided by technology. Not only this, it also stirs up an interest in the common man to learn the technology which facilitates understanding of mundane affairs. An attempt to solve other problems in this GIS environment can also be made by the users of this Election Atlas, thus expanding the potential of this application. This study has sought to interface the technological innovations with societal use. Practical grass root level advantages that can be cited are that if voters can access information about the polling booth, distance and subsequently results of Election, their level of awareness and inclusivity will increase and they will become more responsible and the voter turnout may be more and enlightened, thus adding to the quality of the democratic process. GIS database when integrated with the Electronic Voting Machine information can help voters by guiding them to the correct polling booths and can help polling officials by ensuring that each voter casts his vote only once.

Apart from providing a (Digital) Map Inventory of thematic information pertaining to Andhra Pradesh, the other tangible deliverables of this study has been a massive exercise carried out towards the correction of Mandal, Assembly and Village maps, which have been rectified at the boundaries, transformed and projected. They provide a spatial database for users in the future to map any type of data onto these units in a GIS environment. Also for the first time Constituency – wise Attribute Data has been generated and demographic compatibility with Parliamentary and Assembly Constituencies has been established. Thus the social base for understanding Elections is made available in an objective, statistical manner.

The main inferences which can be drawn after a perusal of the maps in this study are that Hyderabad and Rangareddy stand alone as distinct areas displaying characteristics that go with modernization and development in an otherwise less developed Telangana region. In Coastal Andhra there are pockets of development centred around the Regional urban centre – Visakhapatnam and also over the Delta Districts of E. Godavari, W. Godavari, Krishna and Guntur. Rayalaseema Region of the state exhibits a kind of monotony with regards to low levels of development. A general increase of consciousness on various counts is also witnessed from the west to the east in this state. This is reflected in various ways in the Electoral behaviour of the people. The people in general have a tendency for expecting a change – a change for the betterment of their fate, as every election is on the anvil. They try to use the voting power at their disposal to effect this change. The switch in loyalty from that to a single party to the surfacing of a multiplicity of parties is all too evident and is in keeping with the national trend for regional, communal and other splinter groups to surface.

People in general are happy with the arrangements for elections by the government, the distance to the polling booth, the infrastructure present there etc. This is notwithstanding, complaints of rigging, influencing of voters, buying their allegiance, an increasing tendency of the involvement of big money in getting tickets to contest, violation of the Election code of conduct in select pockets, the role of musclemen and the criminalization of elections in general. These are the things that can be paid heed to by the authorities to nip emerging problems in the bud.

This study has also thrown up certain issues for future work like:

(a) The utility of GIS and Election Information system (EIS) which can help with a reasonable Delimitation policy of Electoral Constituencies.
(b) The use of GIS in monitoring security arrangements in the elections.
(c) Replication of similar work in the case of other states, to help heighten the consciousness of people.
(d) Generation of Street Address based Geocoded files of voters which ensure that invalid addresses are pruned out and a comparison can be made between the spatial data pertaining to constituencies and other administrative units like mandals etc.
(e) GIS can thus help to a considerable extent with the engineering of elections.

REFERENCES

1. Agnew, John (1997), *Political Geography*, Edward Arnold, London.
2. Bardhan, Pranab (1984). *The Political Economy of Development in India.* Oxford: Basil Blackwell.
3. Baxter,Craig. (1969) *District Voting Trends in India.* New York and London: Columbia University Press.
4. Brass, Paul (1997). "General Elections 1996 in Uttar Pradesh."*Economic and Political Weekly,* September 20 : 2403-2421.
5. Chandra, Kanchan (2004). *Why Ethnic Parties Succeed: Patronage and Ethnic Head·Coounts in India,* Cambridge: Cambridge University Press.
6. Chandra, Kanchan, and Chandrika Parmar (1997). Party Strategies in the Uttar Pradesh Assembly Elections 1996. *Economic and political Weekly*, February 1 : 214-222.
7. Cox, Gary (1997). *Making Votes Count.* Cambridge: Cambridge University Press.
8. Dirks, Nicholas B. (2000). *Castes of Mind.* Princeton, NJ: Princeton University Press.
9. Frankel, Francine (1978). *India's Political Economy* 1947-1977. Princeton, NJ: Princeton University Press.
10. Frankel, Francine and M.S.A. Rao (1989). *Dominance and State Power in Modern India,* Vol.I. Delhi: Oxford University Press.
11. Frankel, Francine R and M.S.A.Rao (1990). *Dominance and State Power in Modern India,* Vol. II. Delhi: Oxford University Press.
12. Gould, Harold A. (2001). *Grassroots Politics in India.* New Delhi: Oxford and IBH Publishing, 1994.
13. Government of India, Census.
14. Jaffrelot, Christophe, (2003). *India"s silent Revolution: The Rise of the low castes in North Indian politics*, Delhi: Permnent Black.
15. Jayal, Niraja Gopal (2006). *Representing India: Ethnic Diversity and the Governance of Public Institutions,* Houndmitls: Palgrave Macmillan.
16. Kohli, Atul. *India's Democracy.* Princeton, NJ: Princeton University press, 1988.
17. Kondo, Norio (2003). *Indian Parliament Elections after Independence: Social changes and Electoral participation,* Chiba (Japan): Institute of Developing Economies (JETRO).
18. Kothari, Rajni, ed.*Caste in Indian Politics.* Hyderabad: Orient Longman, 1970.
19. Lama-Rewal, Stephanie Tawa (2005). *Electoral Reservations, Political Representation and Social change in India*, New Delhi: Manohar.
20. Lyngdoh, James Michael (2004). *Chronicle of an Impossible Election: The Election Commission and the 2002 Jammu and Kashmir Assembly Elections,* New Delhi: Penguin Viking.
21. Markandey, Kalpana and S. Simhadri (2006). GIS in Mapping Election Information System : Technology – Society Interface, Unpublished DST Project Report.
22. McMillan, Alistair (2005). *Standing at the Margins: Representation and Electoral Reservation in India,* New Delhi: Oxford University Press.
23. Meyer, Ralph. (1989). "How Do Indians Vote?"*Asian Survey,* Vol. 29, No. 12: 1111-1122.
24. Murali Manohar, K, (2008). Andhra Pradesh Politics (in Telugu), Forum for Empowerment of Weaker Sections, Hyderabad.
25. Newell, James L. (1998). "The Scottish National Party: Development and Change."In Lieven de Winter and Huri Tursan, eds. *Regionalist Parties in Western Europe.* London: Routledge: 105-124.
26. Popkin, Samuel L. (1991). *The Reasoning Voter.* Chicago: University of Chicago Press.

27. 16) Putnum, Robert (1993). *Making Democracy Work.* Princeton, NJ: Princeton University Press.
28. Puttuswamy Commission Report on Backward Classes, AP (unpublished)
29. Roy, Meenu (2000). Electoral Politics in India-Election Process and Outcomes, Voting behaviour and Current trends, Deep and Deep, New Delhi.
30. Shah, Ghanshyam (1991). Tenth Lok Sabha Elections: BJP's Victory in Gujarat. *Economic and political Weekly*, December 21: 2921-2924.
31. Shastri, Sandeep (1995). *Towards Explaining the Voter's Mandate: An analysis of the Karnataka Assembly Elections.* Bangalore.
32. Simhadri, S.(2008). Development Politics under the shadow of Caste (in Telugu), FEWS, Hyderabad.
33. Singh, V.B., and Shankar Bose (1987-88). *State Elections in India.* Delhi: Sage.
34. Stoll, Heather (2004). Another Endogeneity Problem and More in Electoral Studies: Social Cleavages Revisited Prepared for the SCR Graduate Retreat, Stanford University, May.
35. Sudeepta Adikari (1997), Political Geography, Rawat, Jaipur.
36. Taylor, Peter J. (1985), Political Geography, Longman, London.
37. Varshney, Ashutosh (2002). *Ethnic Conflict and Civic Life: Hindus and Muslims in India,* New York: Oxford University Press.
38. Visvanathan, Shiv (April 1996). "Thinking about Elections."*Seminar,* Vol. 440: 72-75.
39. Wallace, Paul and Ramashray Roy (Ed). (2003). *India's 1999 Elections and 20th Century Politics,* New Delhi: Sage.
40. Wilkinson, Steven I. (2004). *Votes and Violence: Electoral Competition and Communal Riots in India,* Cambridge: Cambridge University Press.
41. Weiner, Myron (1967). *Party Building in a New Nation: The Indian National Congress.* Chicago: University of Chicago Press.
42. Wood, John R. (1984) "Congress Restored? The" Kham "Strategy and Congress (1) Recruitment in Gujarat. In John R.Wood, ed. *State Politics in Contemporary India.* Boulder, CO: Westview Press: 197-227.
43. Yadav, Yogendra (2004). "The Elusive Mandate of 2004", *Economic and Political Weekly,* December 18.
44. Yadav, Yogendra. (1996). "Reconfiguration in Indian Politics." *Economic and Political Weekly,* January 13-20: 95-104.

(Contd.)

Coloured Maps

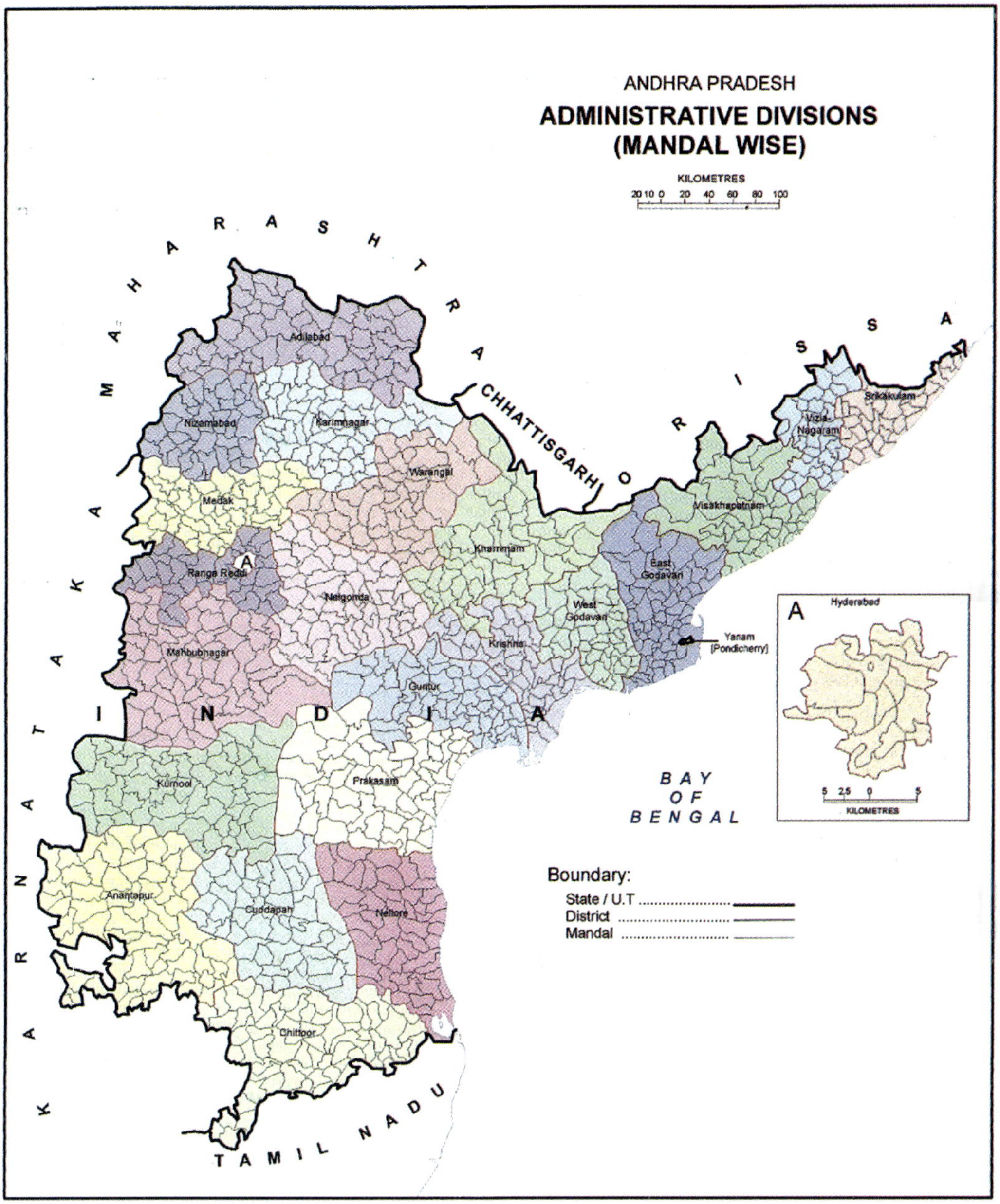

Map 1.1: Mandals of Andhra Pradesh

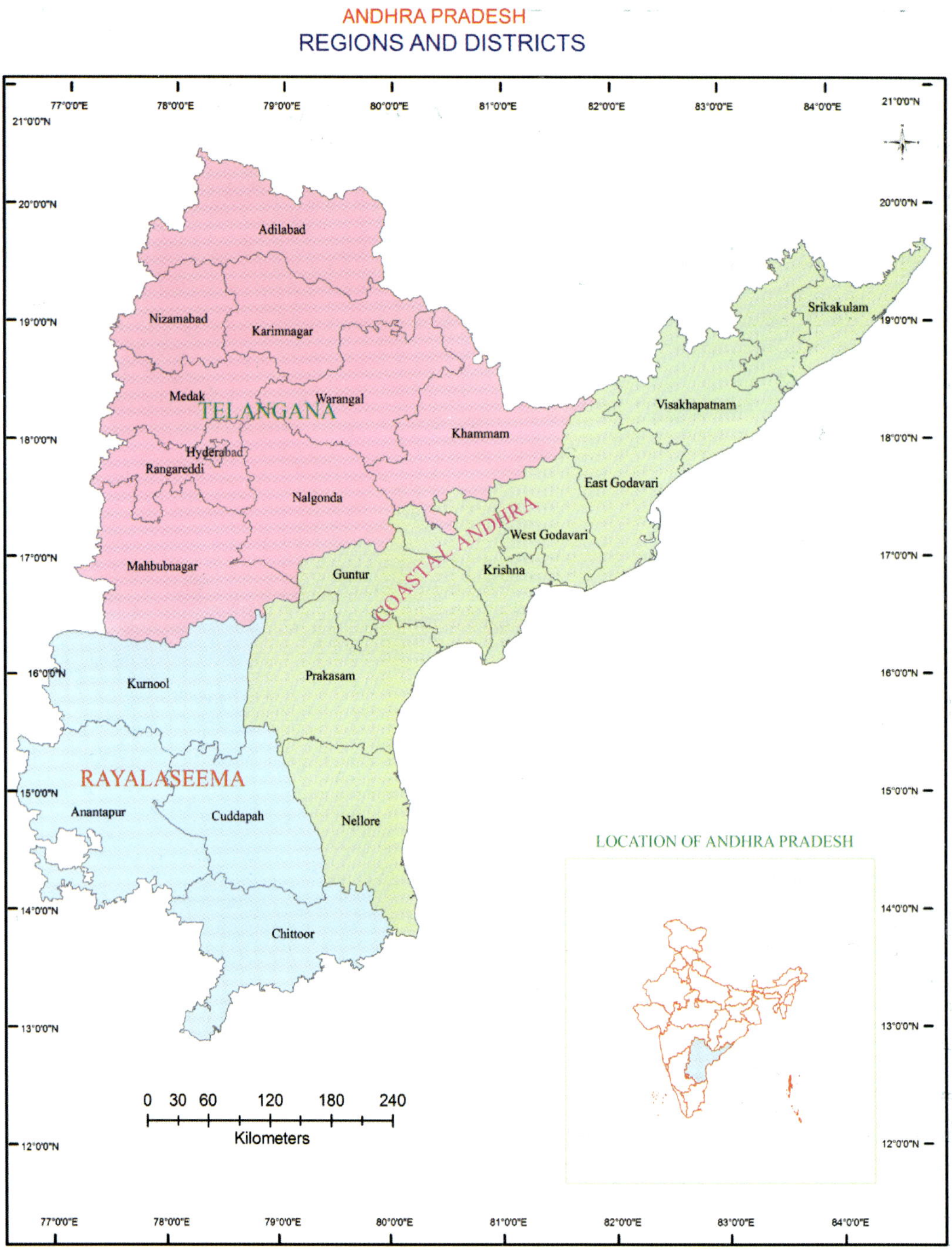

Map 1.2: Andhra Pradesh: Administrative divisions – Regions and Districts: 2004

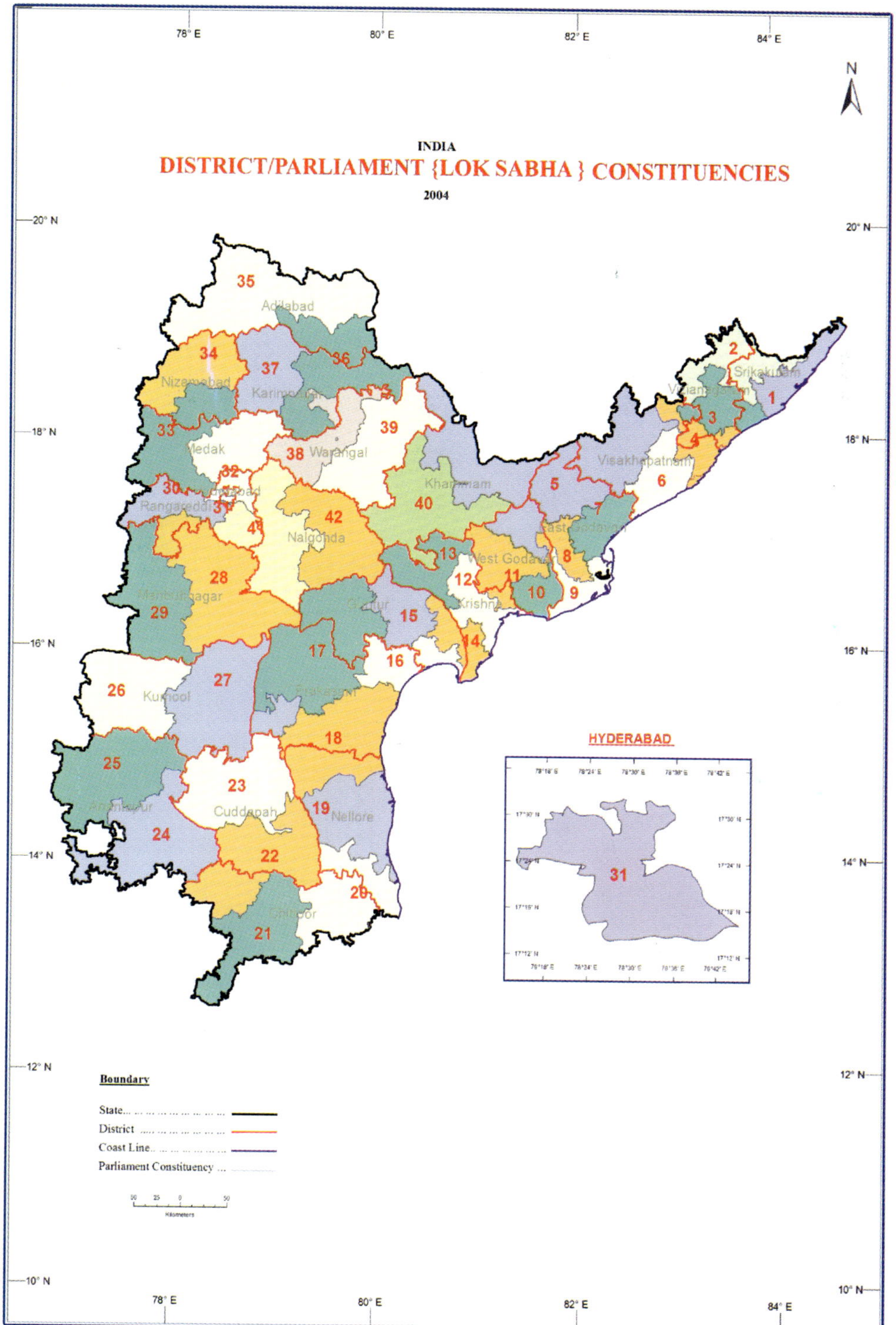

Map 1.3: Andhra Pradesh: District/Parliament (Lok Sabha) Constituencies: 2004

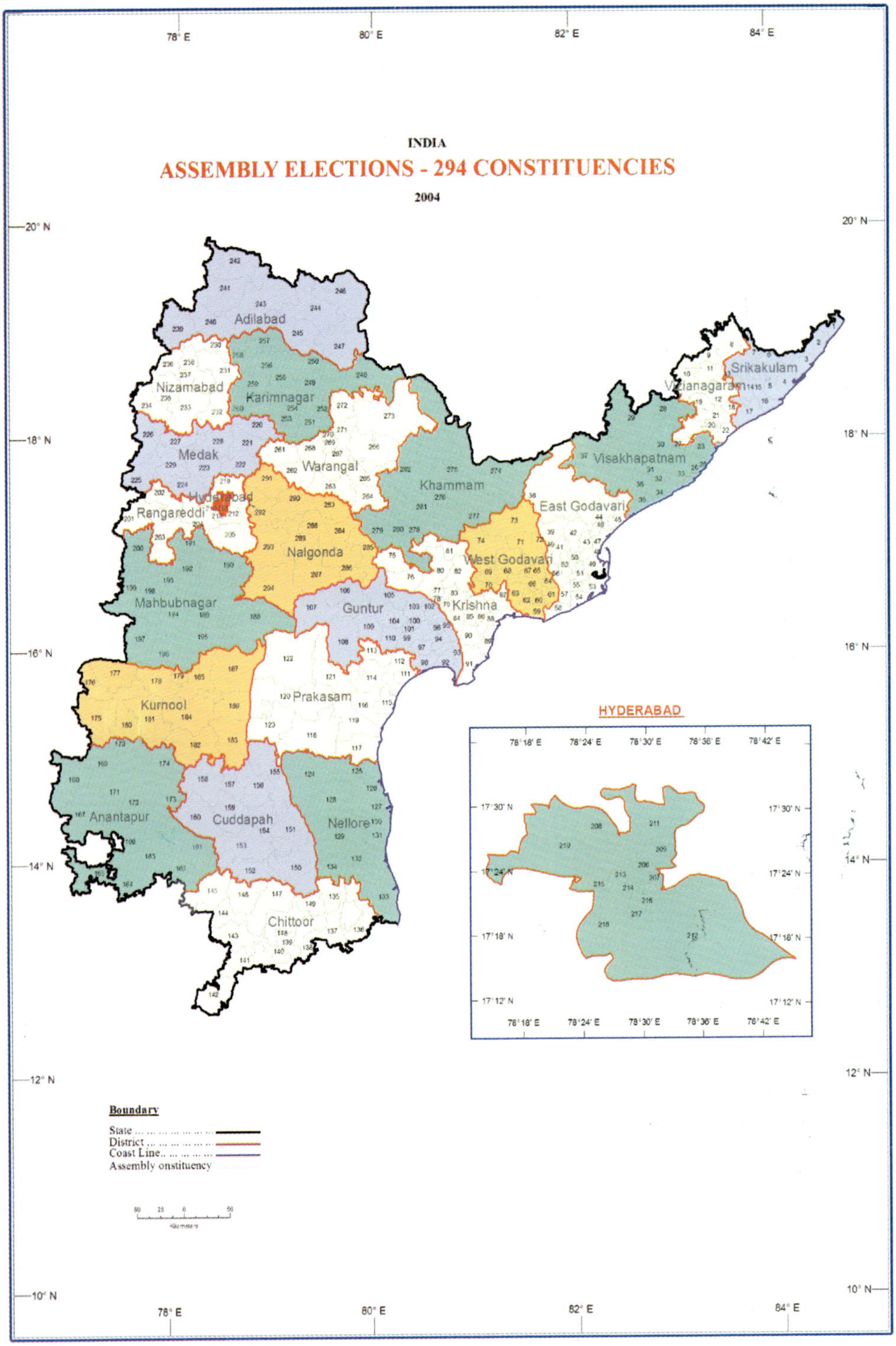

Map 1.4: Andhra Pradesh: Assembly Elections – 294 Constituencies: 2004

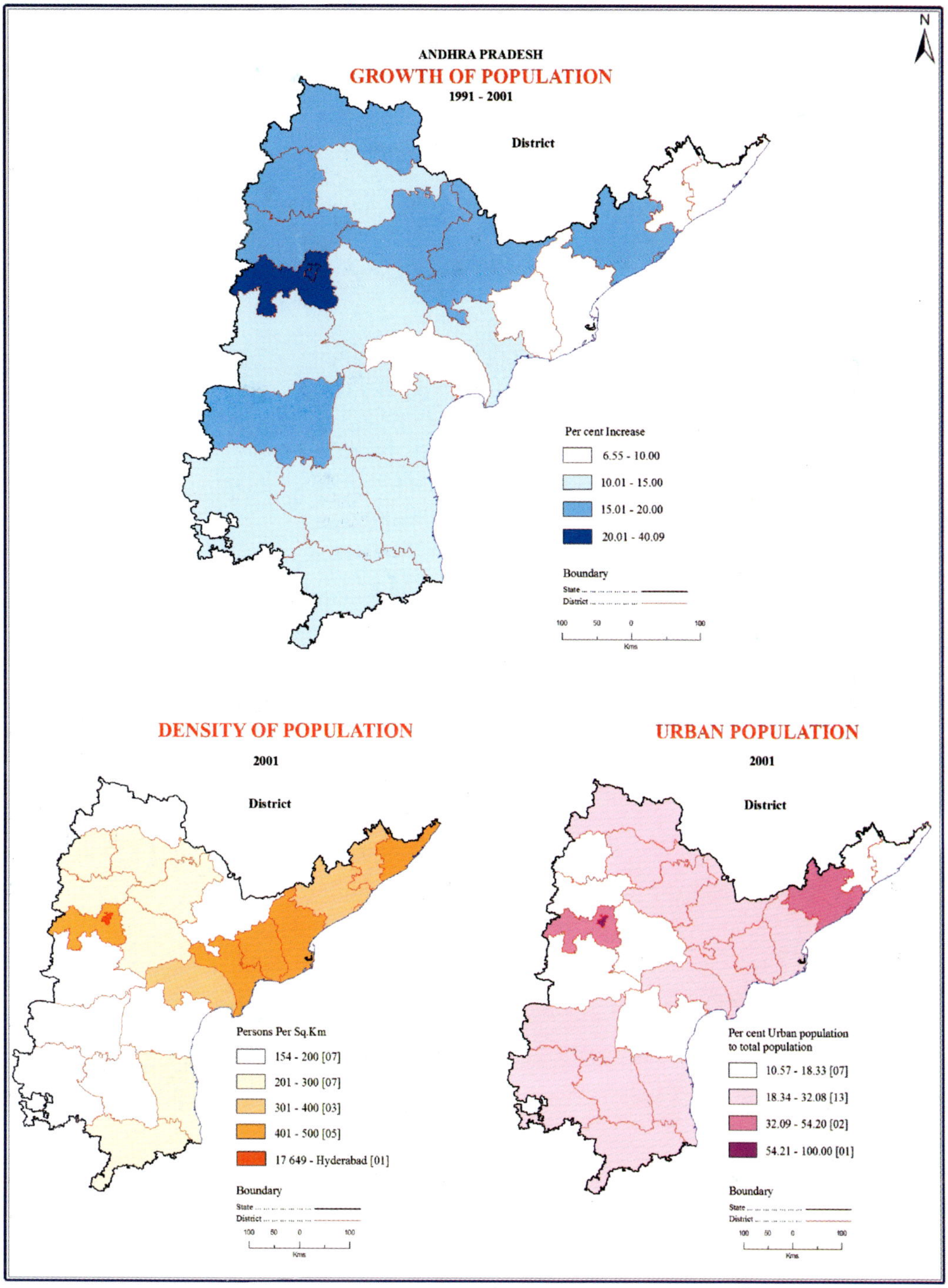

Map 1.5: Andhra Pradesh: Growth of Population, 1991-2001, Density of Population and Urban Population

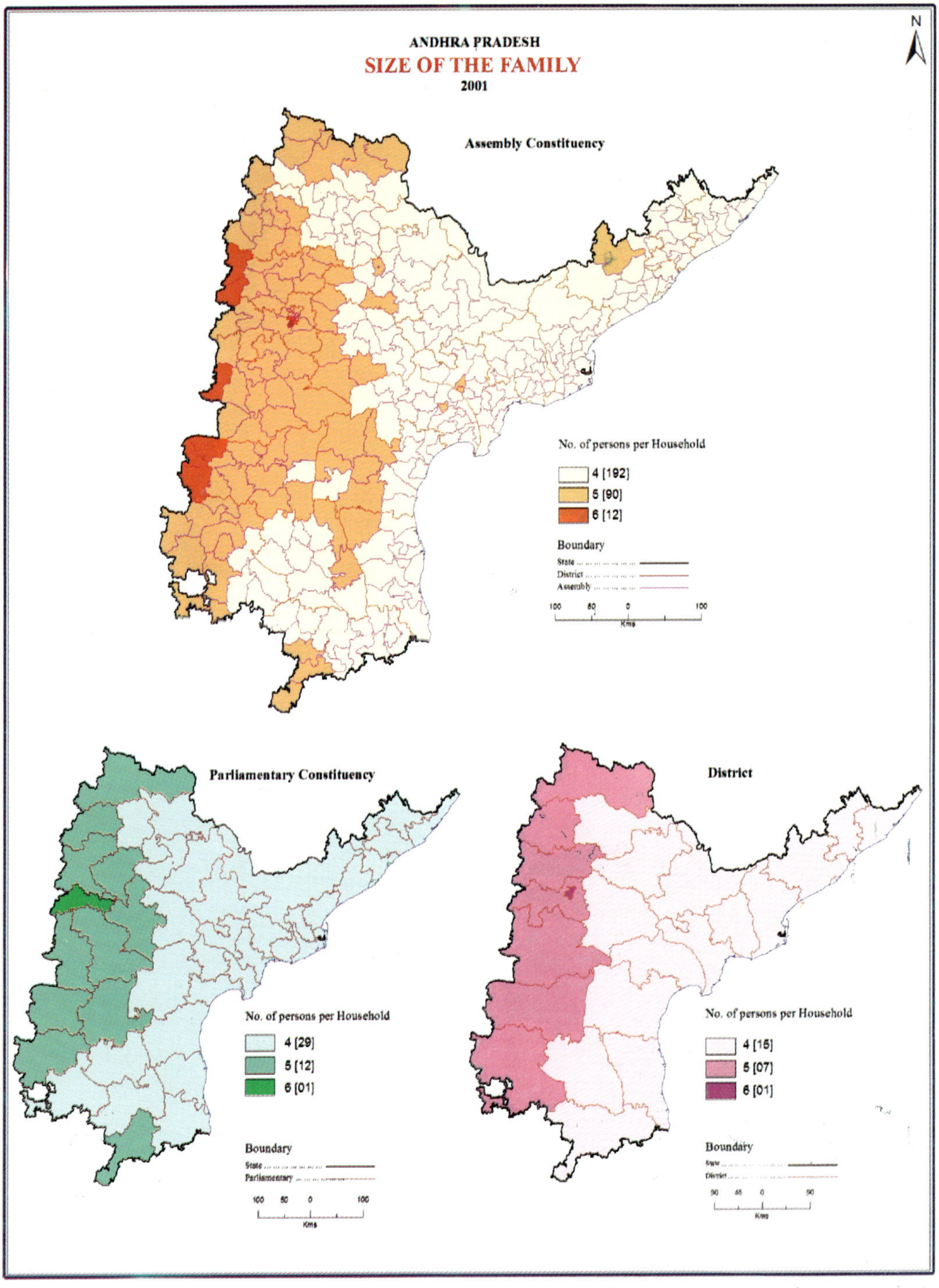

Map 1.6: Andhra Pradesh: Size of the Family, 2001

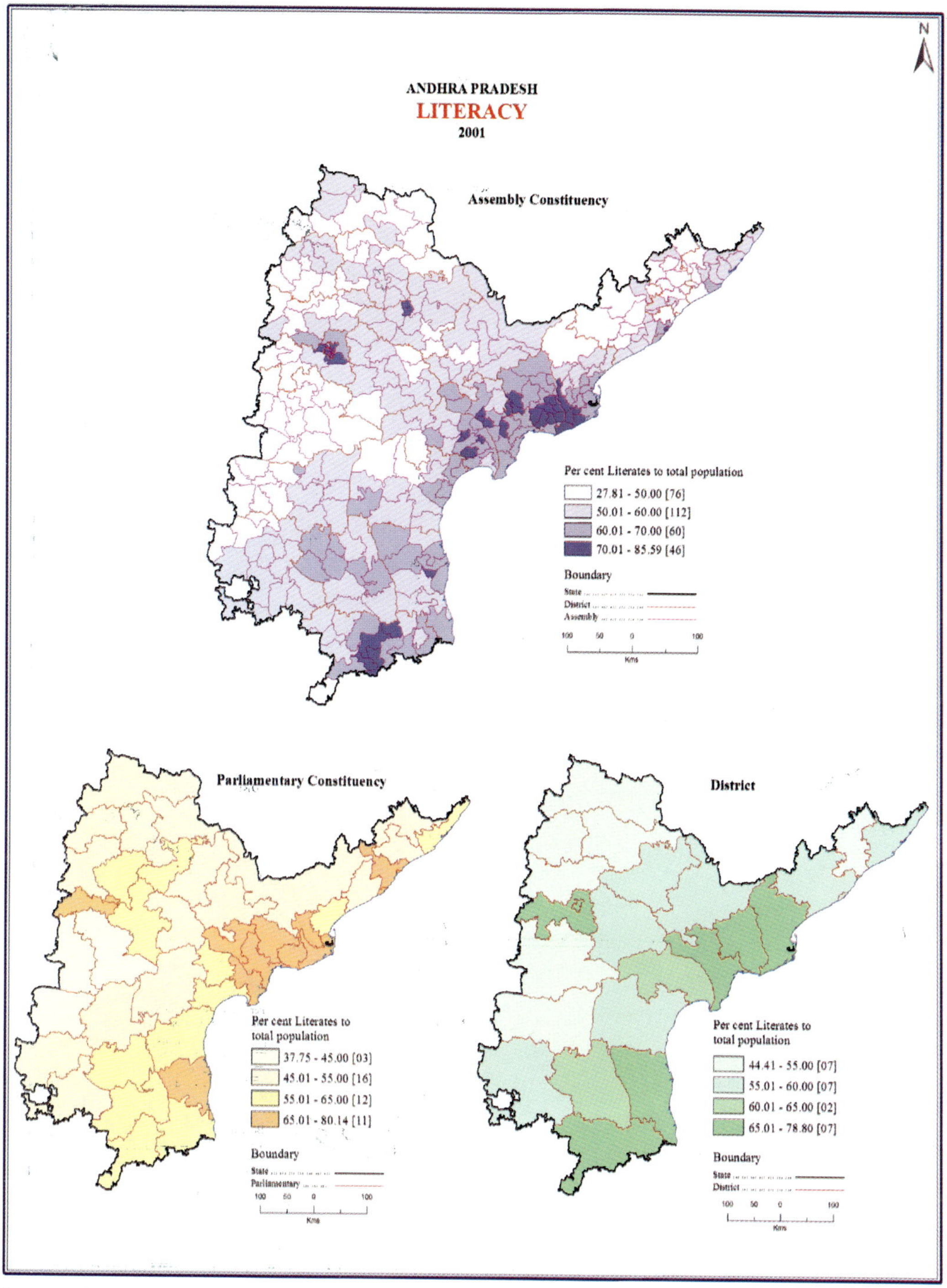

Map 1.7: Andhra Pradesh: Literacy, 2001

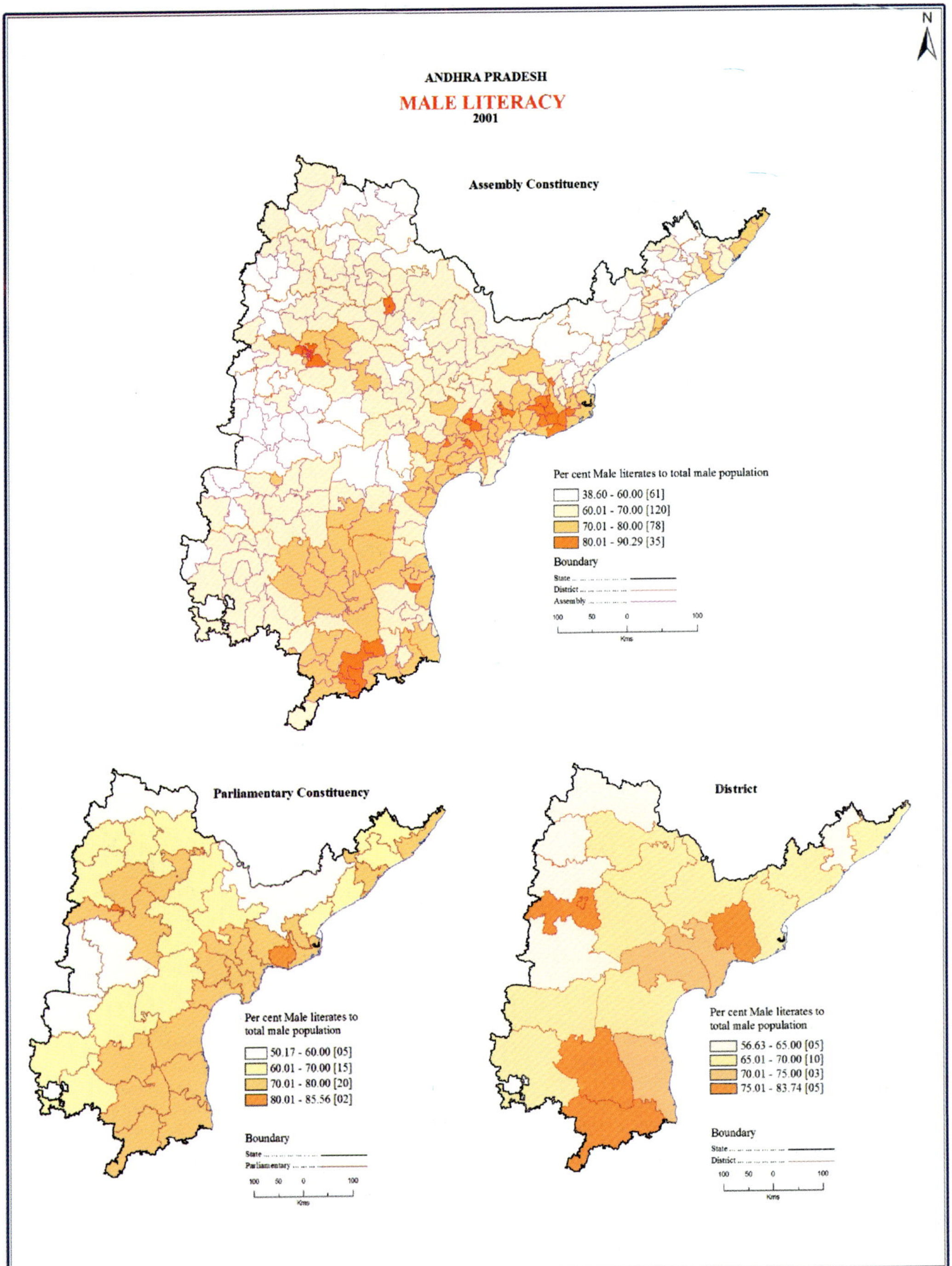

Map 1.8: Andhra Pradesh: Male Literacy, 2001

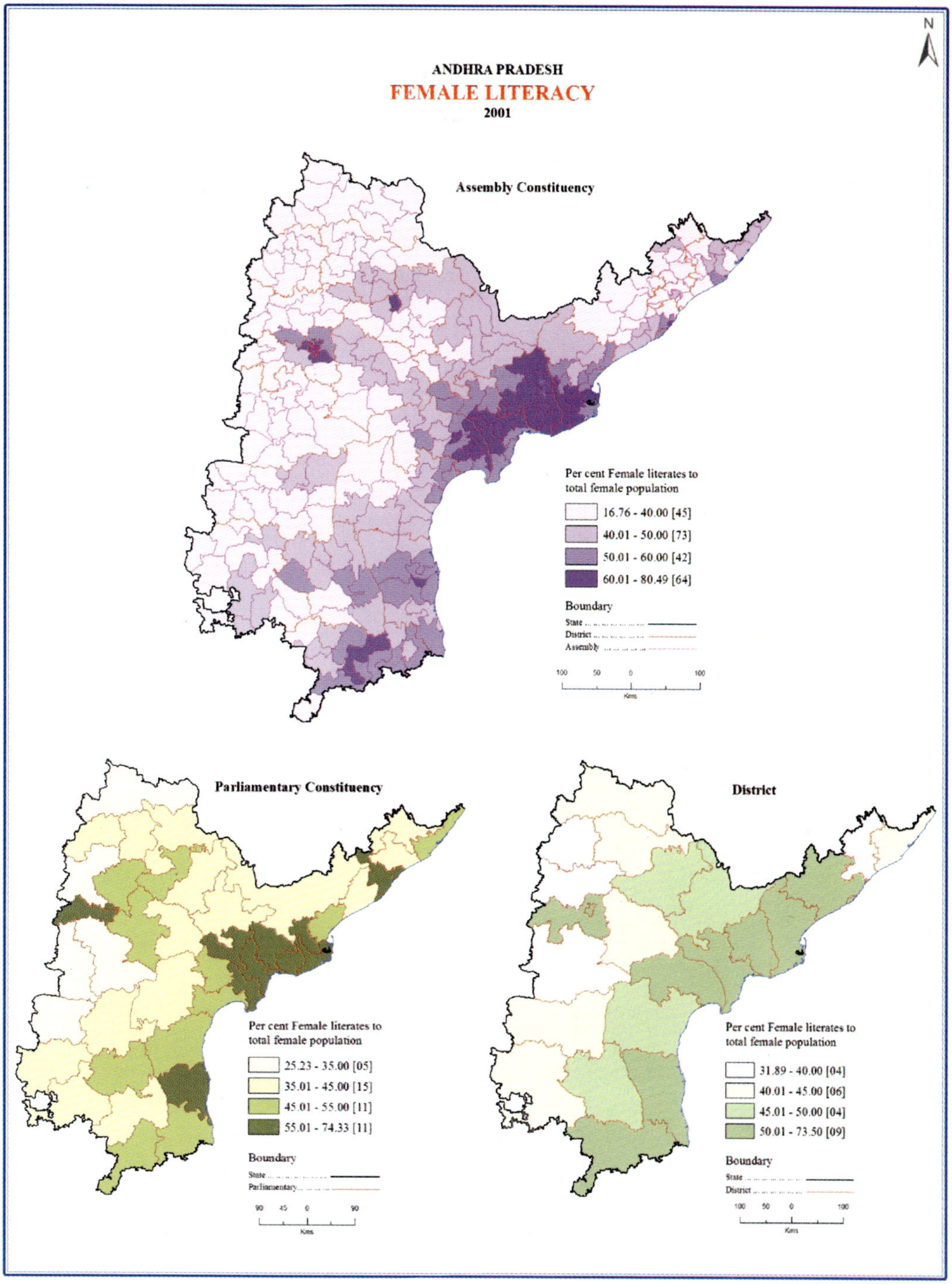

Map 1.9: Andhra Pradesh: Female Literacy, 2001

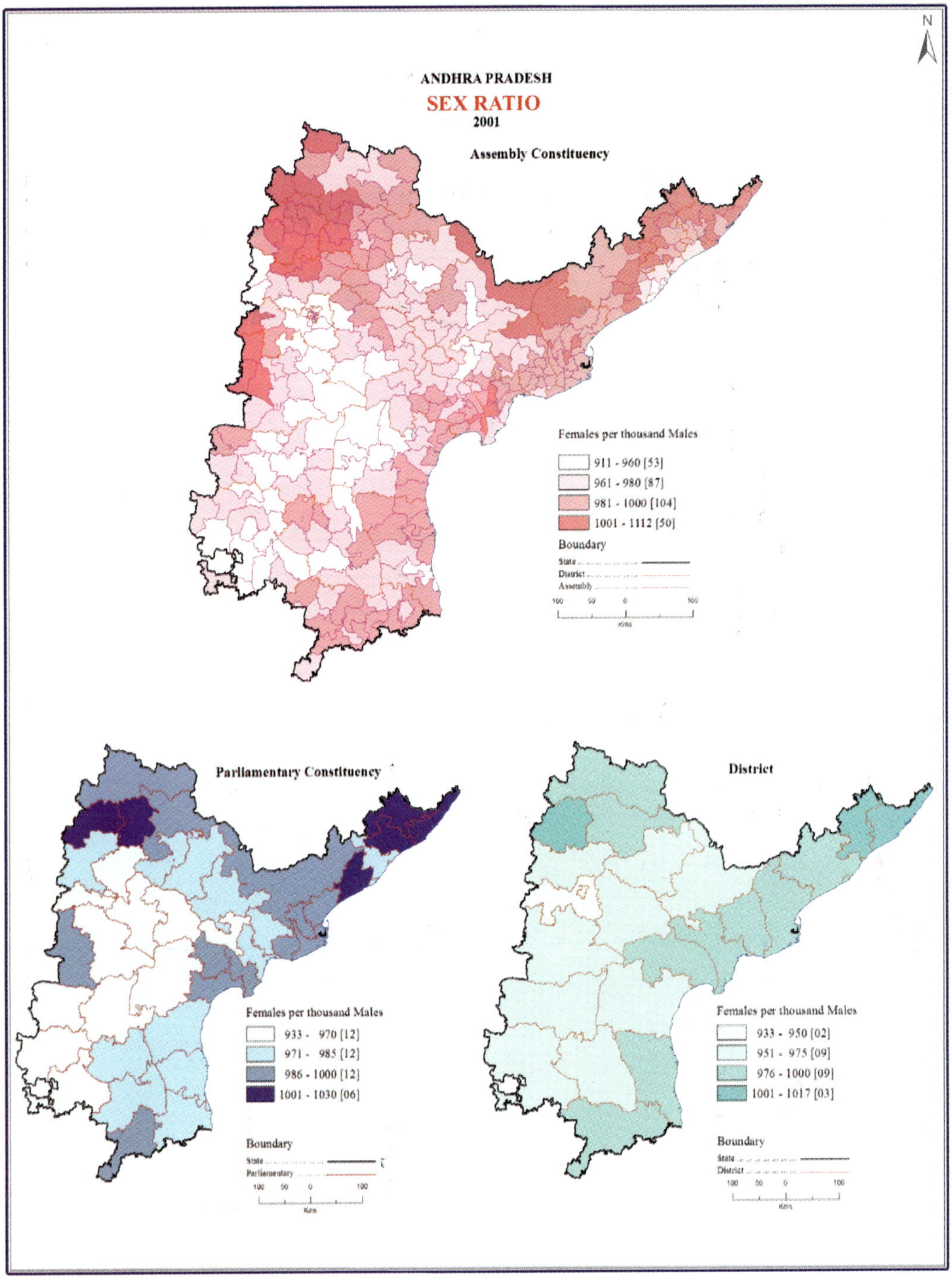

Map 1.10: Andhra Pradesh: Sex Ratio, 2001

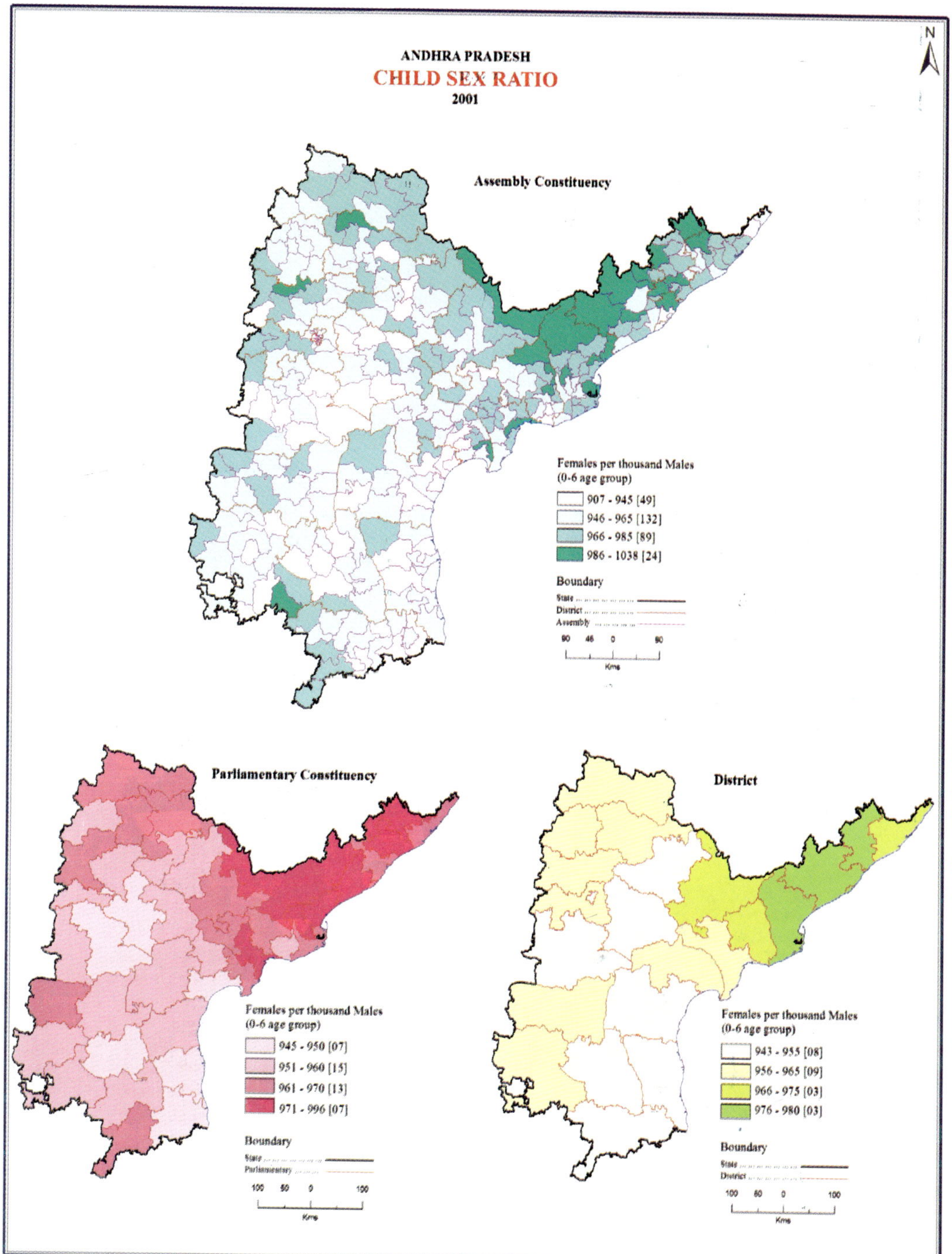

Map 1.11: Andhra Pradesh: Child Sex Ratio: 2001

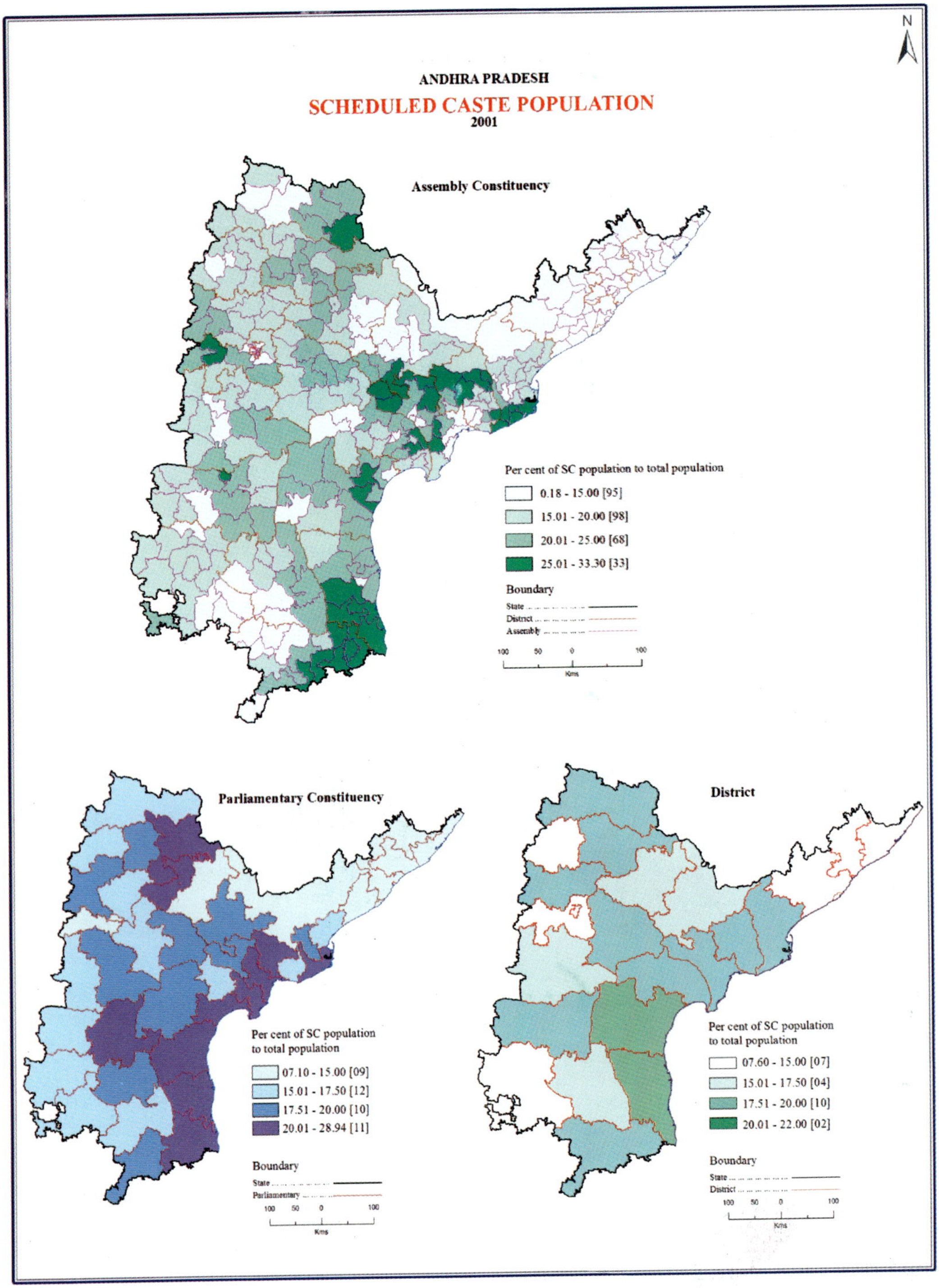

Map 1.12: Andhra Pradesh: Scheduled Caste Population: 2001

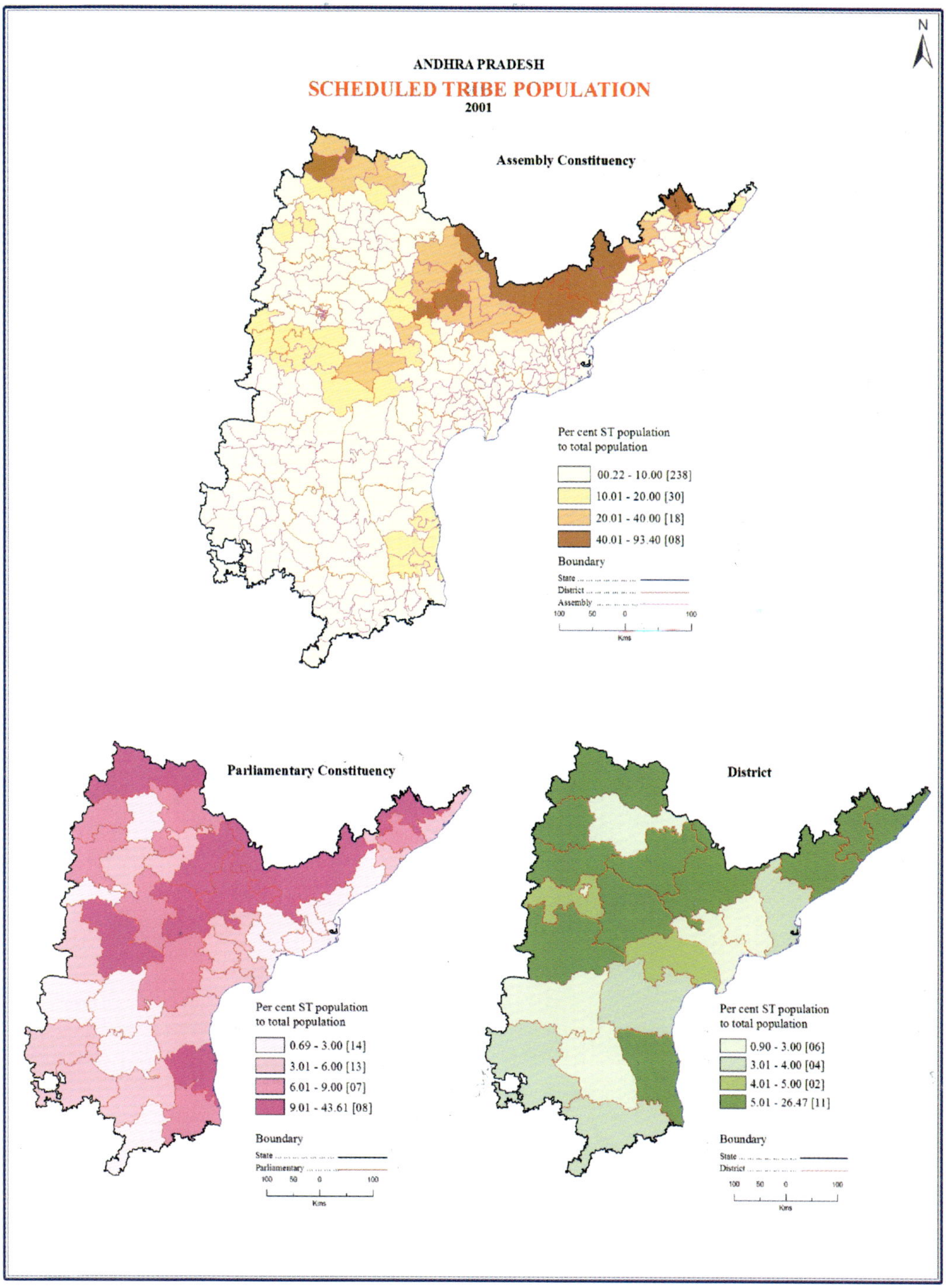

Map 1.13: Andhra Pradesh: Scheduled Tribe Population: 2001

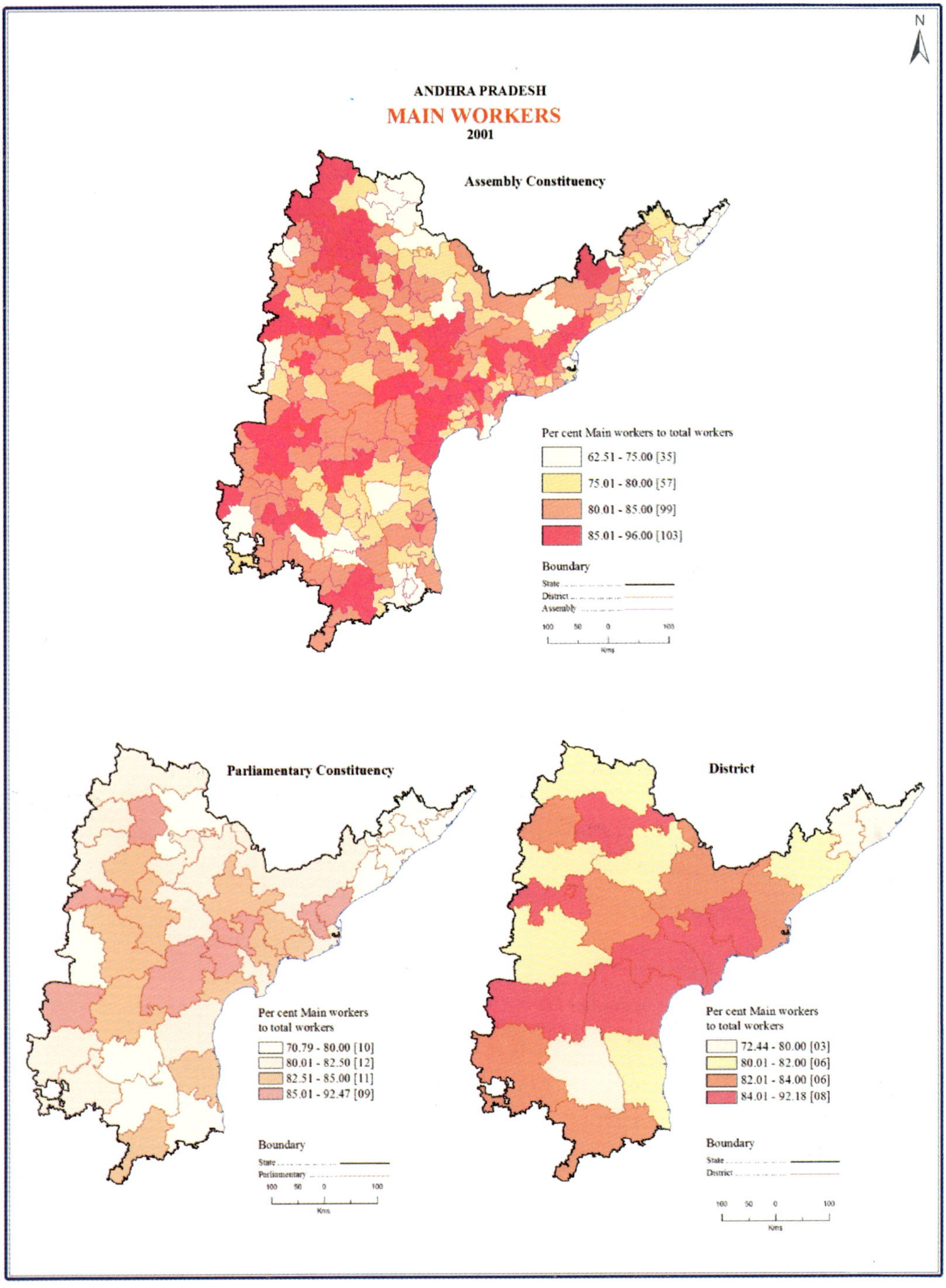

Map 1.14: Andhra Pradesh: Main Workers: 2001

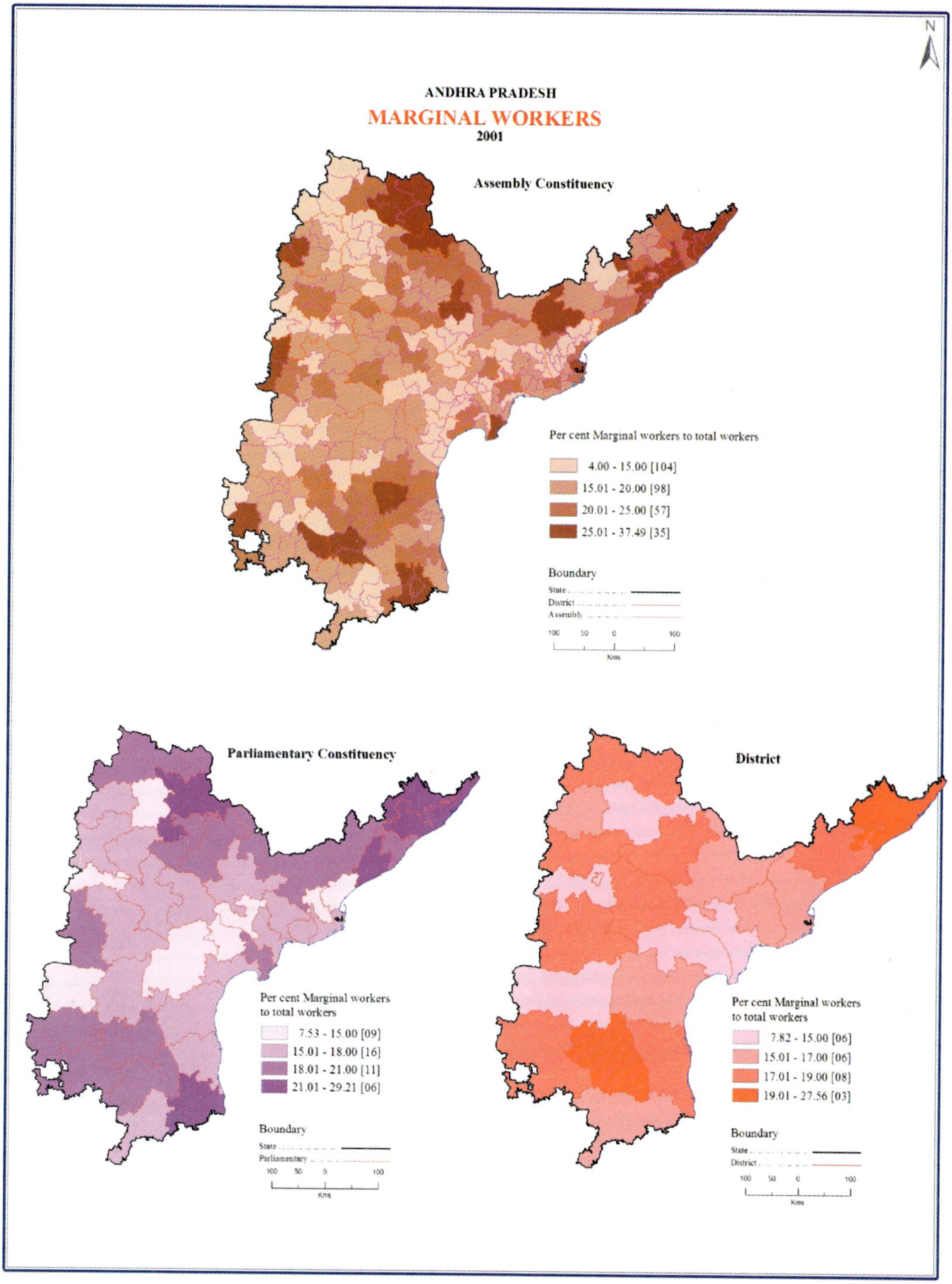

Map 1.15: Andhra Pradesh: Marginal Workers: 2001

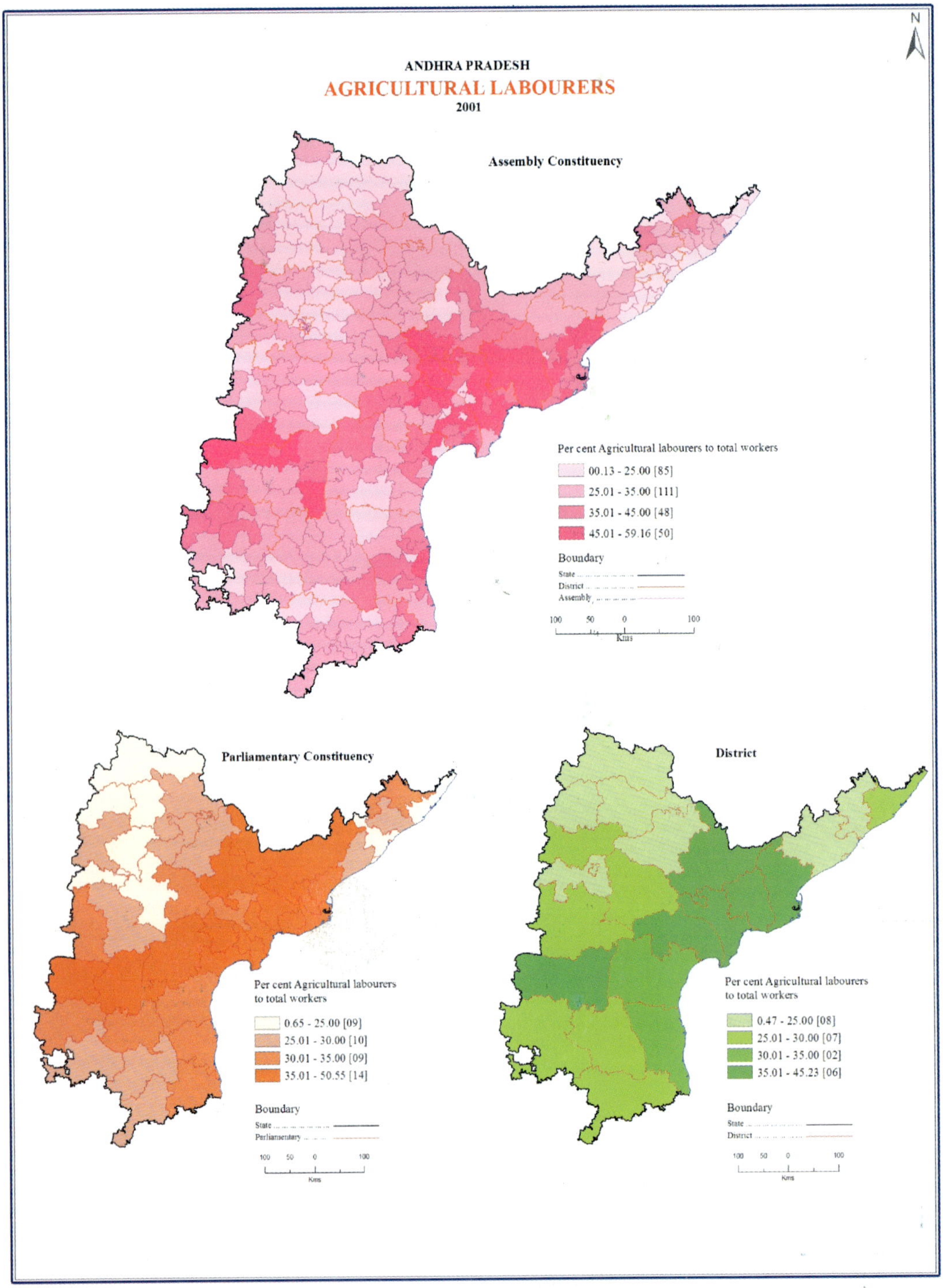

Map 1.16: Andhra Pradesh: Agricultural Laborers: 2001

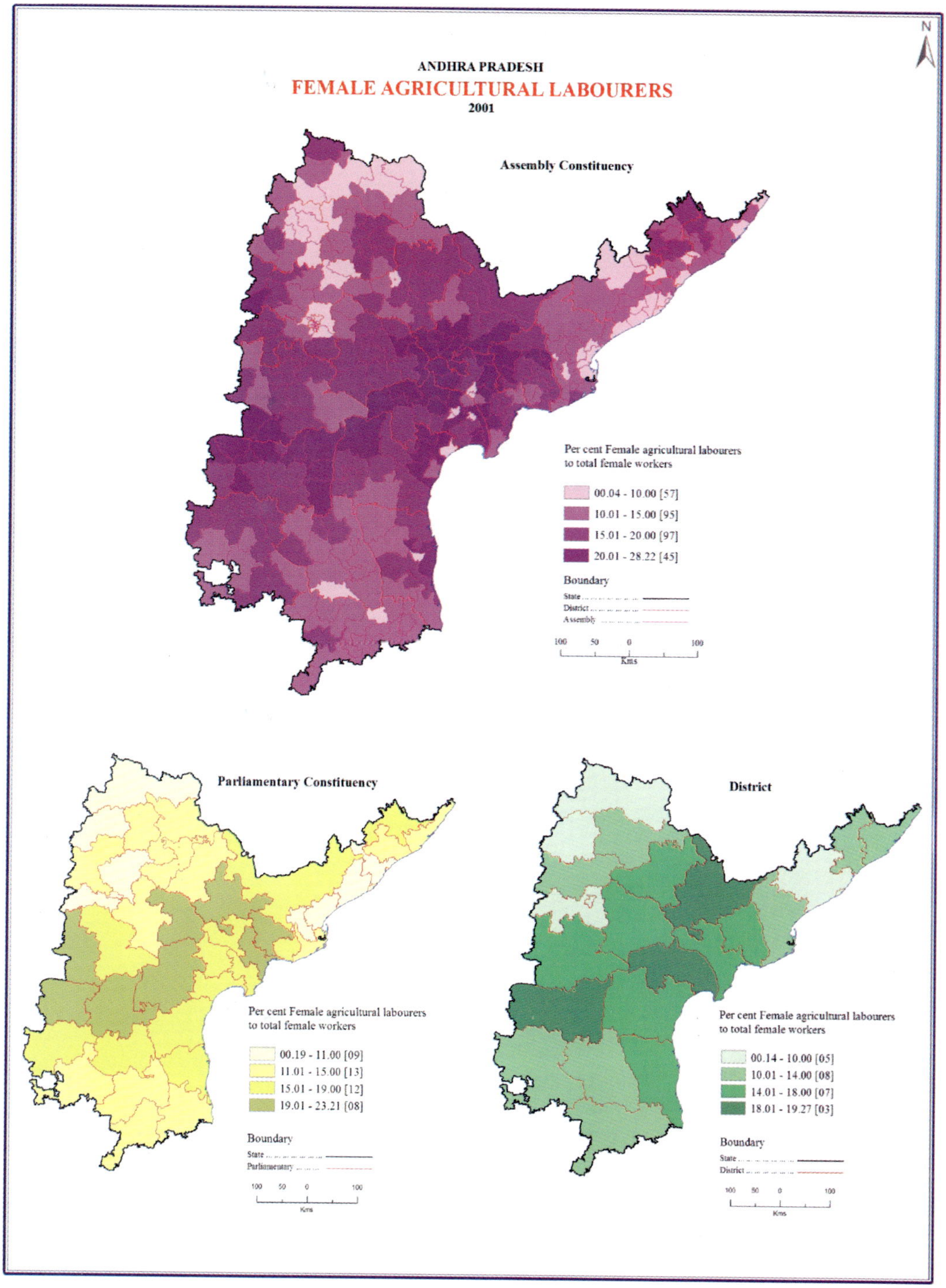

Map 1.17: Andhra Pradesh: Female Agricultural Labourers: 2001

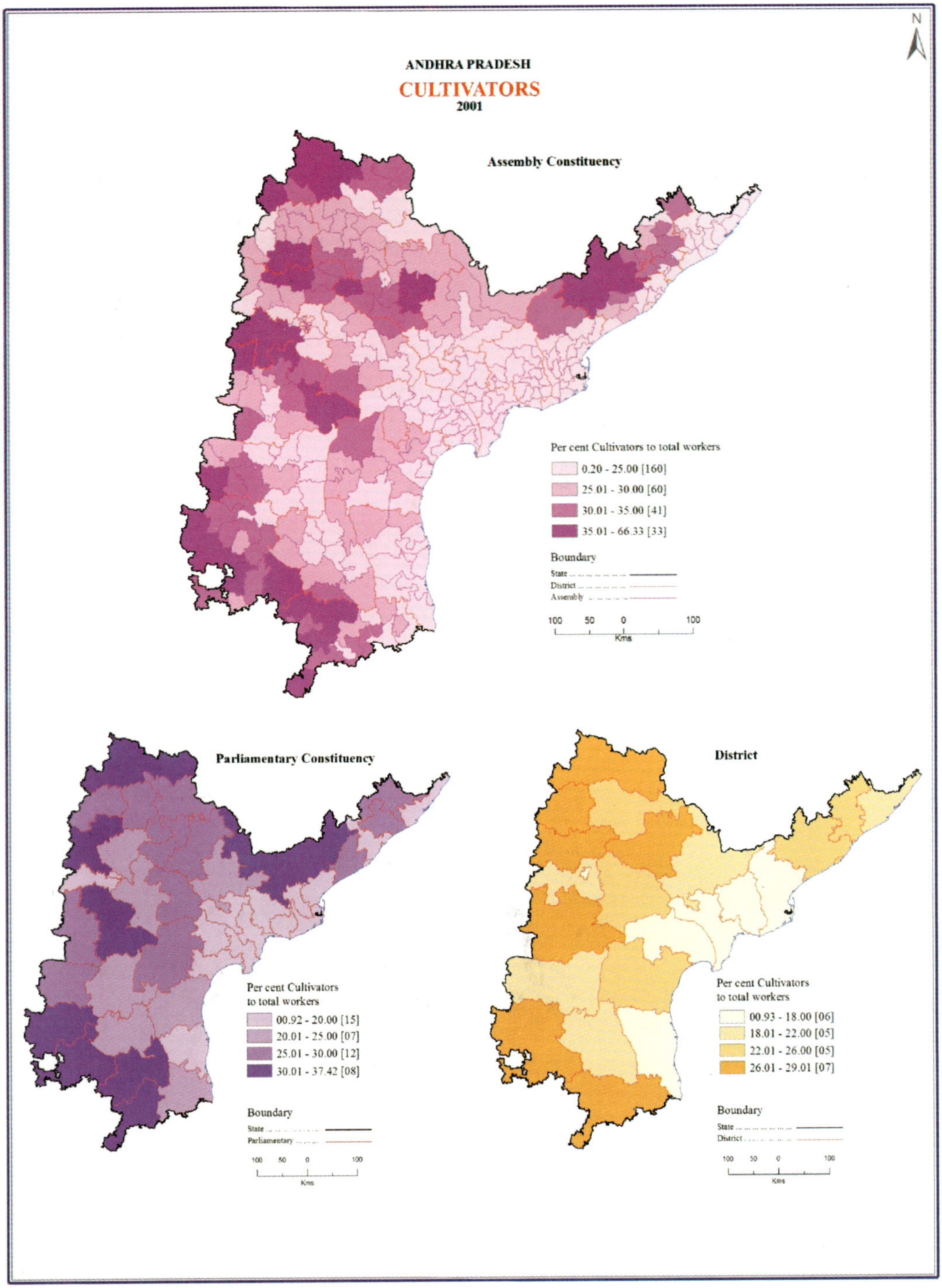

Map 1.18: Andhra Pradesh: Cultivators: 2001

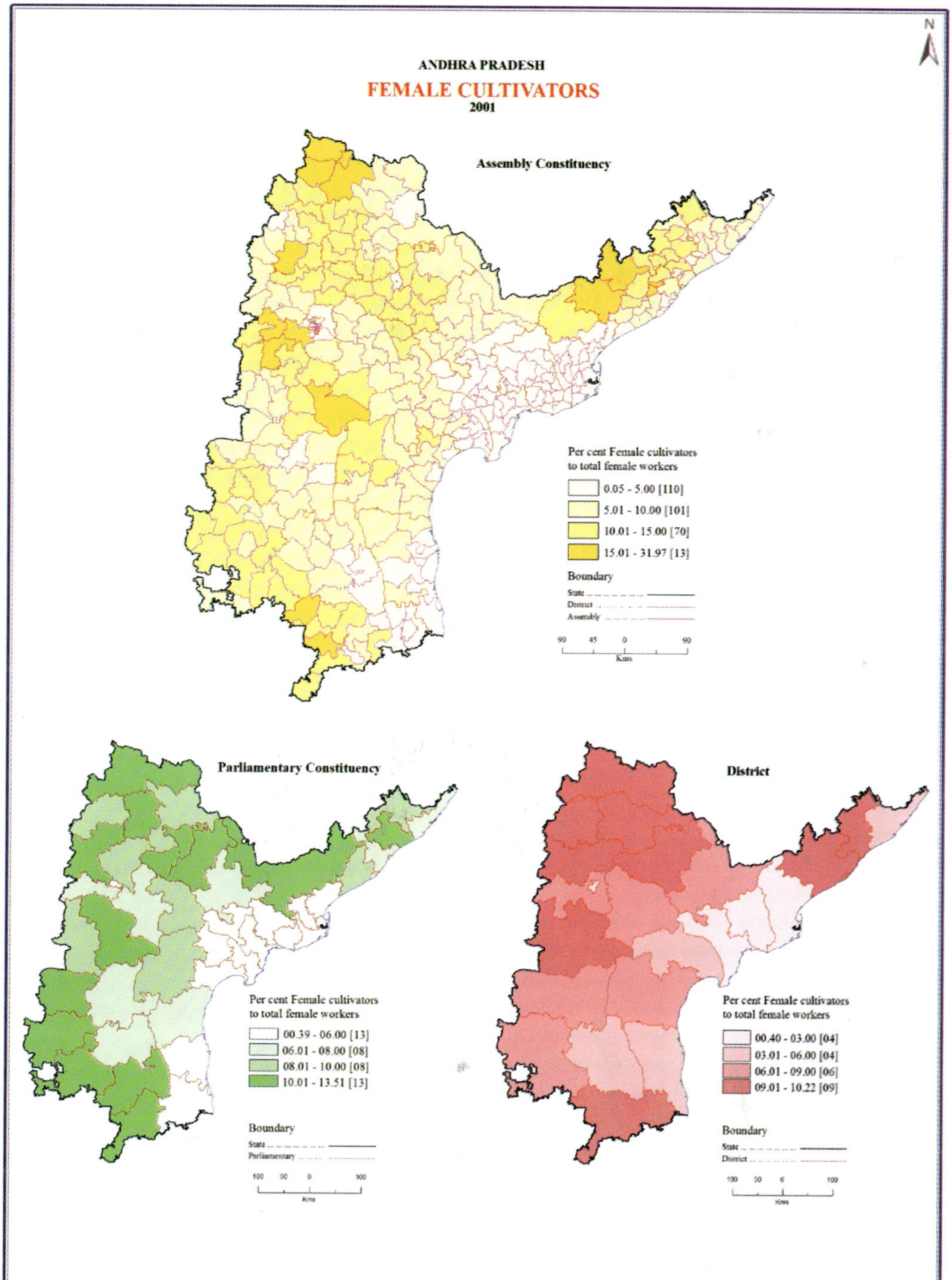

Map 1.19: Andhra Pradesh: Female Cultivators: 2001

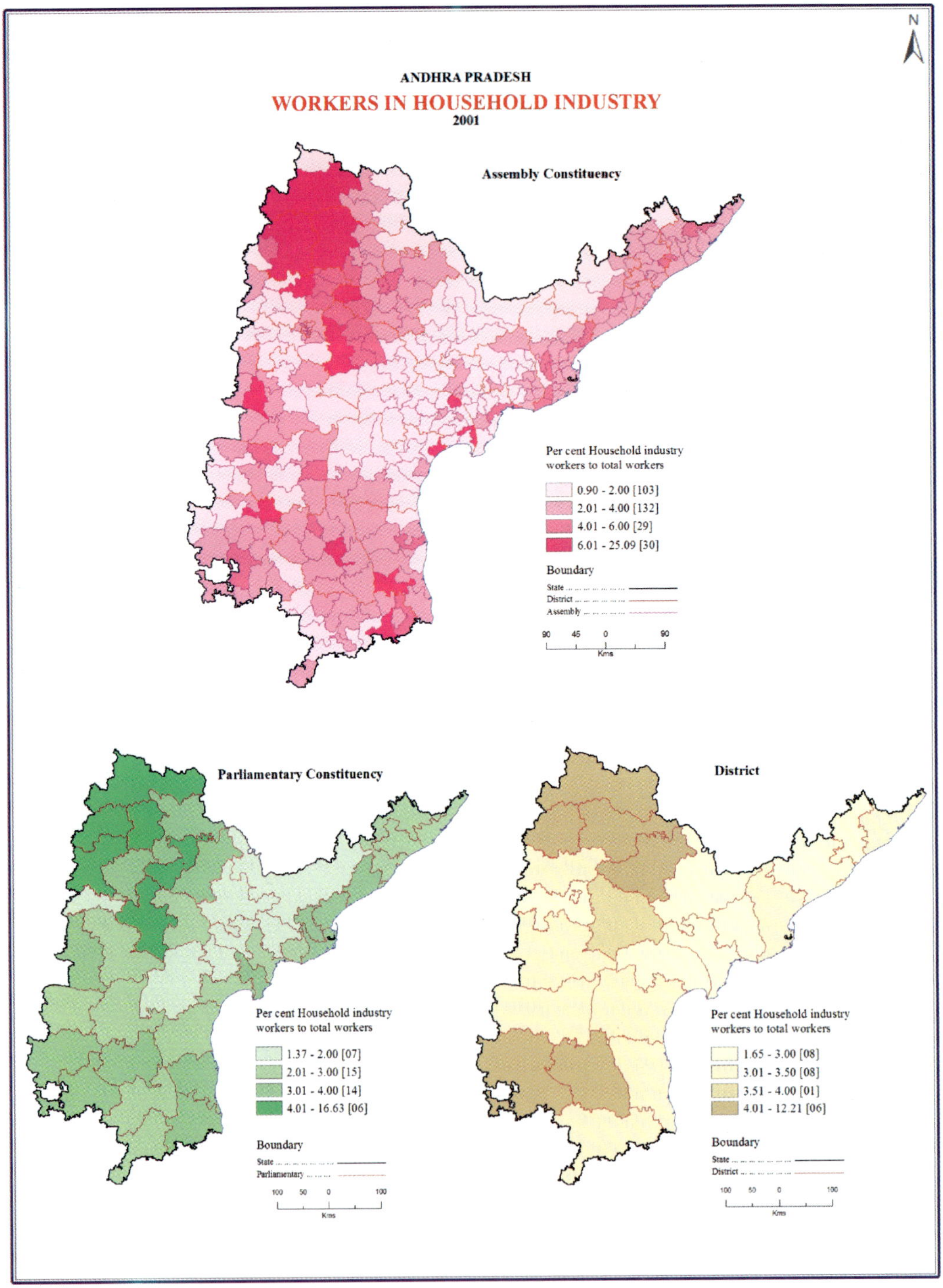

Map 1.20: Andhra Pradesh: Workers in Household Industry: 2001

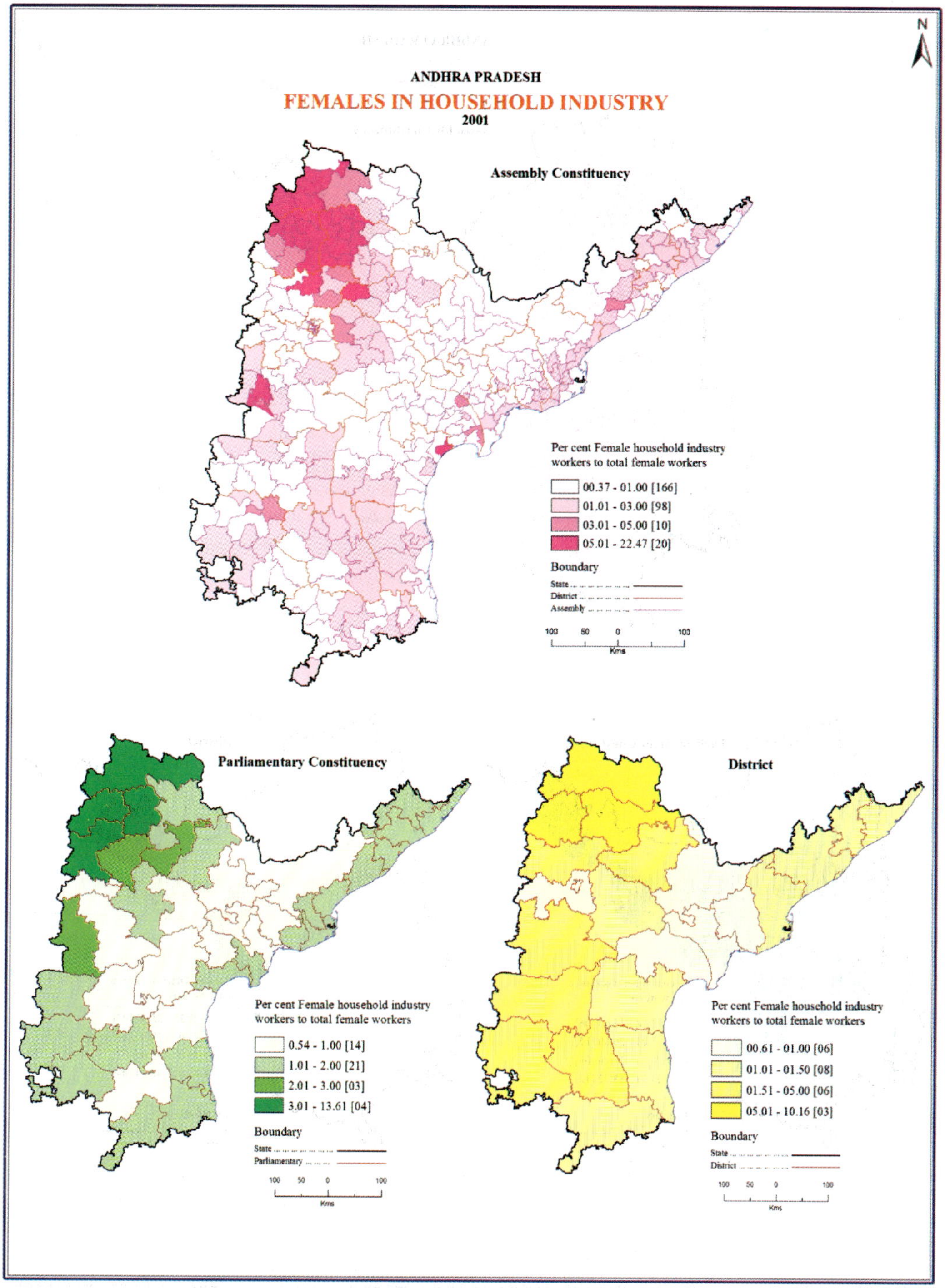

Map 1.21: Andhra Pradesh: Females in Household Industry: 2001

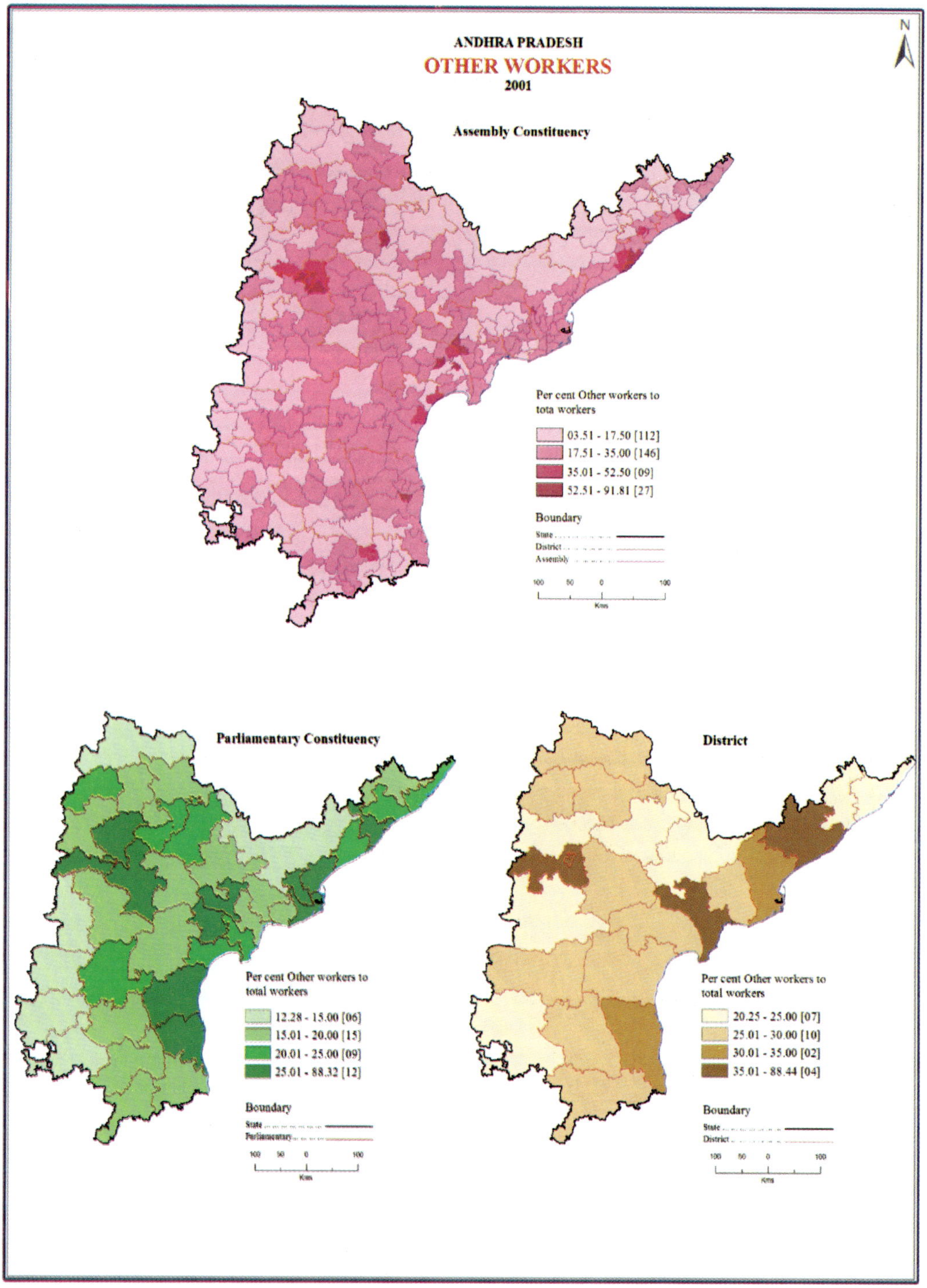

Map 1.22: Andhra Pradesh: Other Workers: 2001

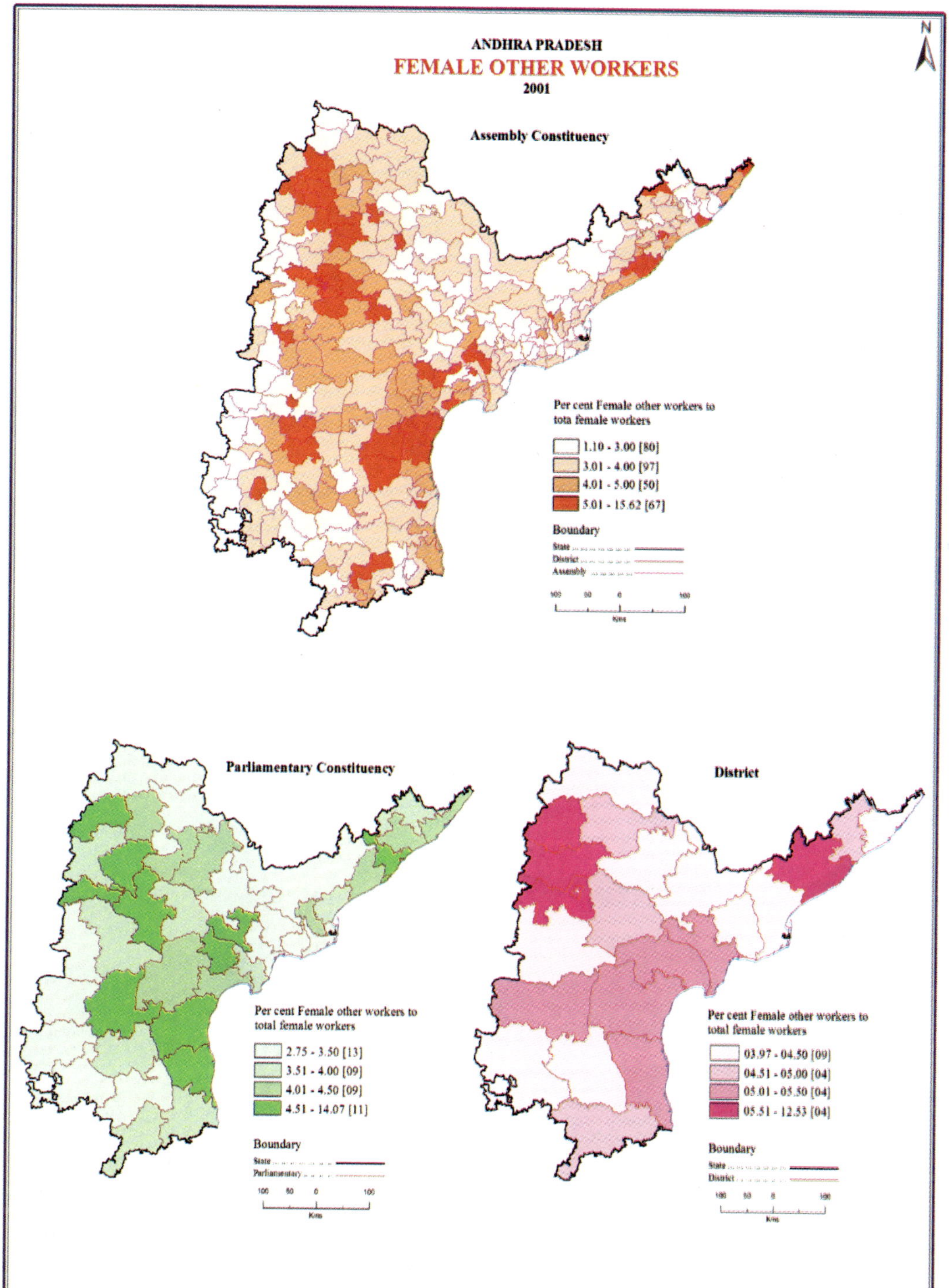

Map 1.23: Andhra Pradesh: Female Other Workers: 2001

Map 2.1: India: Parliament Divisions-543: 2004

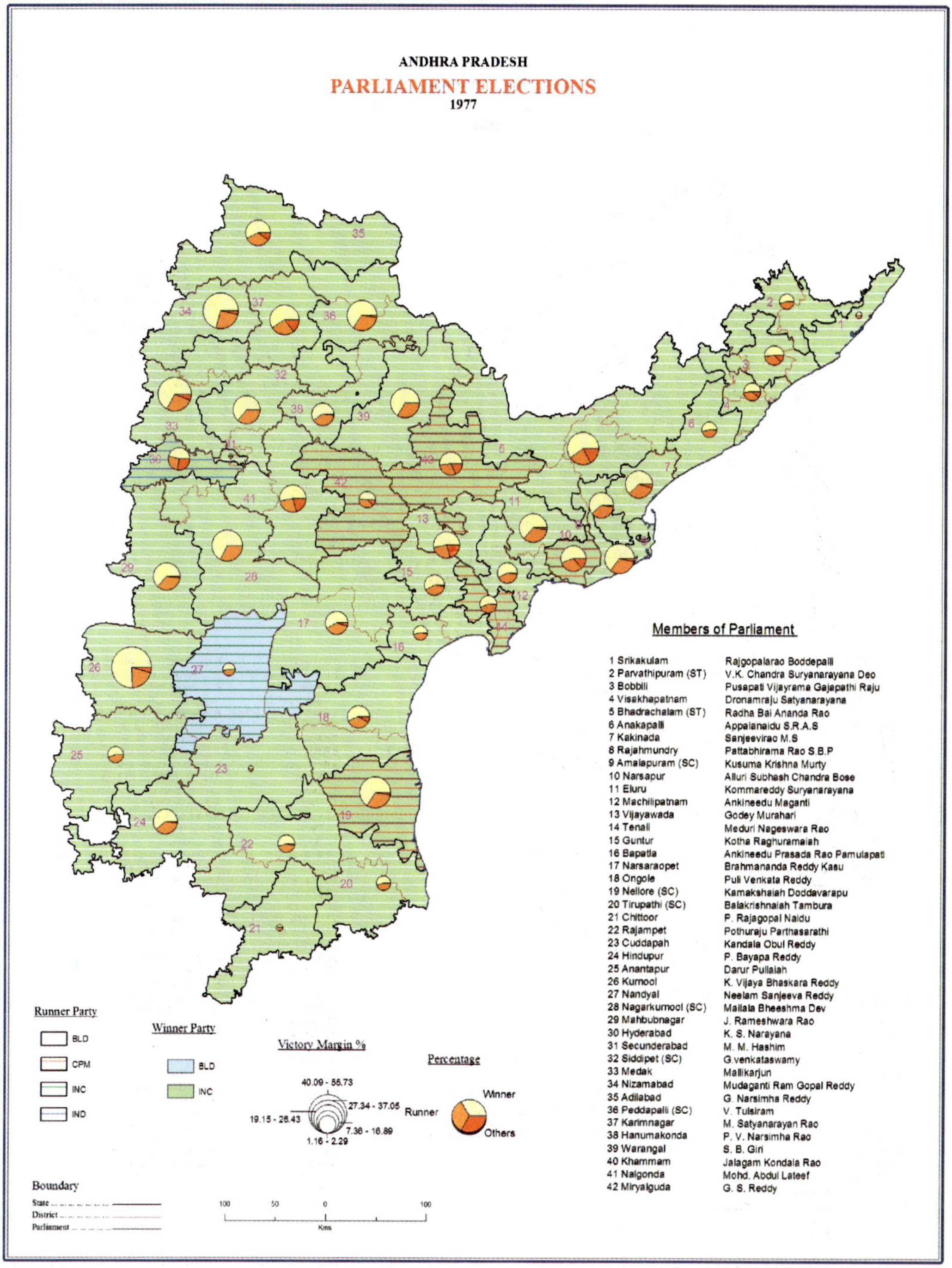

Map 2.2: Andhra Pradesh: Parliament Elections: 1977

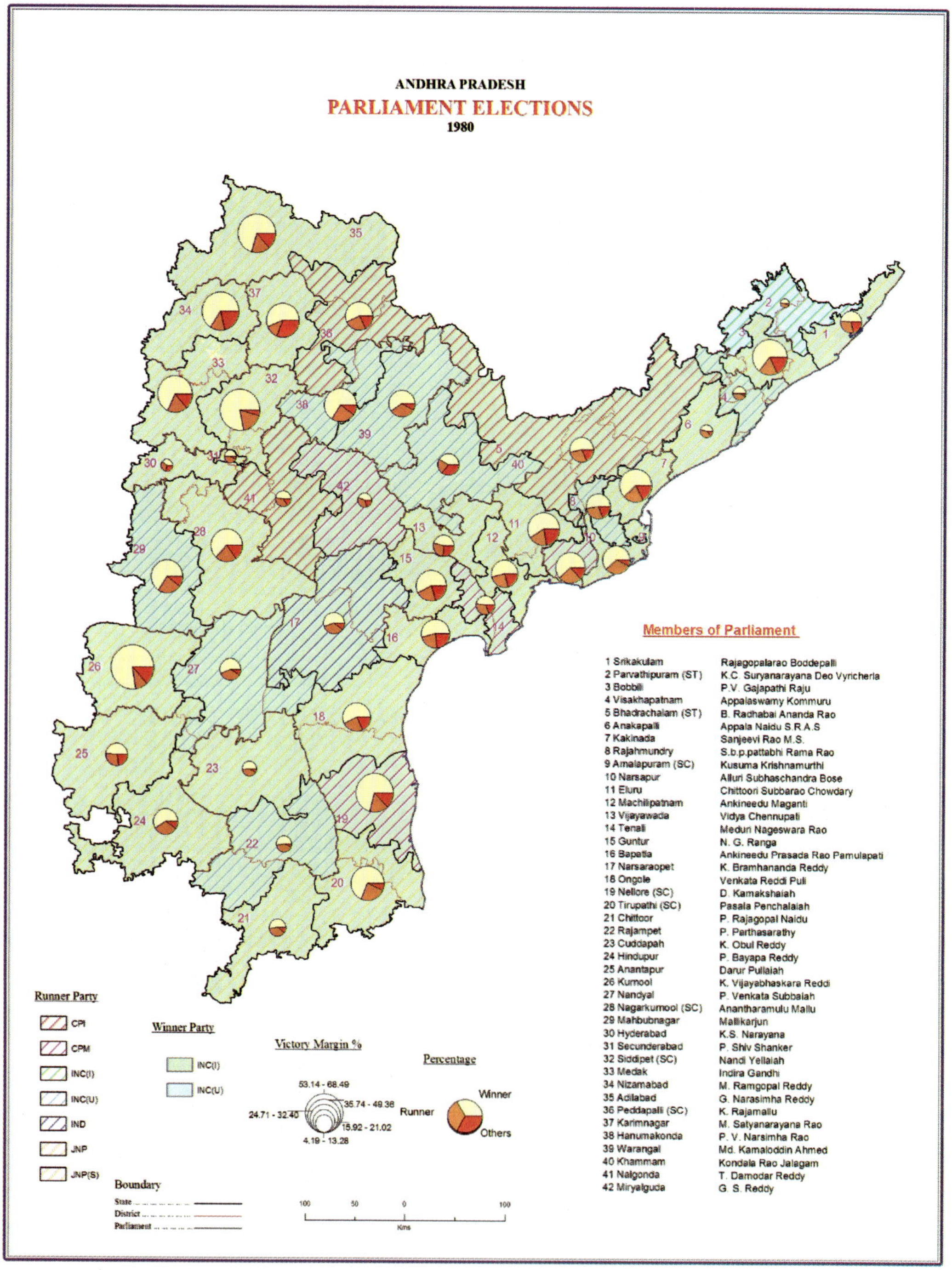

Map 2.3: Andhra Pradesh: Parliament Elections: 1980

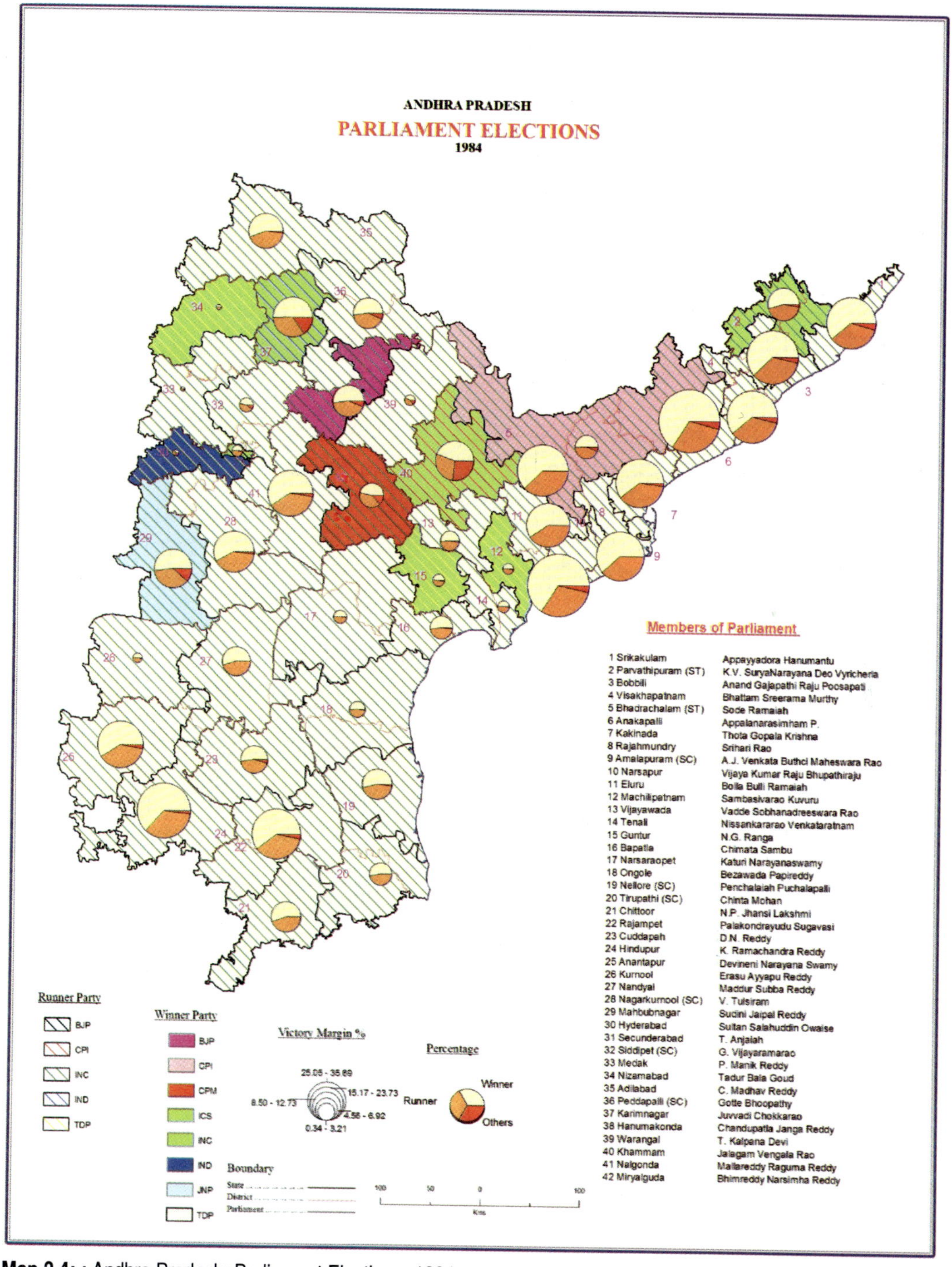

Map 2.4: : Andhra Pradesh: Parliament Elections: 1984

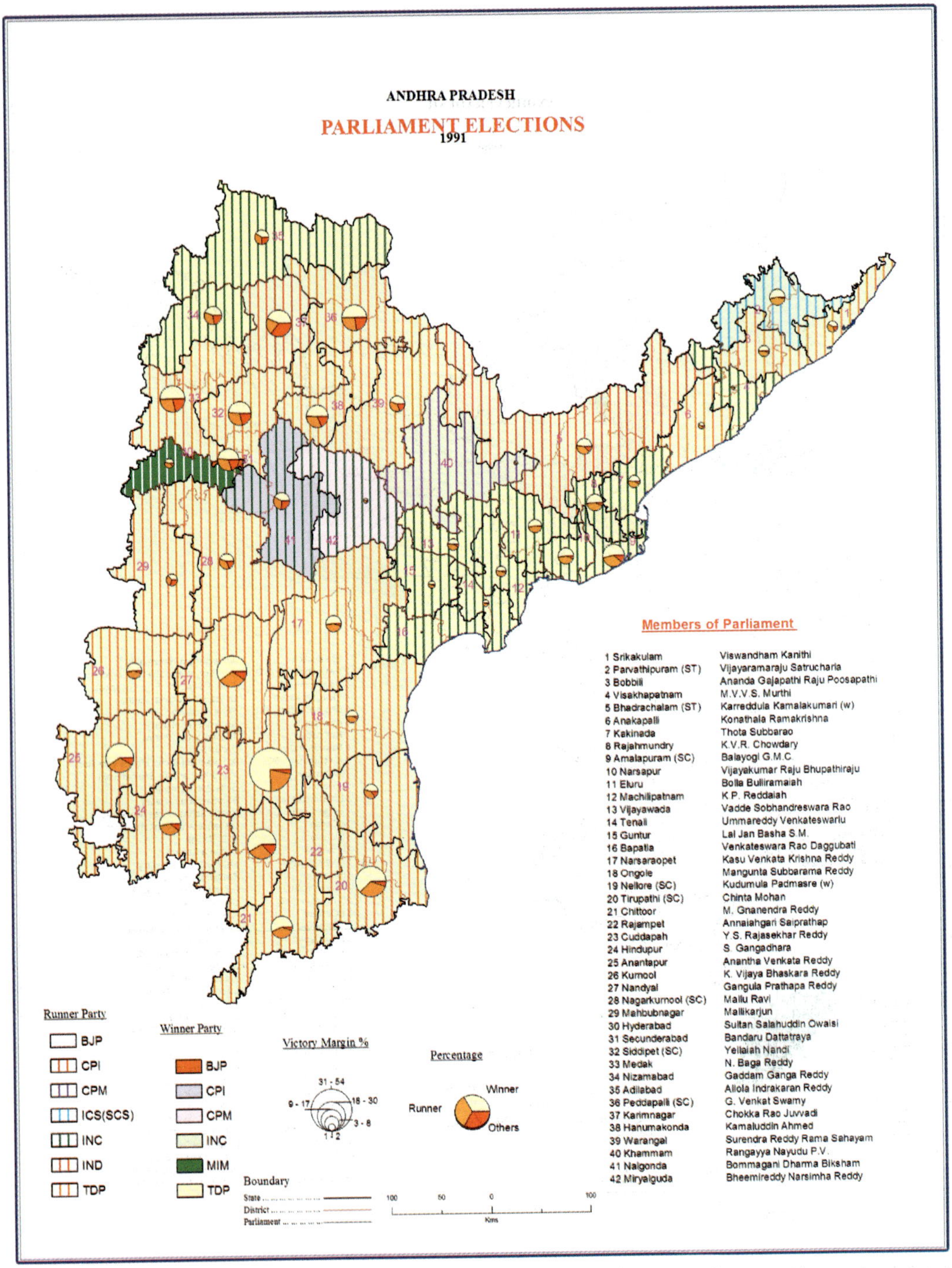

Map 2.5: Andhra Pradesh: Parliament Elections: 1991

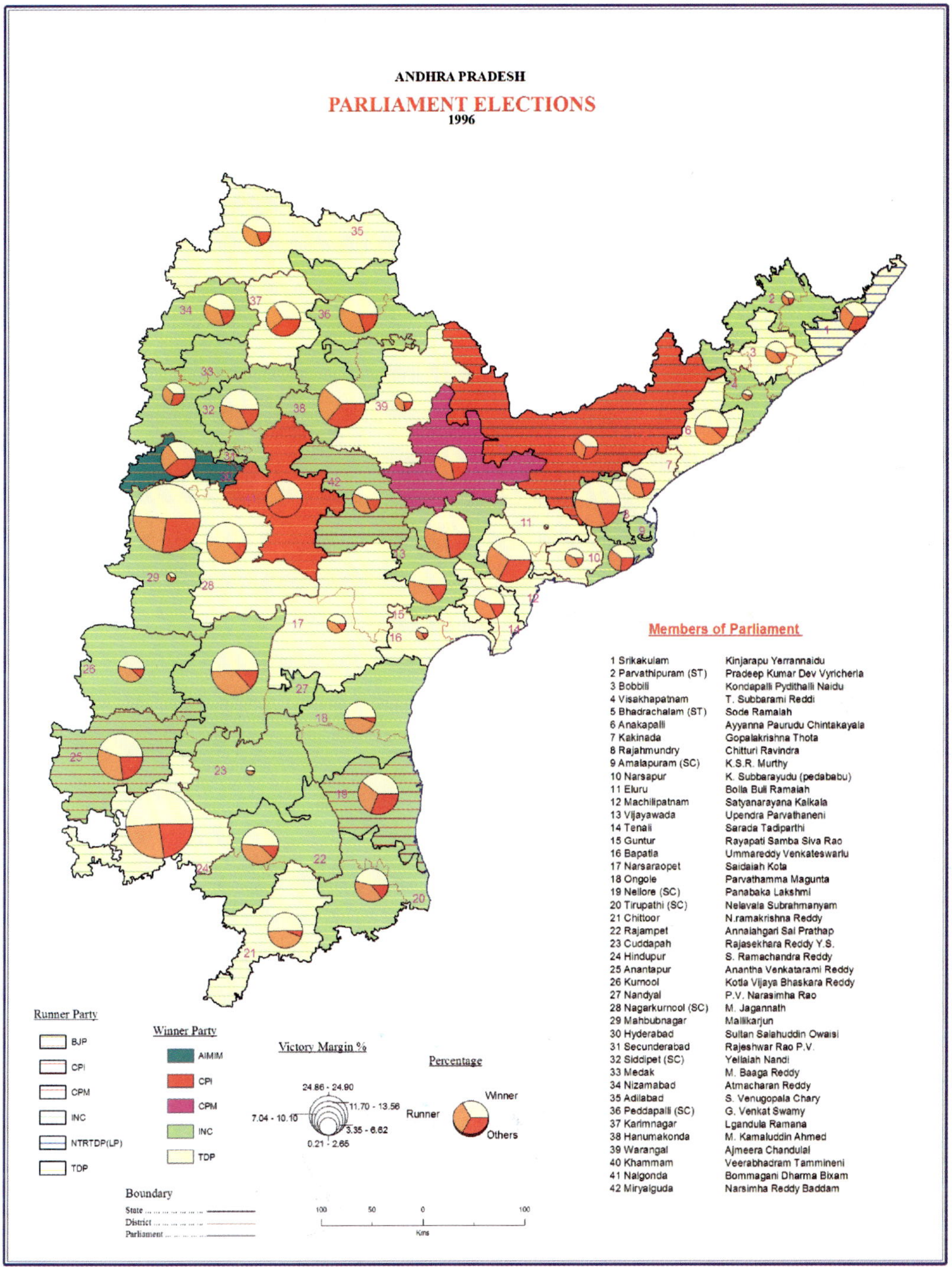

Map 2.6: Andhra Pradesh: Parliament Elections: 1996

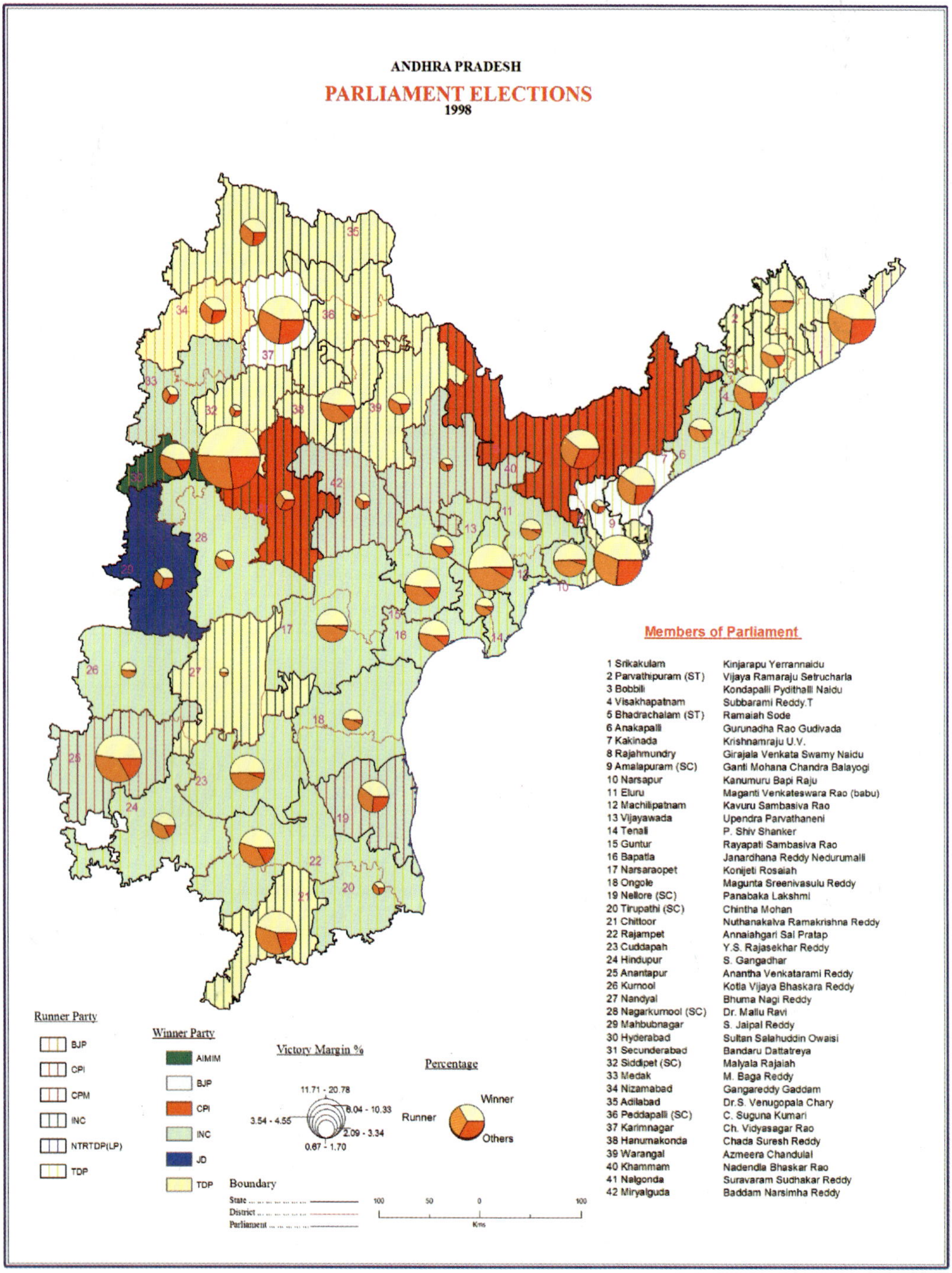

Map 2.7: Andhra Pradesh: Parliament Elections: 1998

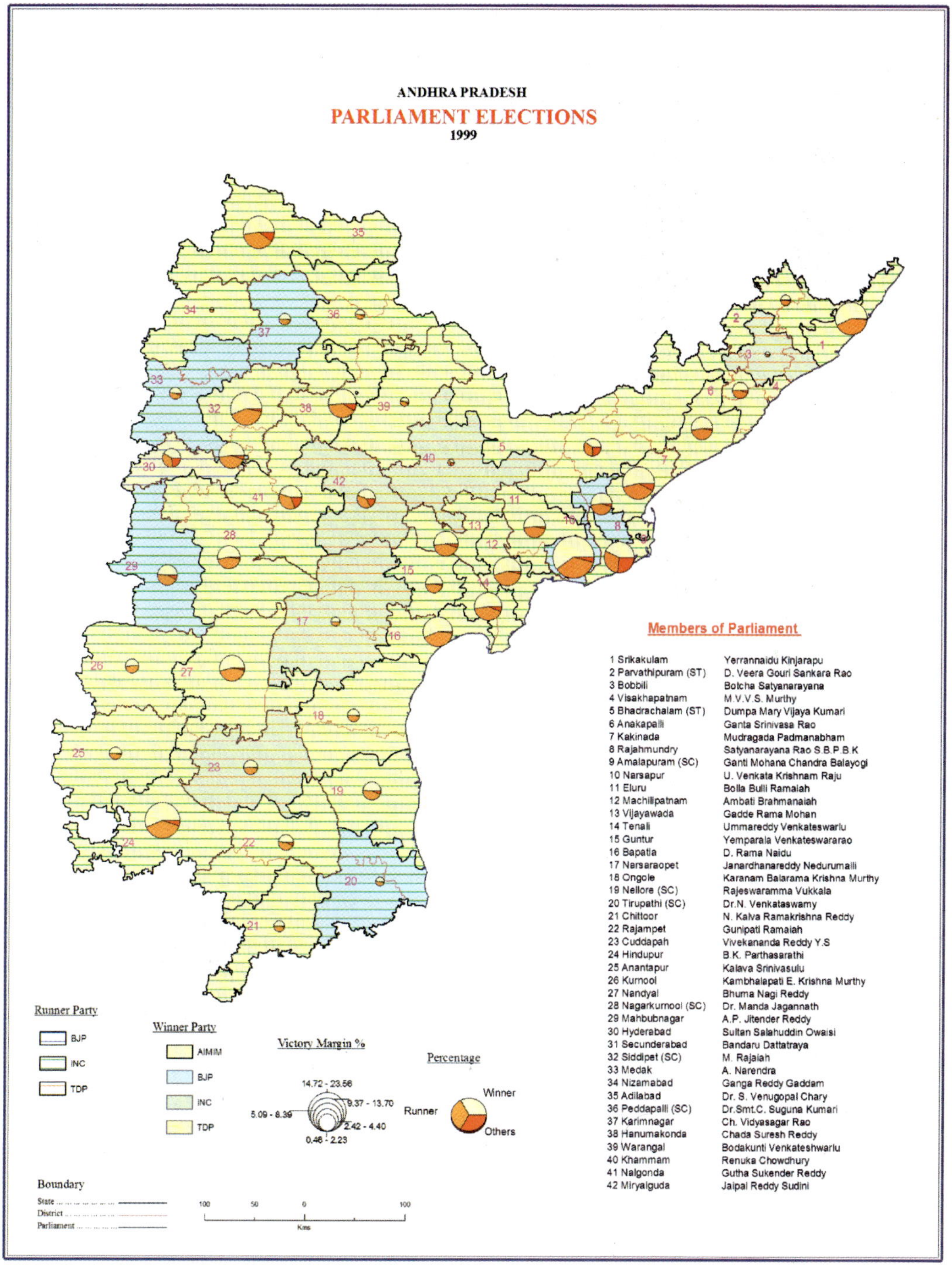

Map 2.8: Andhra Pradesh: Parliament Elections: 1999

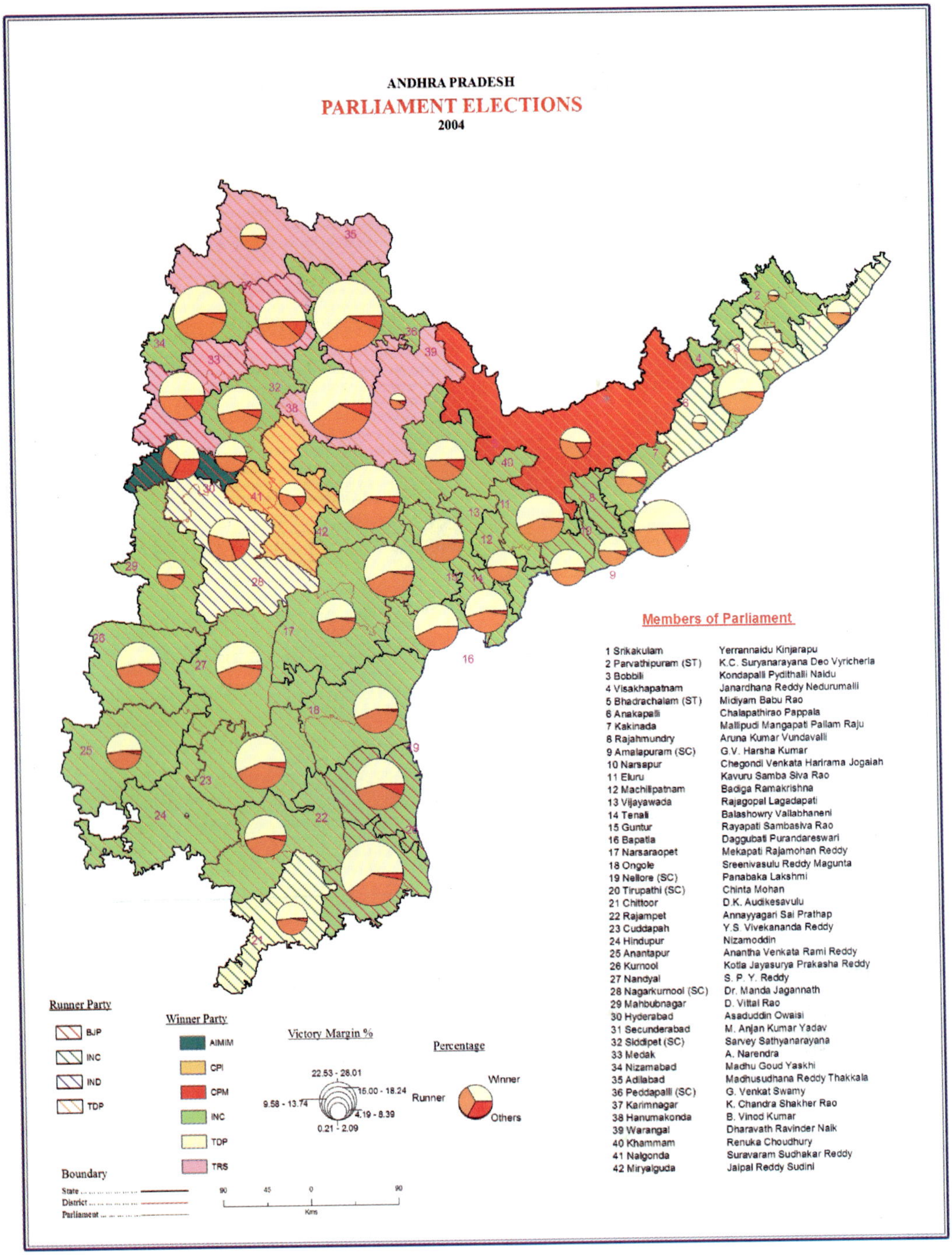

Map 2.9: Andhra Pradesh: Parliament Elections, 2004

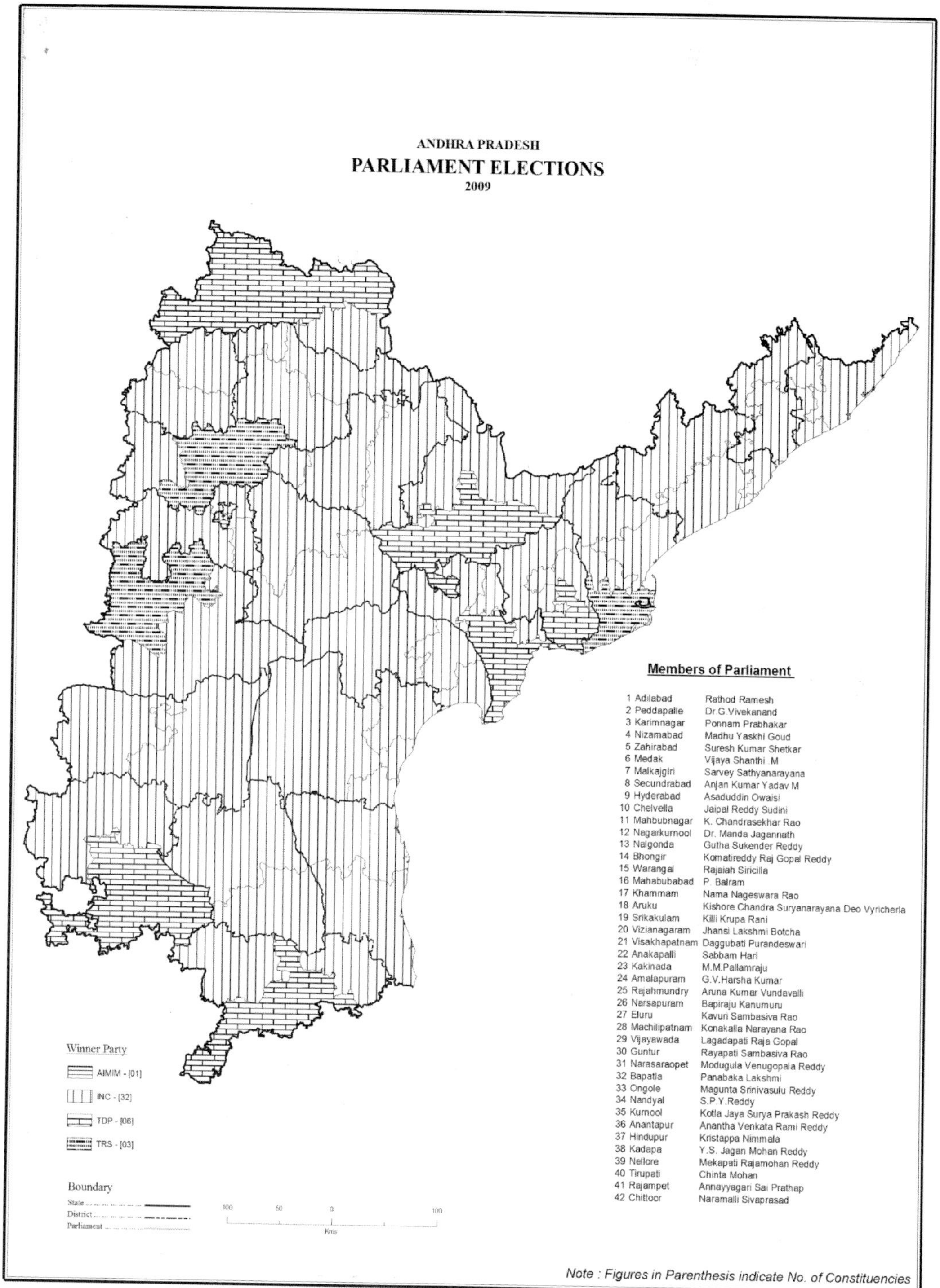

Map 2.10: Andhra Pradesh: Parliament Elections, 2009

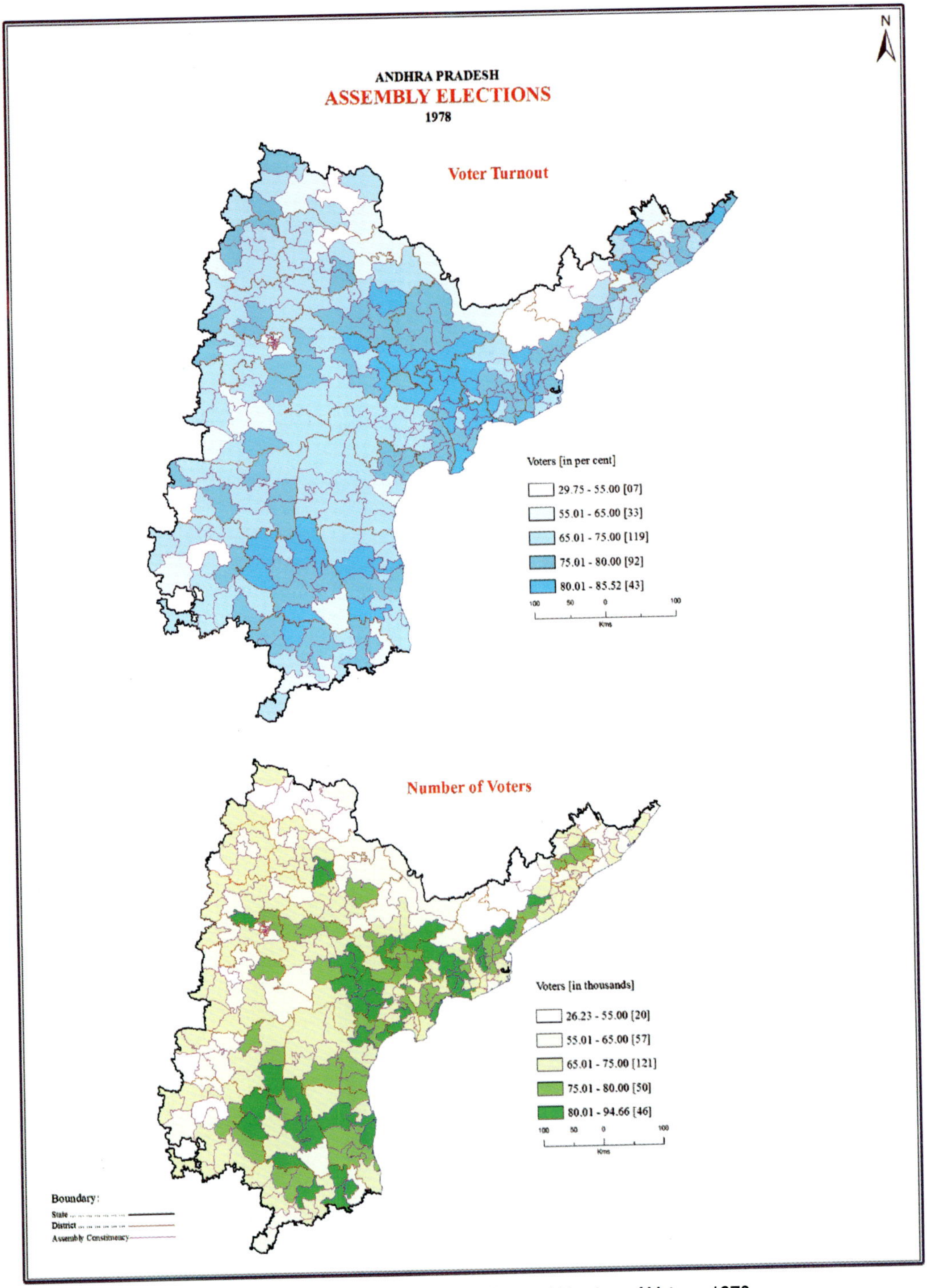

Map 3.1: Andhra Pradesh: Assembly Elections: Voter Turn Out and Number of Voters: 1978

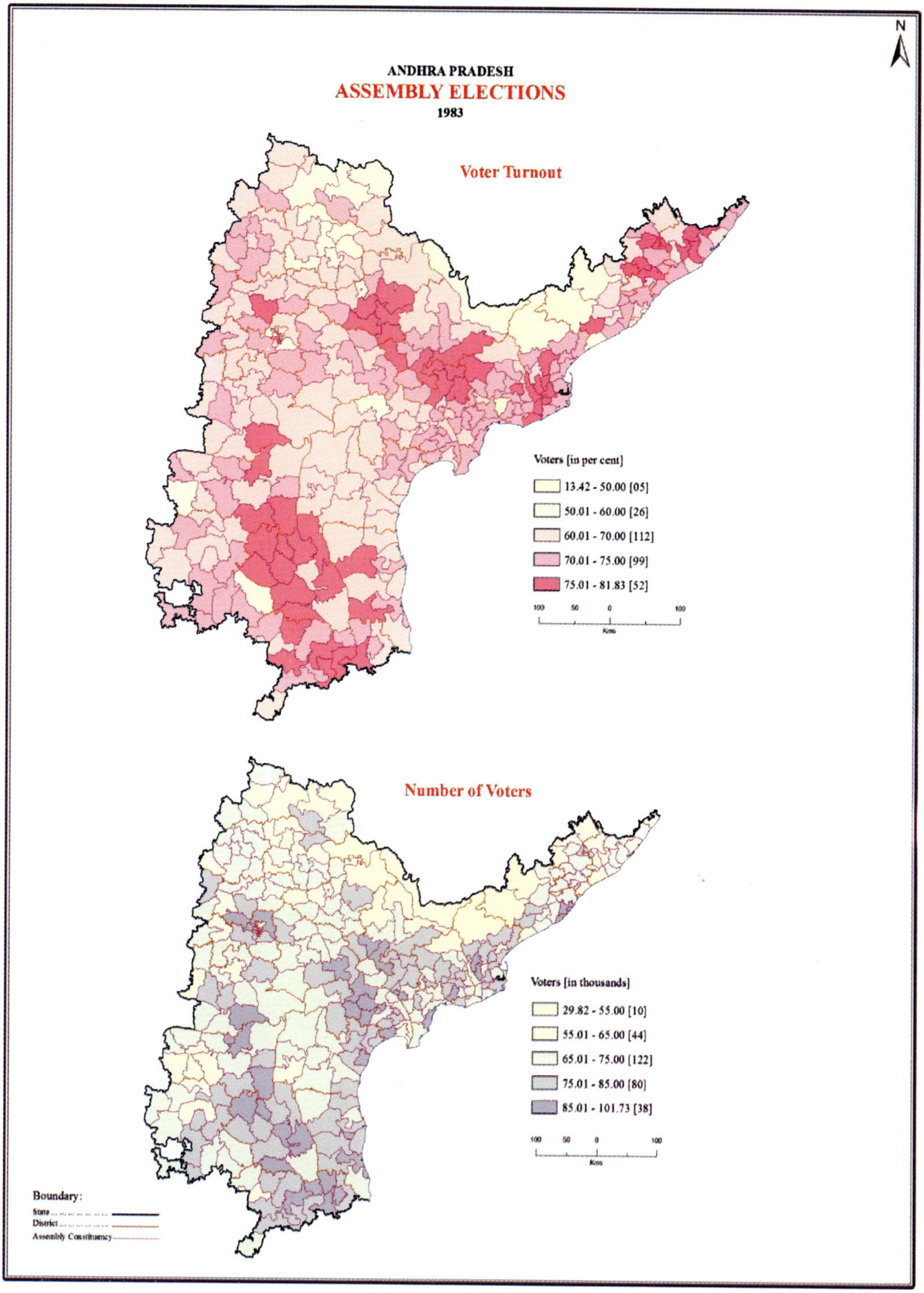

Map 3.2: Andhra Pradesh: Assembly Elections :Voter Turn Out and Number of Voters: 1983

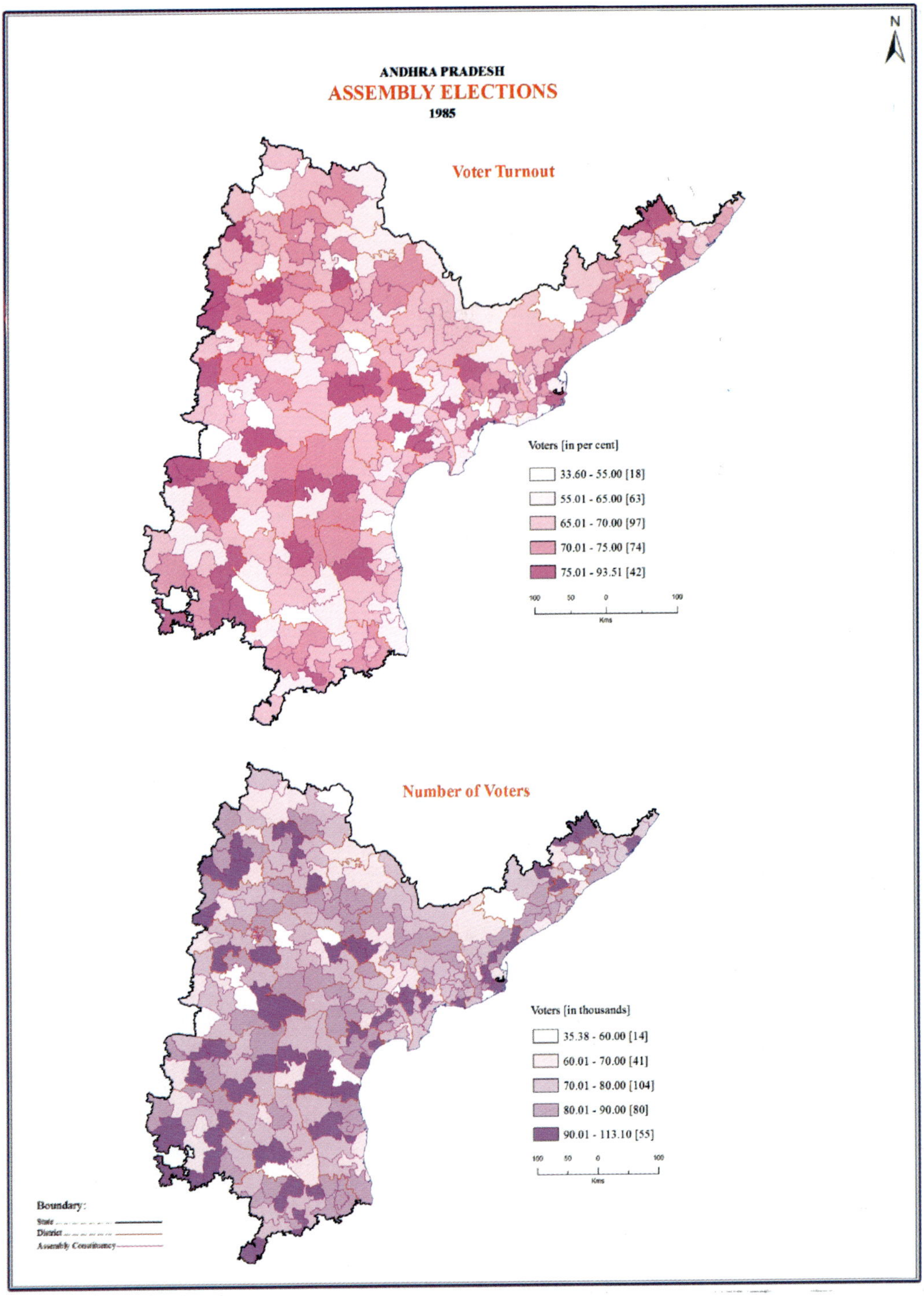

Map 3.3: Andhra Pradesh: Assembly Elections : Voter Turn Out and Number of Voters: 1985

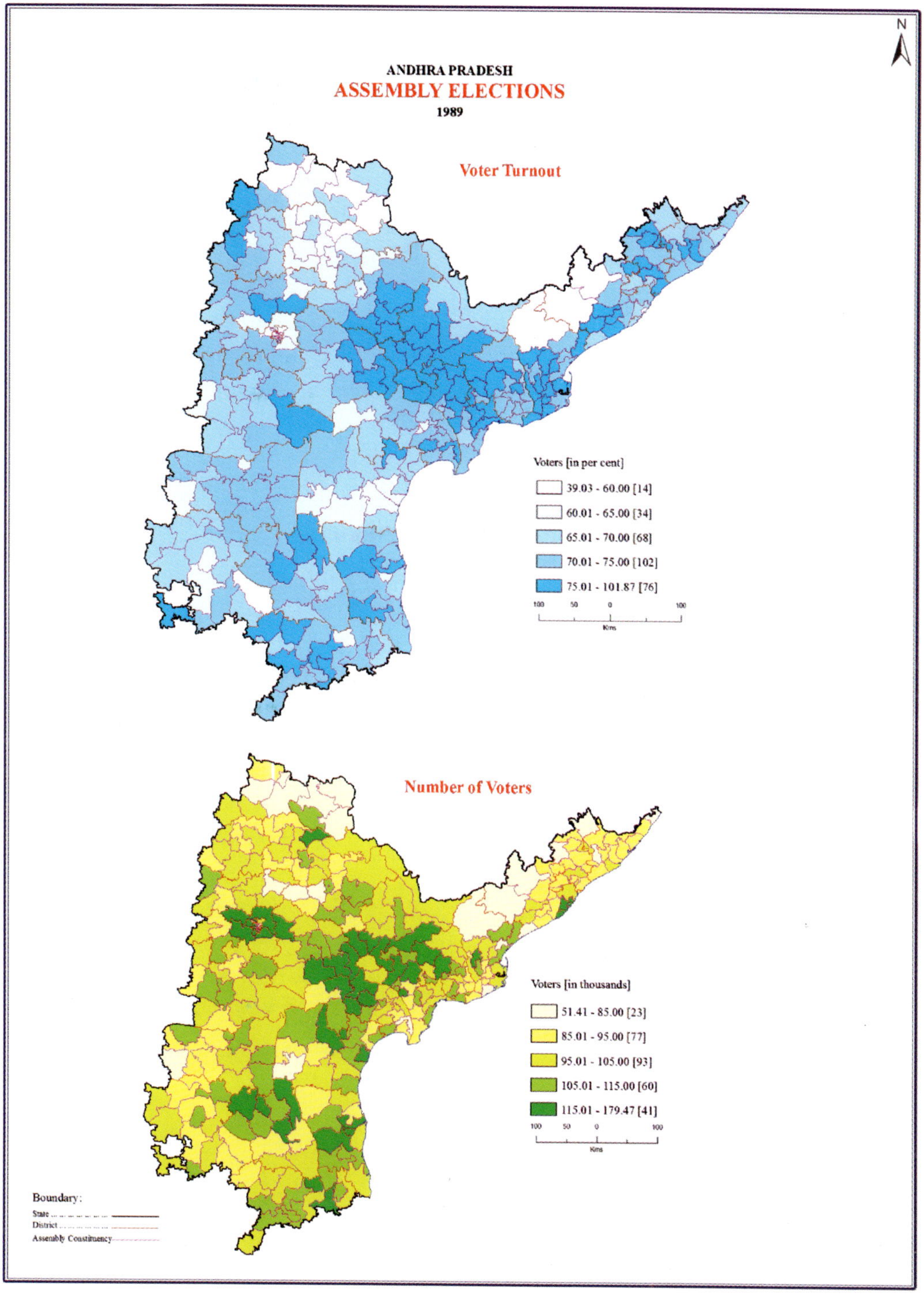

Map 3.4: Andhra Pradesh: Assembly Elections : Voter Turn Out and Number of Voters: 1989

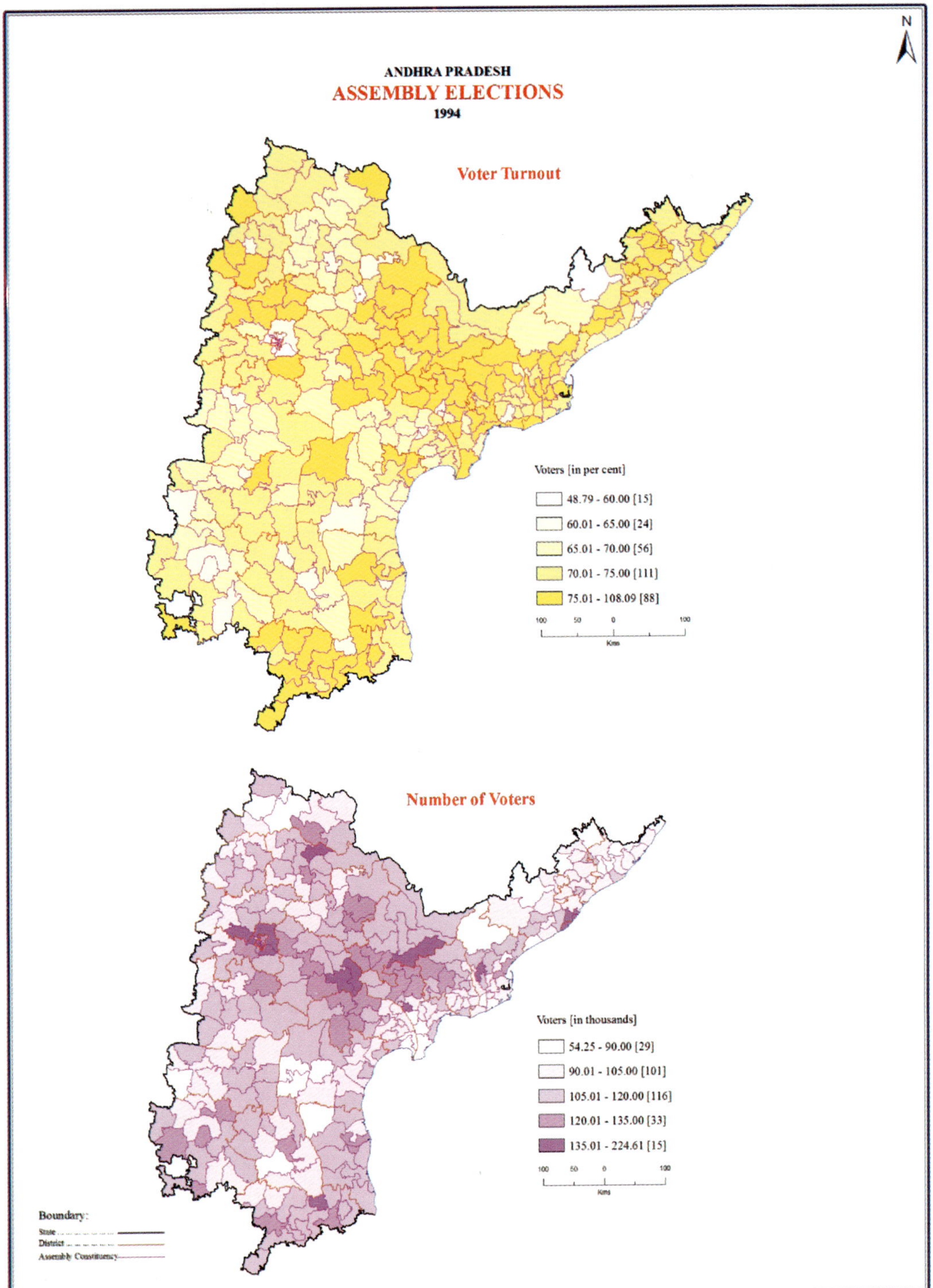

Map 3.5: Andhra Pradesh: Assembly Elections : Voter Turn Out and Number of Voters : 1994

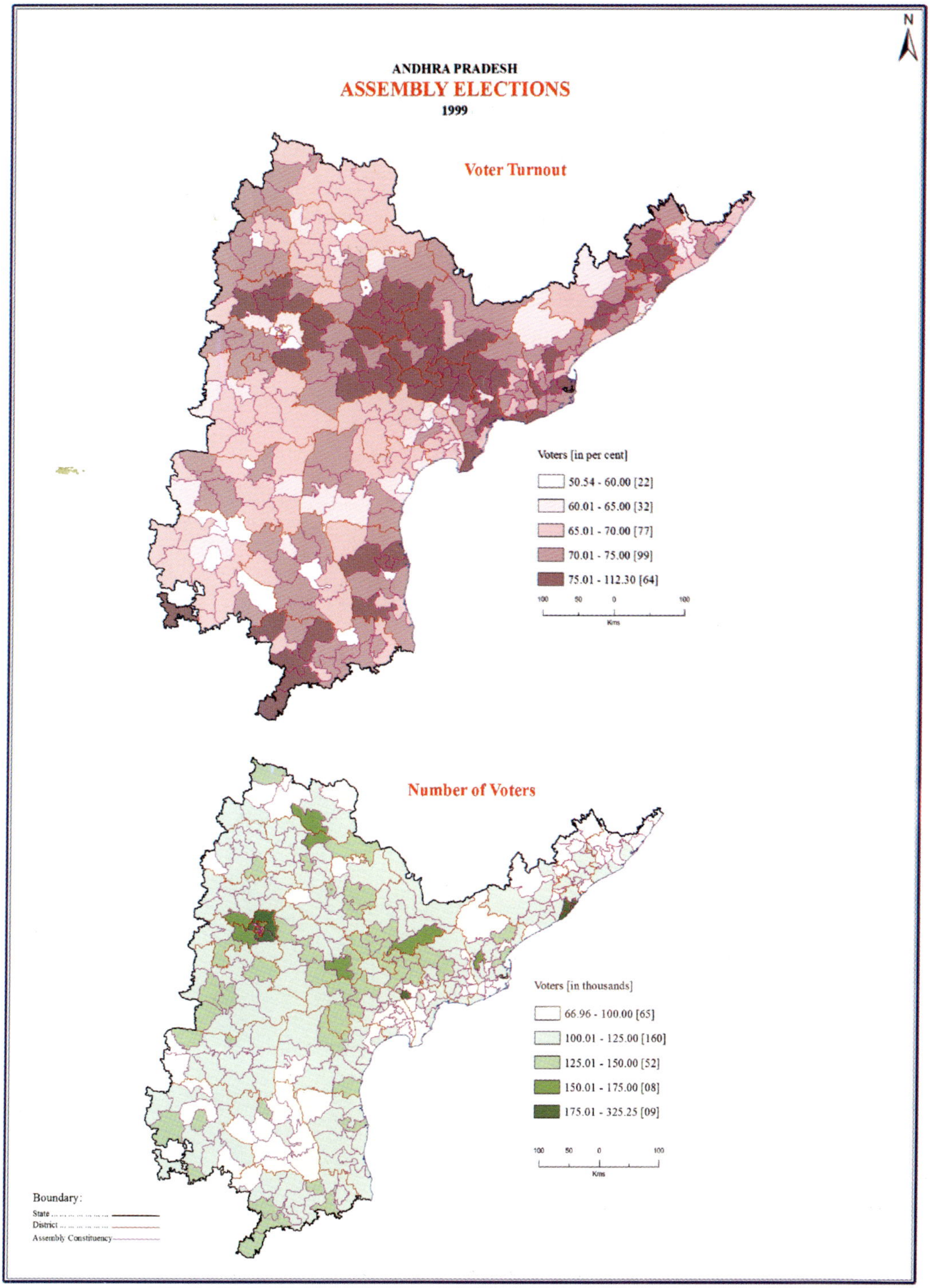

Map 3.6: Andhra Pradesh: Assembly Elections : Voter Turn Out and Number of Voters: 1999

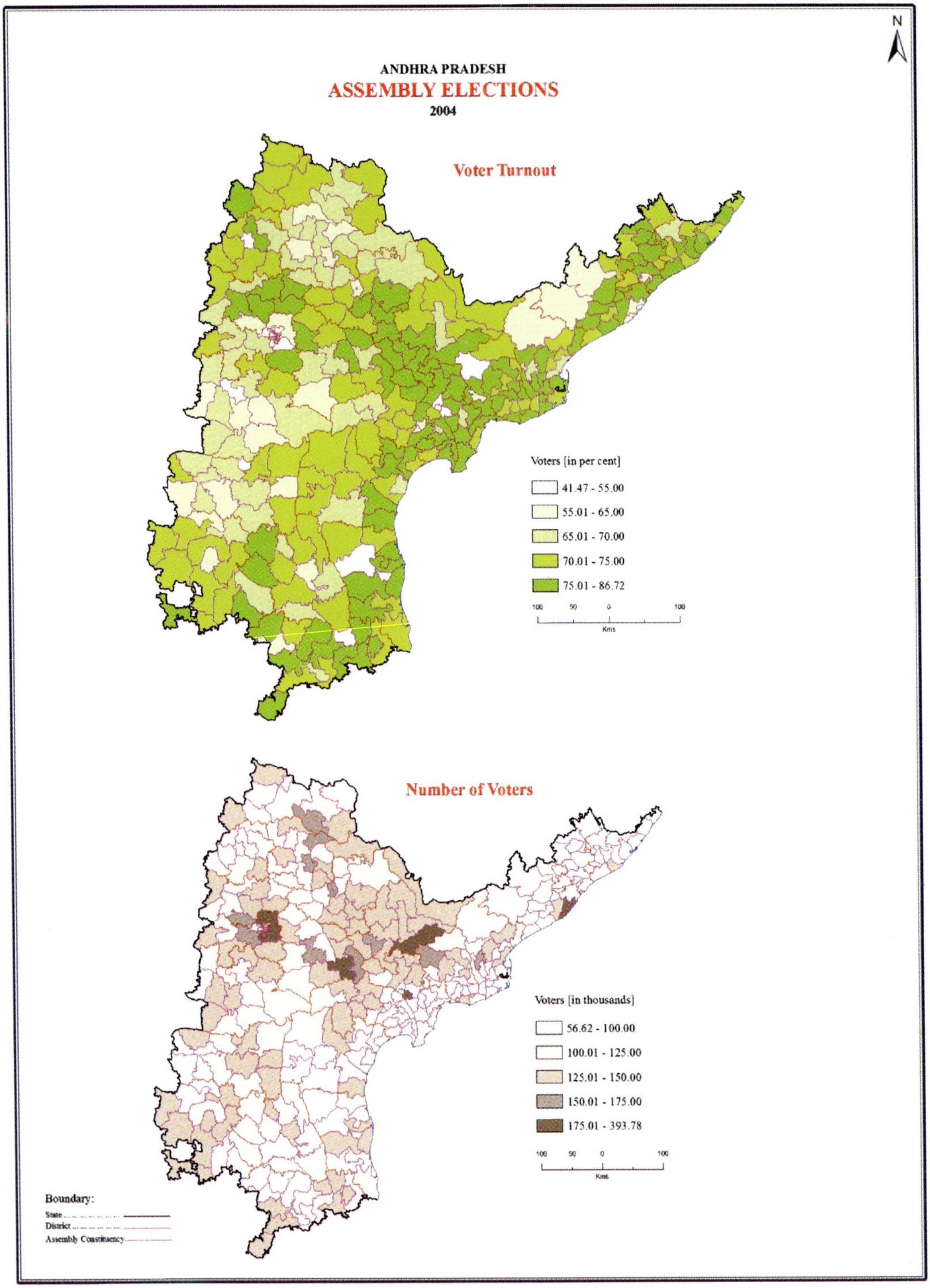

Map 3.7: Andhra Pradesh: Assembly Elections : Voter Turnout and Number of Voters: 2004

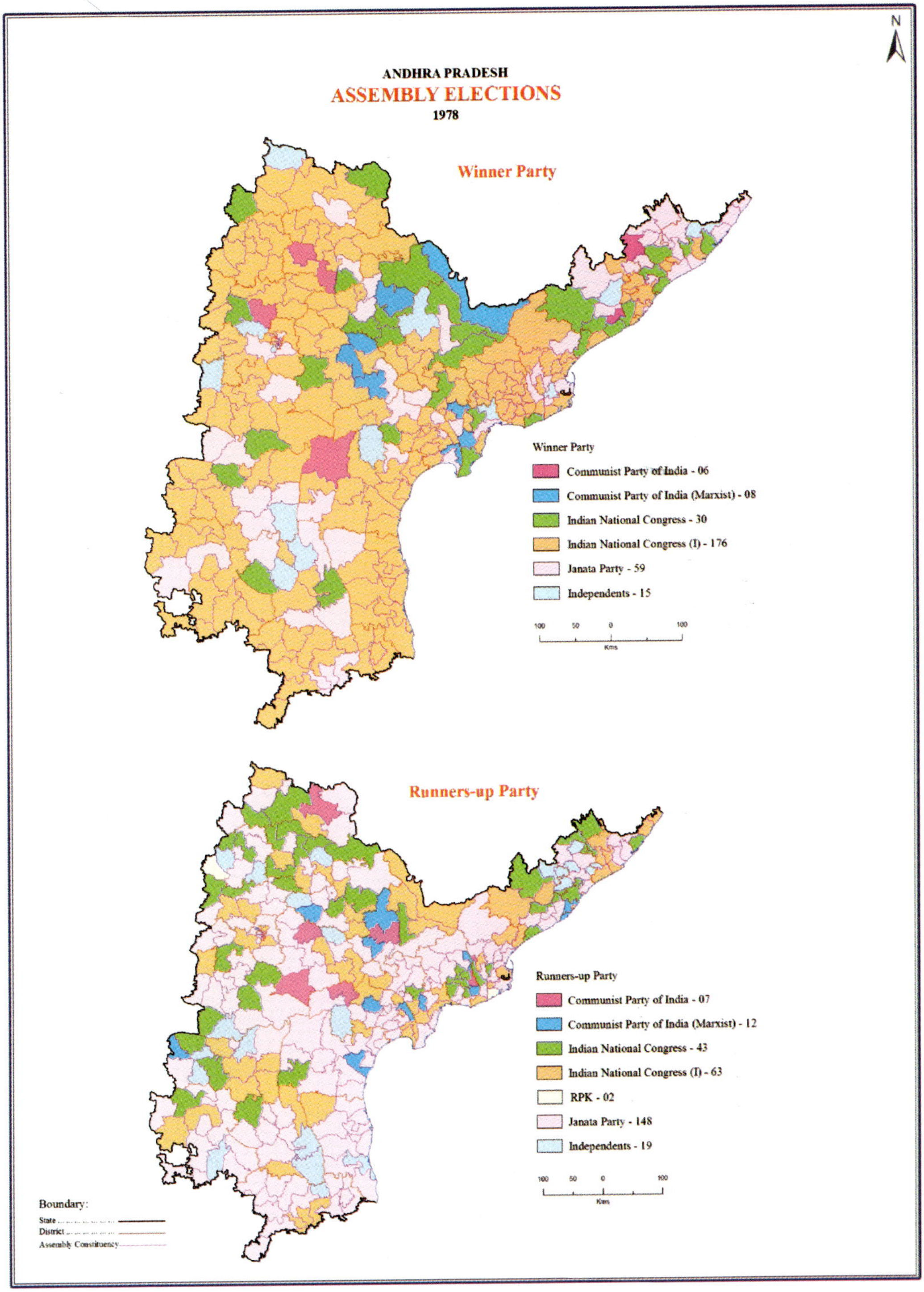

Map 3.8: Andhra Pradesh: Assembly Elections: Winner Party and Runners-up Party: 1978

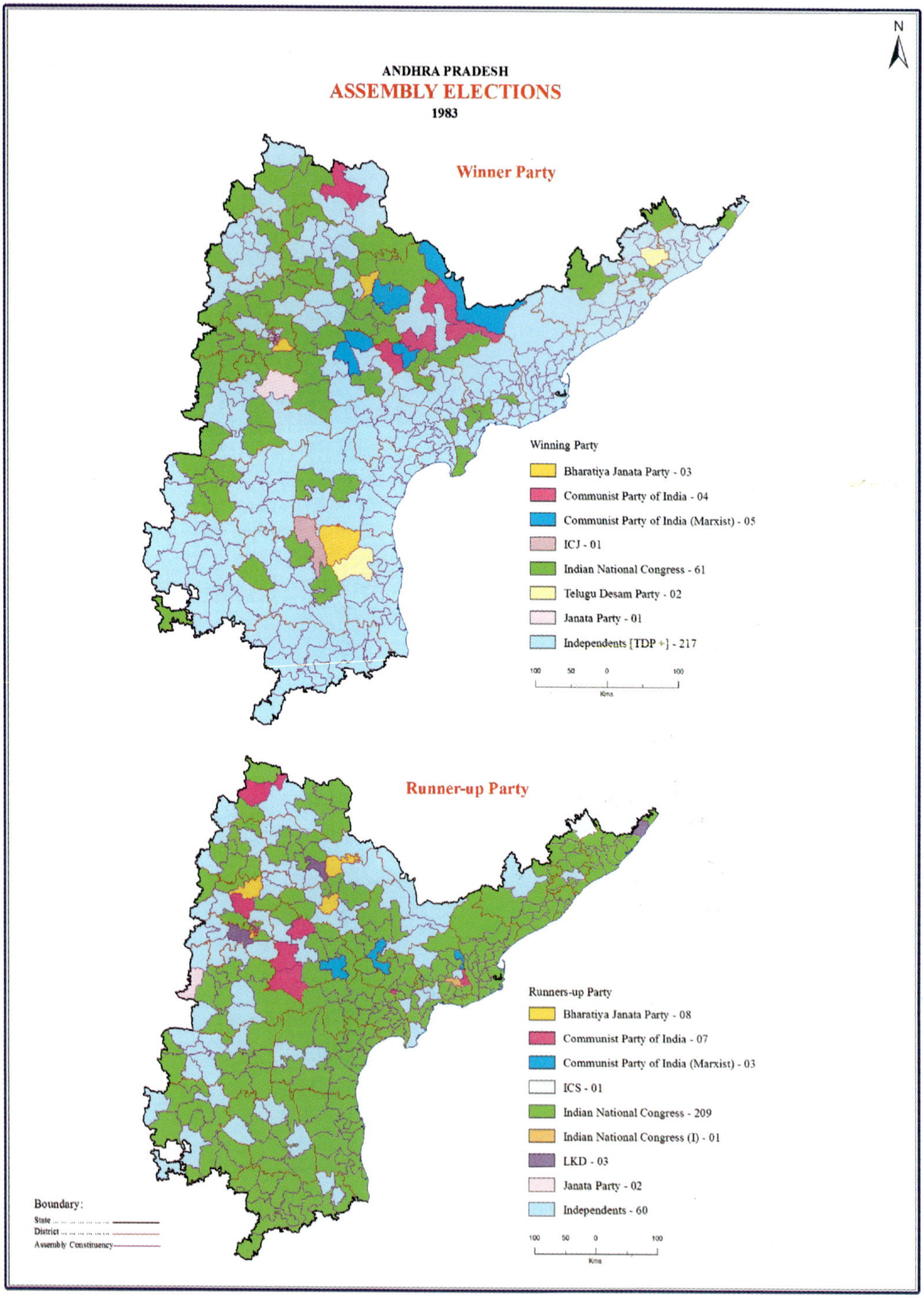

Map 3.9: Andhra Pradesh: Assembly Elections: Winner Party and Runners-up Party: 1983

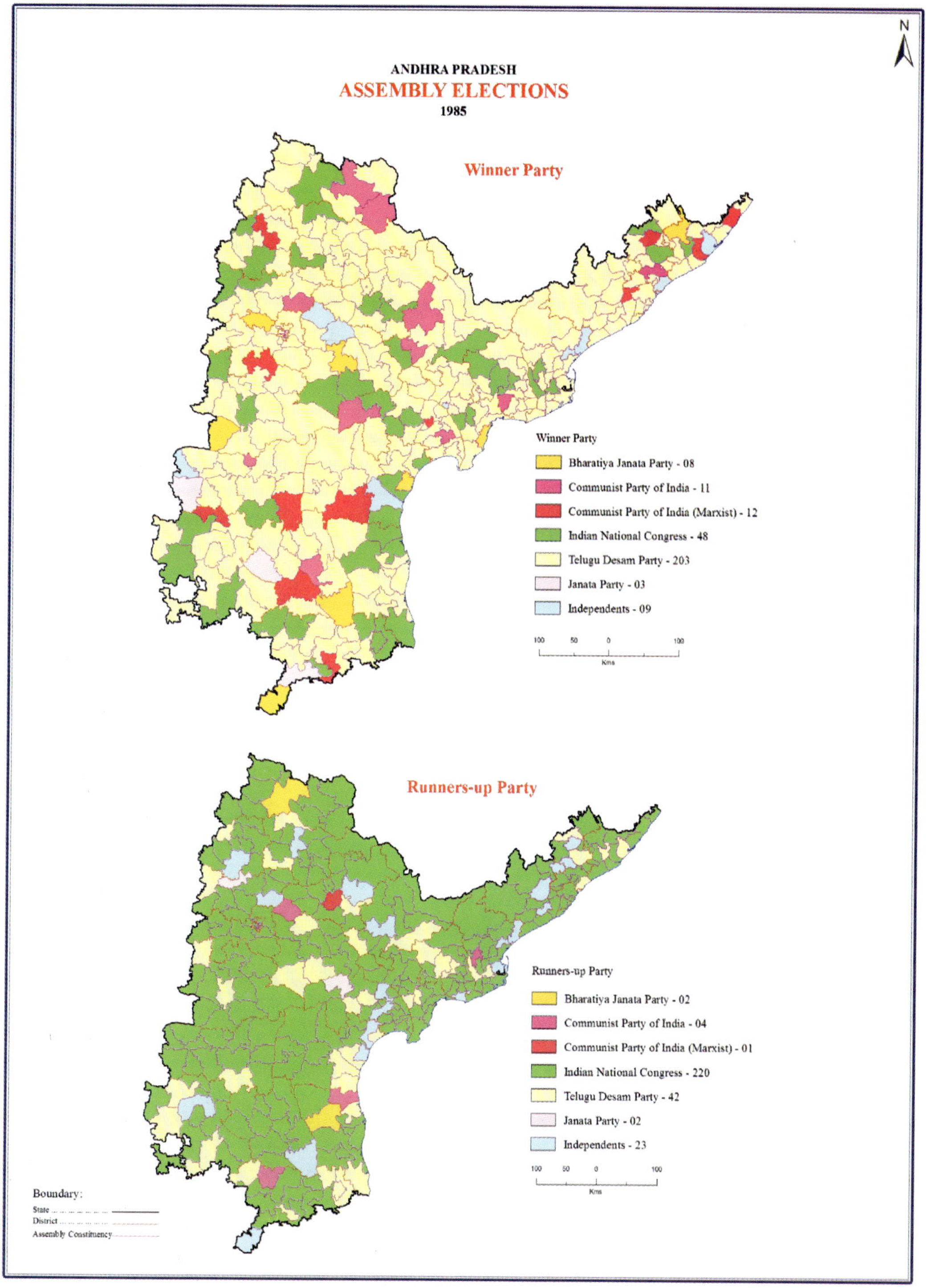

Map 3.10: Andhra Pradesh: Assembly Elections: Winner Party and Runners-up Party: 1985

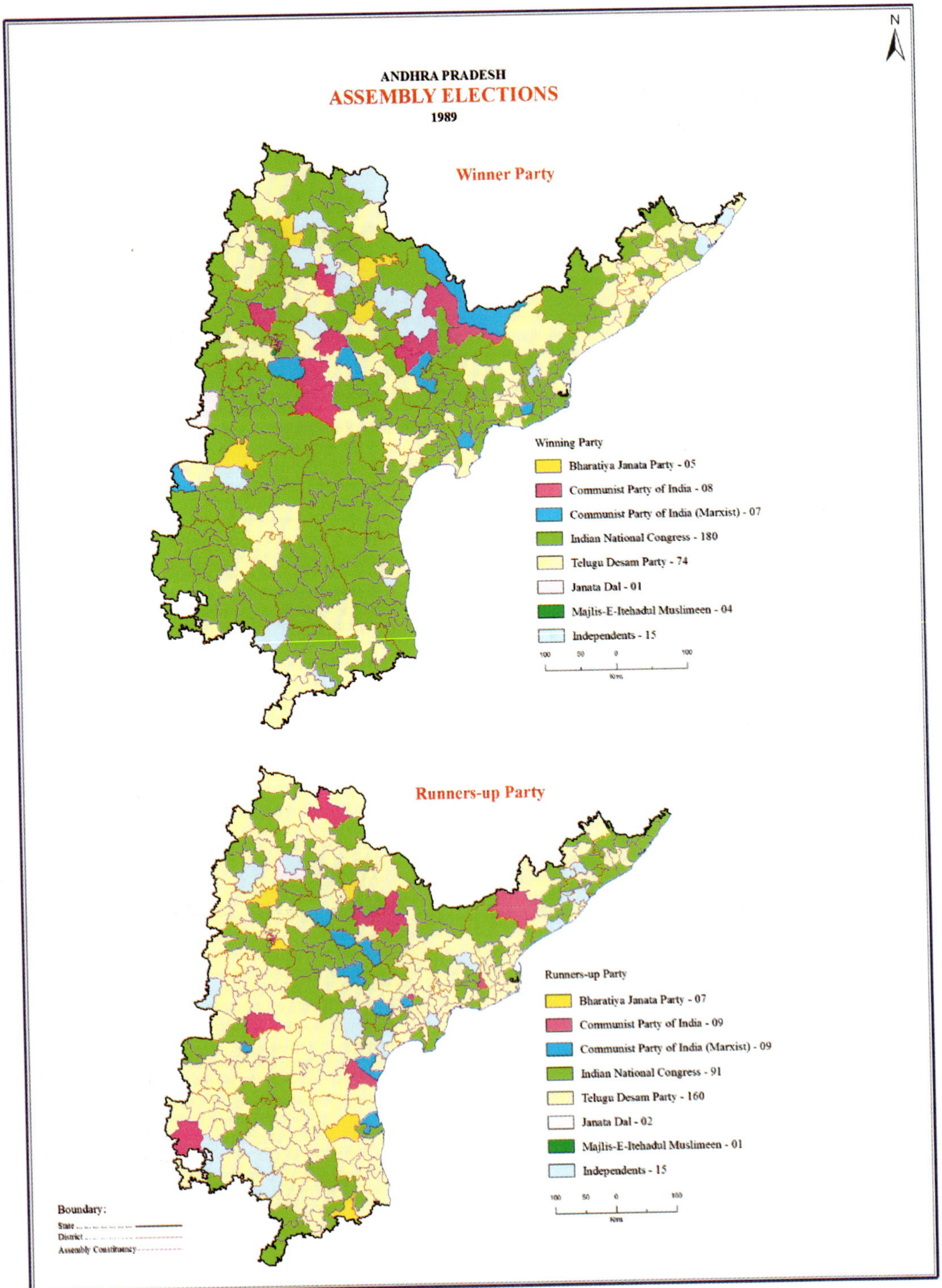

Map 3.11: Andhra Pradesh: Assembly Elections: Winner Party and Runners-up Party: 1989

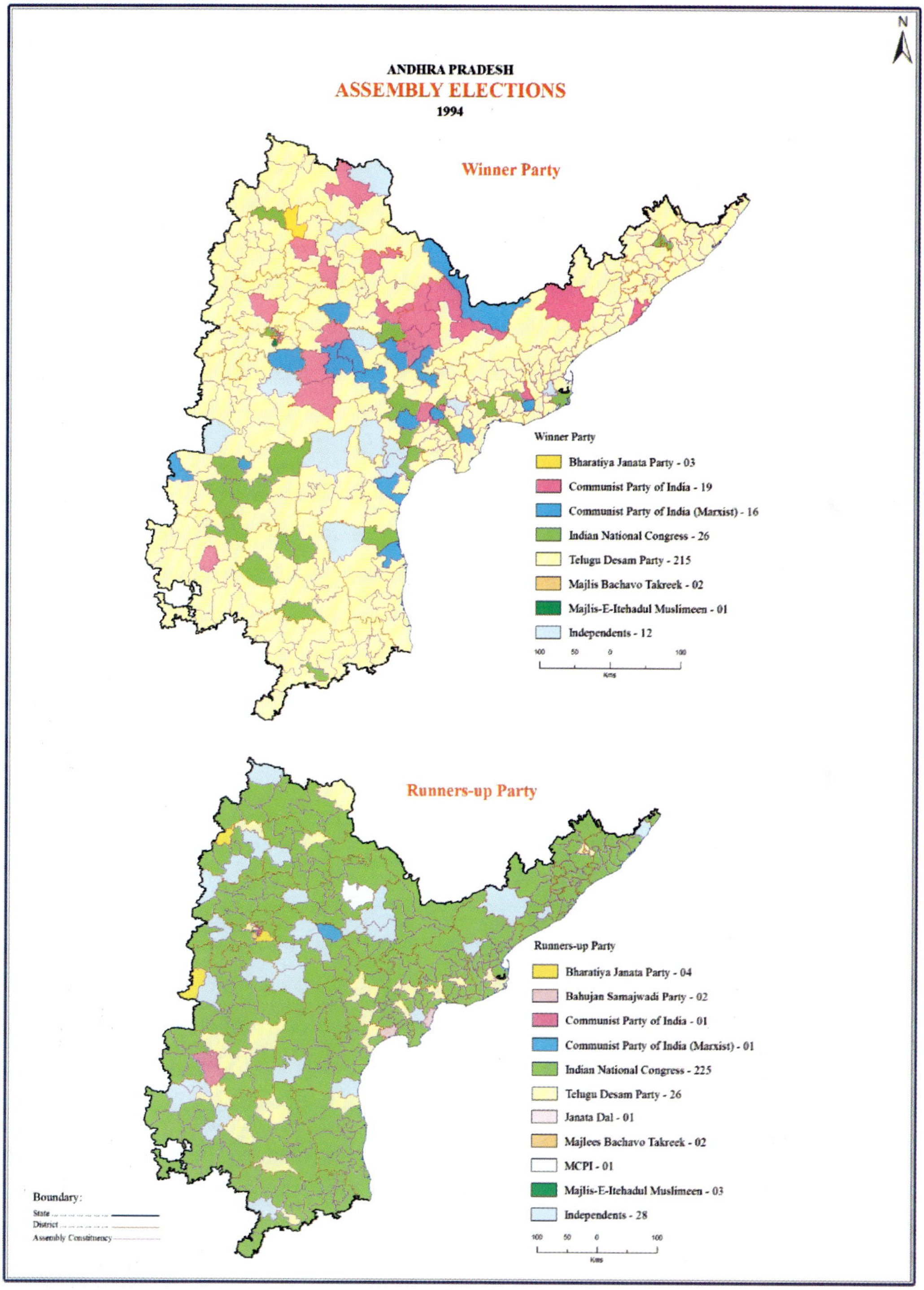

Map 3.12: Andhra Pradesh: Assembly Elections: Winner Party and Runners-up Party: 1994

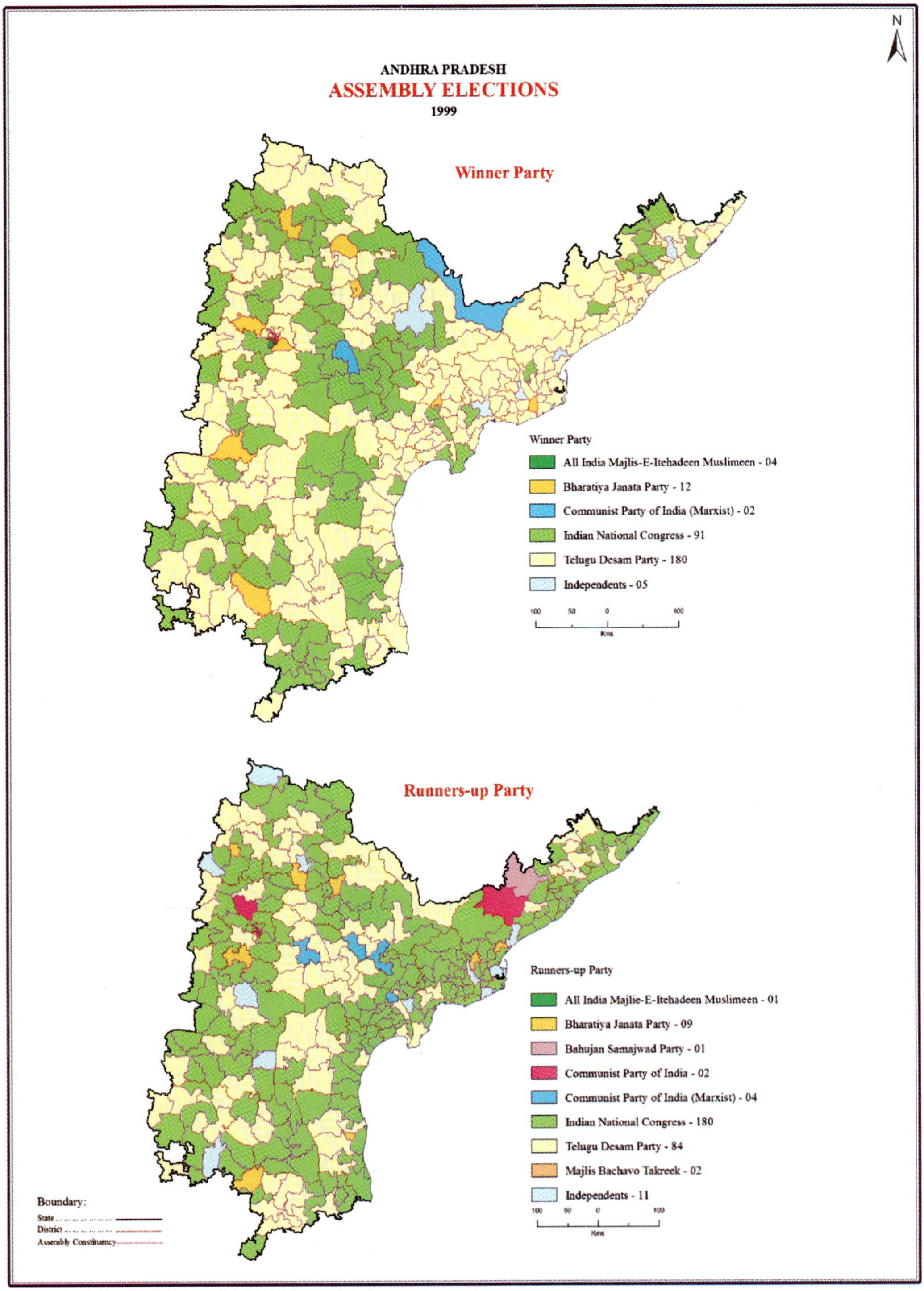

Map 3.13: Andhra Pradesh: Assembly Elections: Winner Party and Runners-up Party: 1999

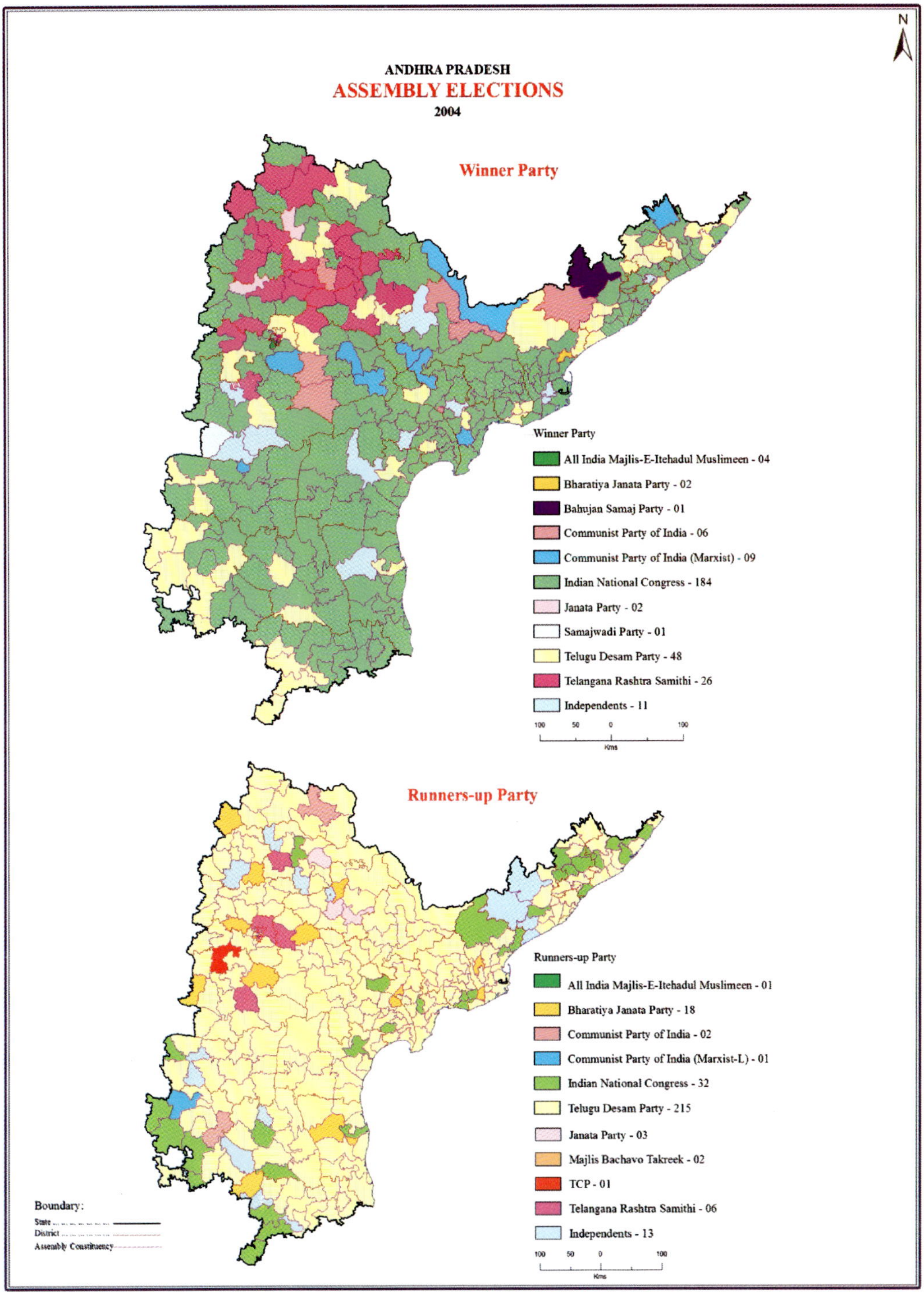

Map 3.14: Andhra Pradesh: Assembly Elections: Winner Party and Runners-up Party: 2004

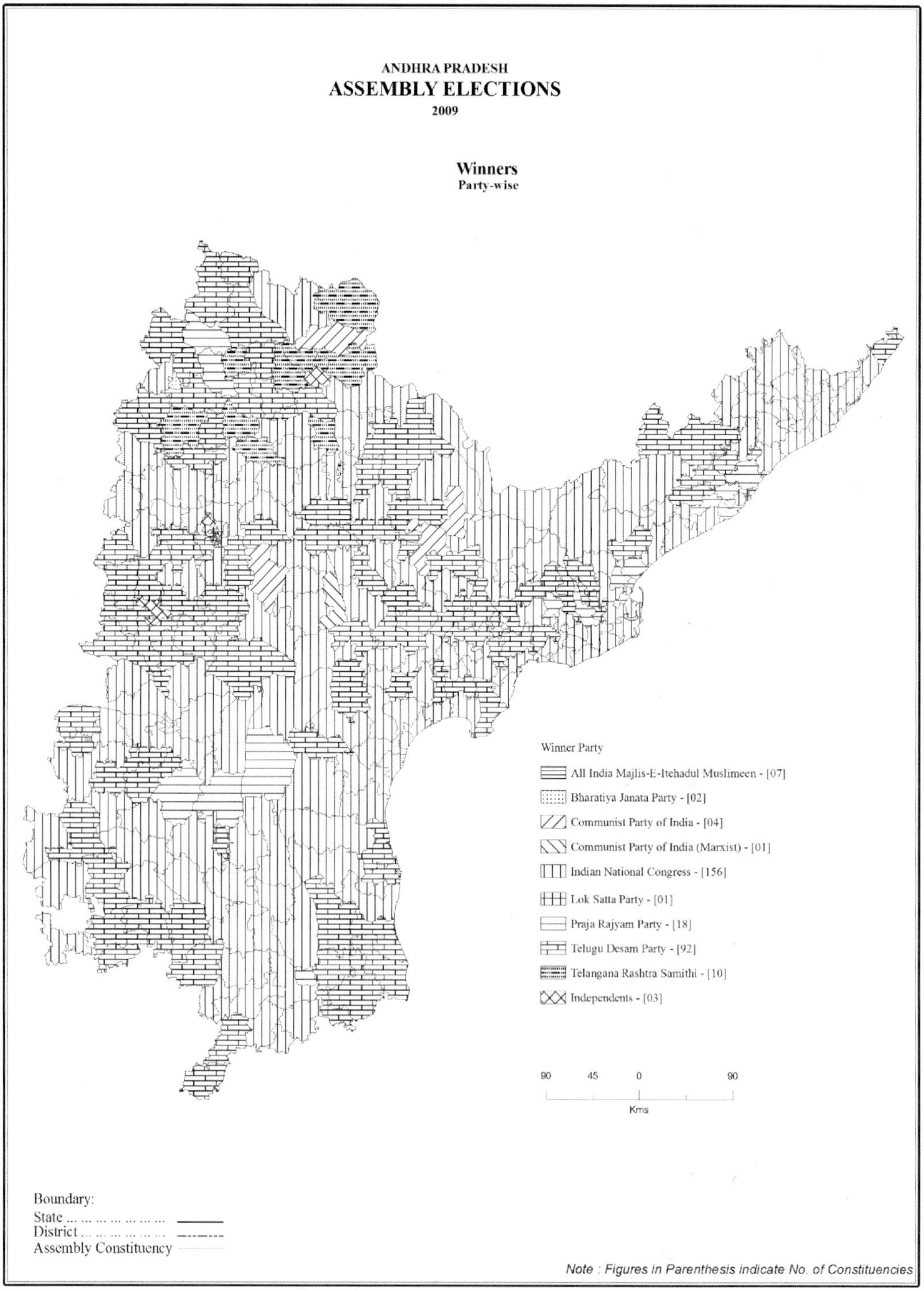

Map 3.15: Andhra Pradesh: Assembly Elections: Winners Party-Wise: 2009

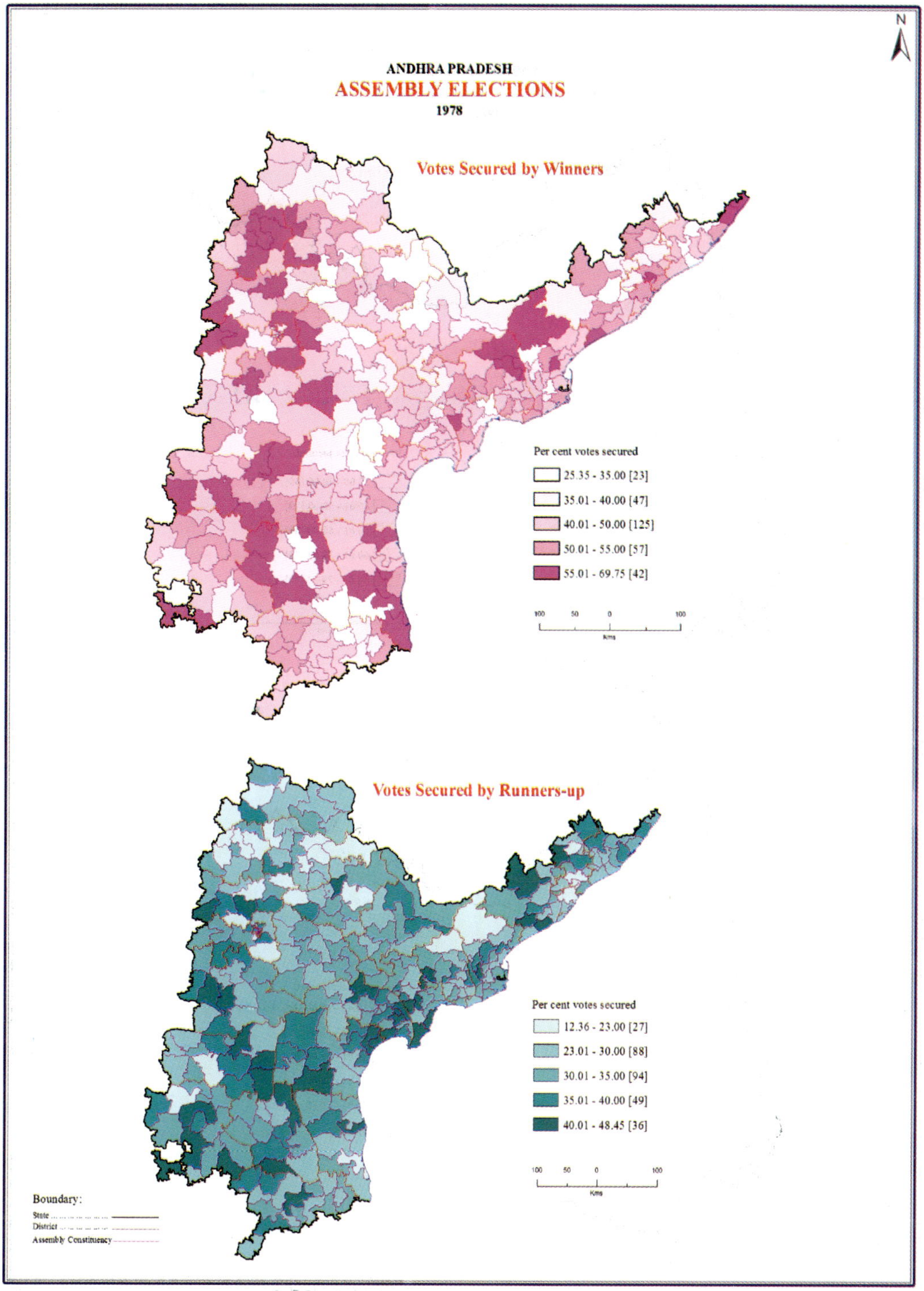

Map 3.16: Andhra Pradesh: Assembly Elections: Votes Secured by winners and Votes Secured by Runners-up: 1978

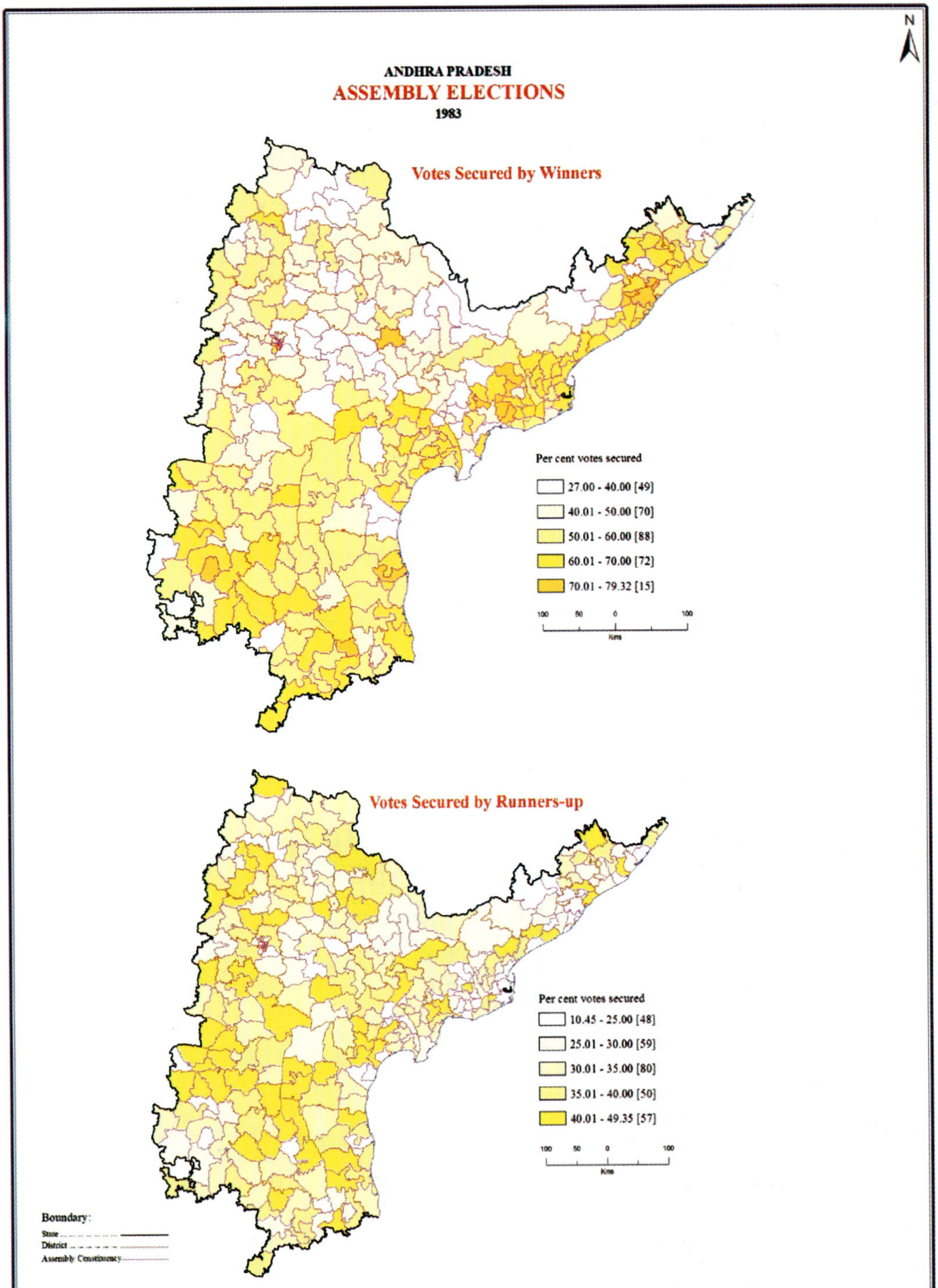

Map 3.17: Andhra Pradesh: Assembly Elections: Votes Secured by Winners and Votes Secured by Runners-up:1983

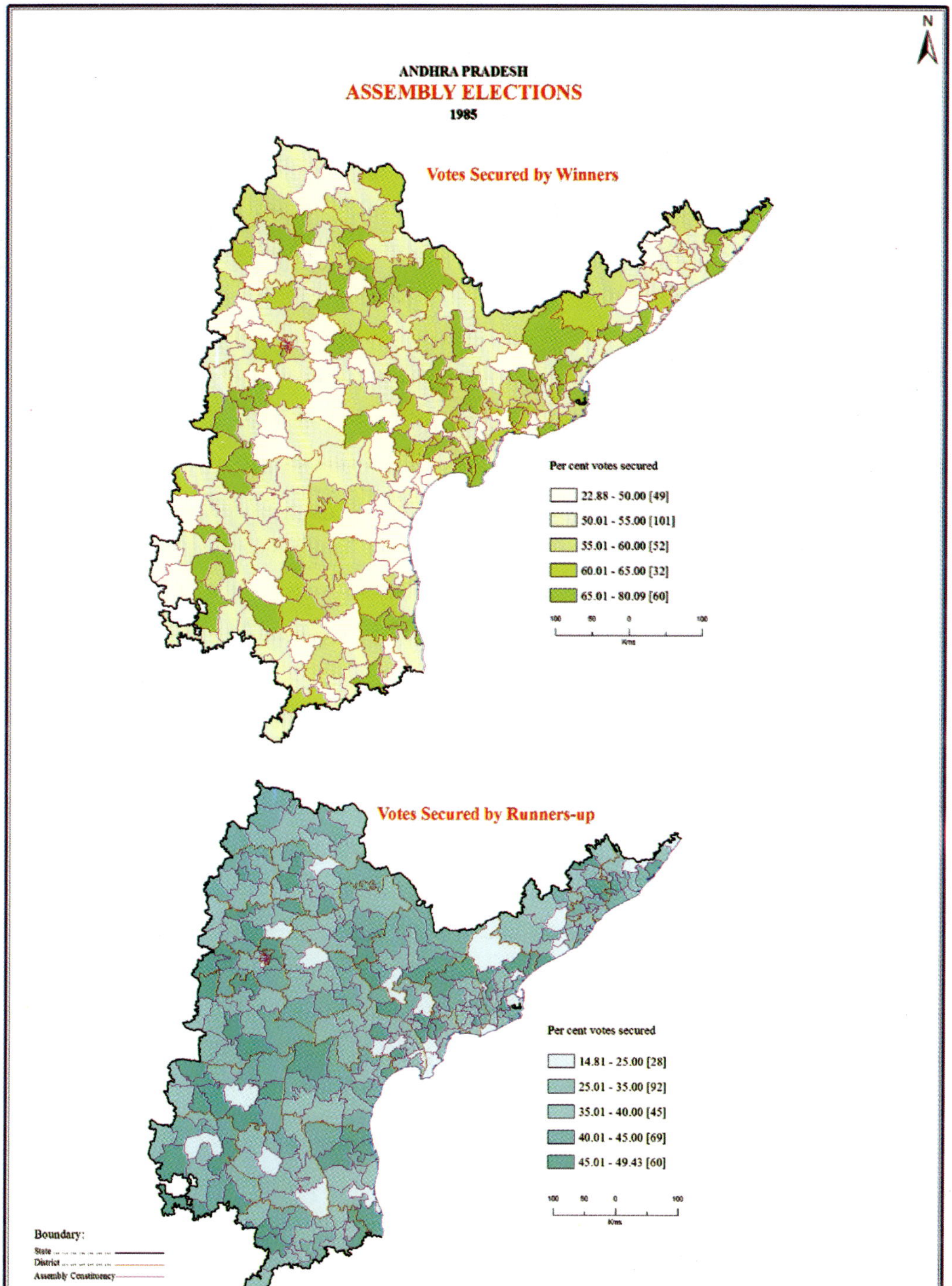

Map 3.18: Andhra Pradesh: Assembly Elections: Votes Secured by Winners and Votes Secured by Runners-up: 1985

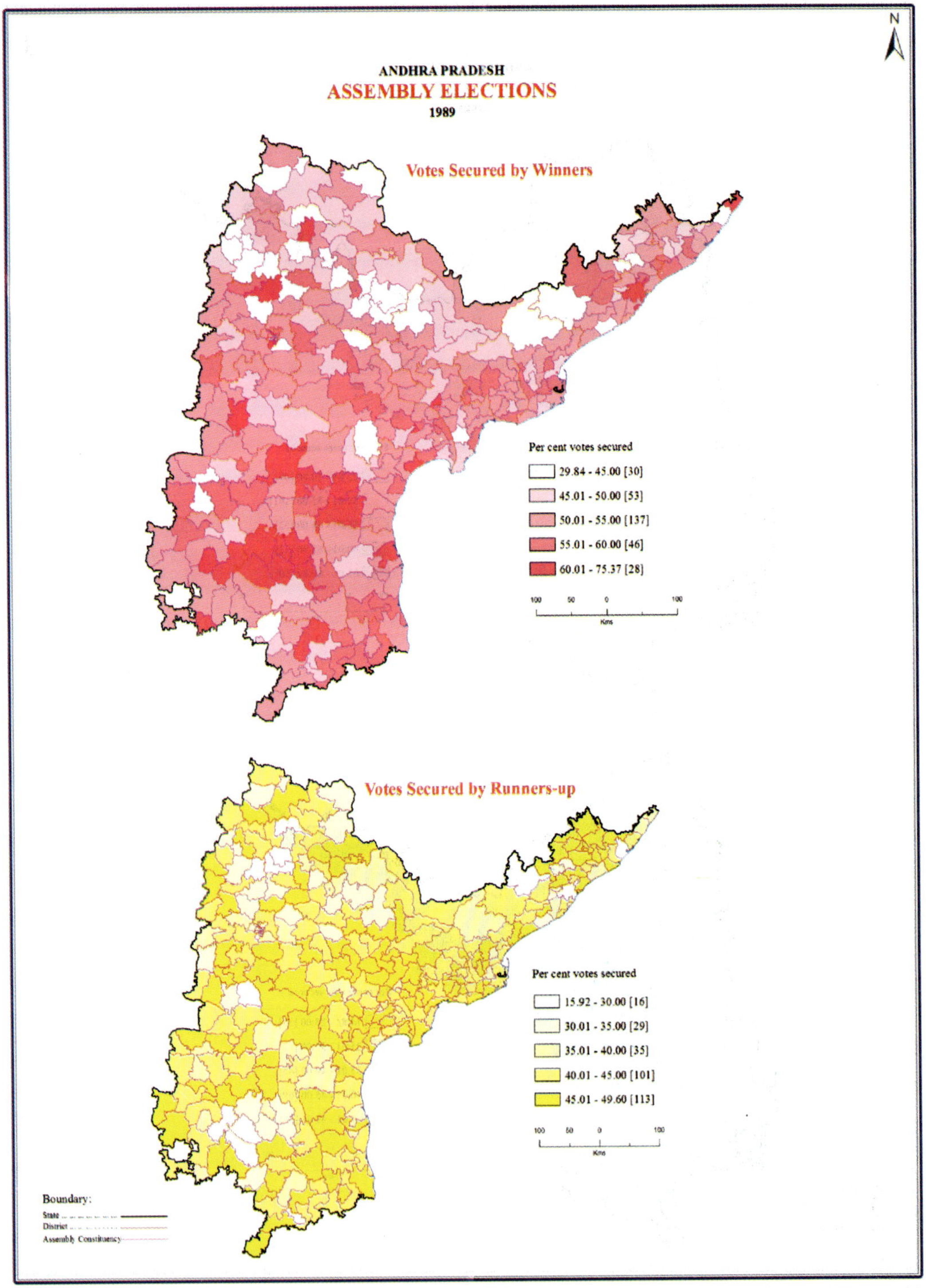

Map 3.19: Andhra Pradesh: Assembly Elections: Votes Sec ured by Winners and Votes Secured by Runners-up: 1989

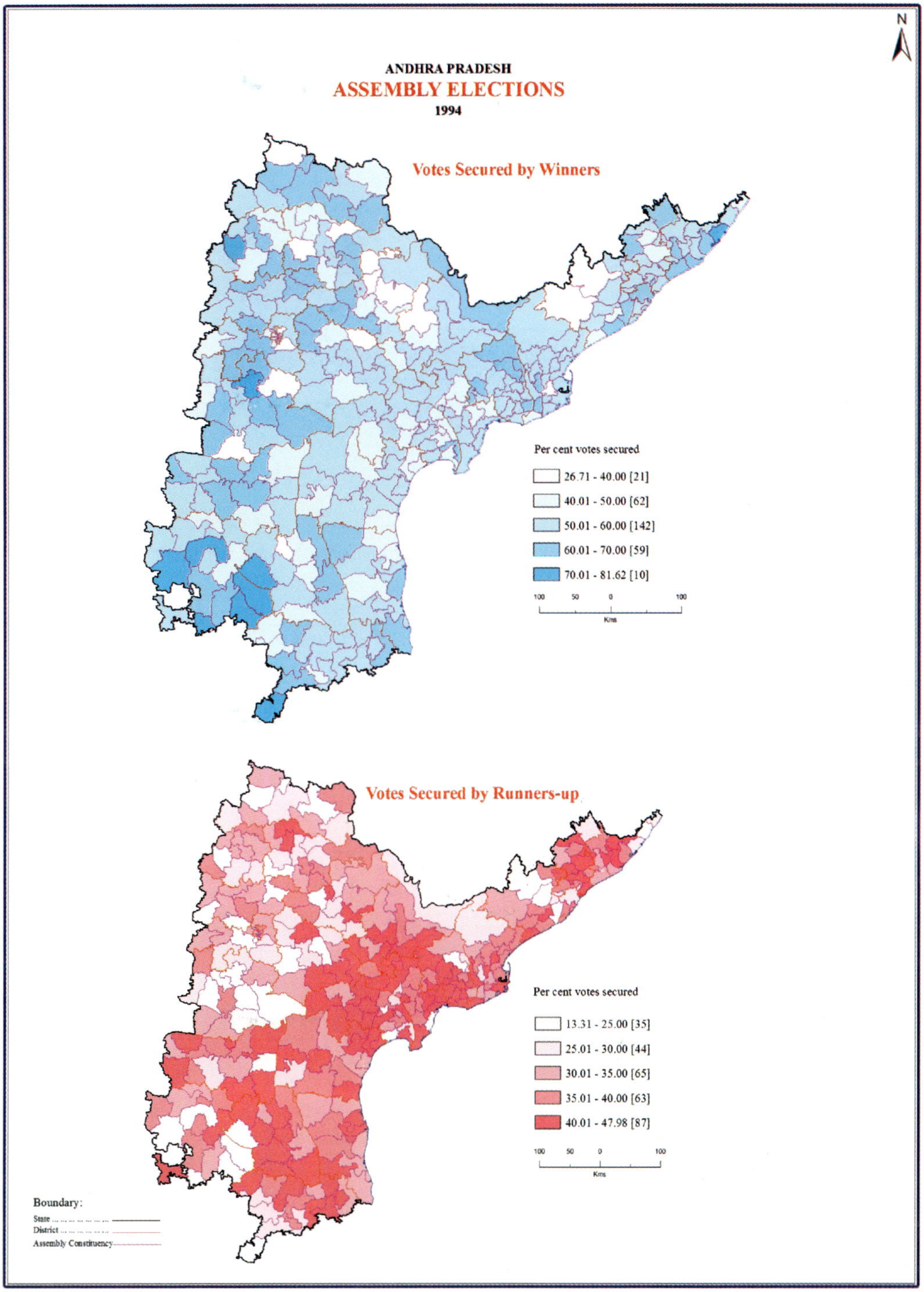

Map 3.20: Andhra Pradesh: Assembly Elections: Votes Secured by Winners and Votes Secured by Runners-up: 1994

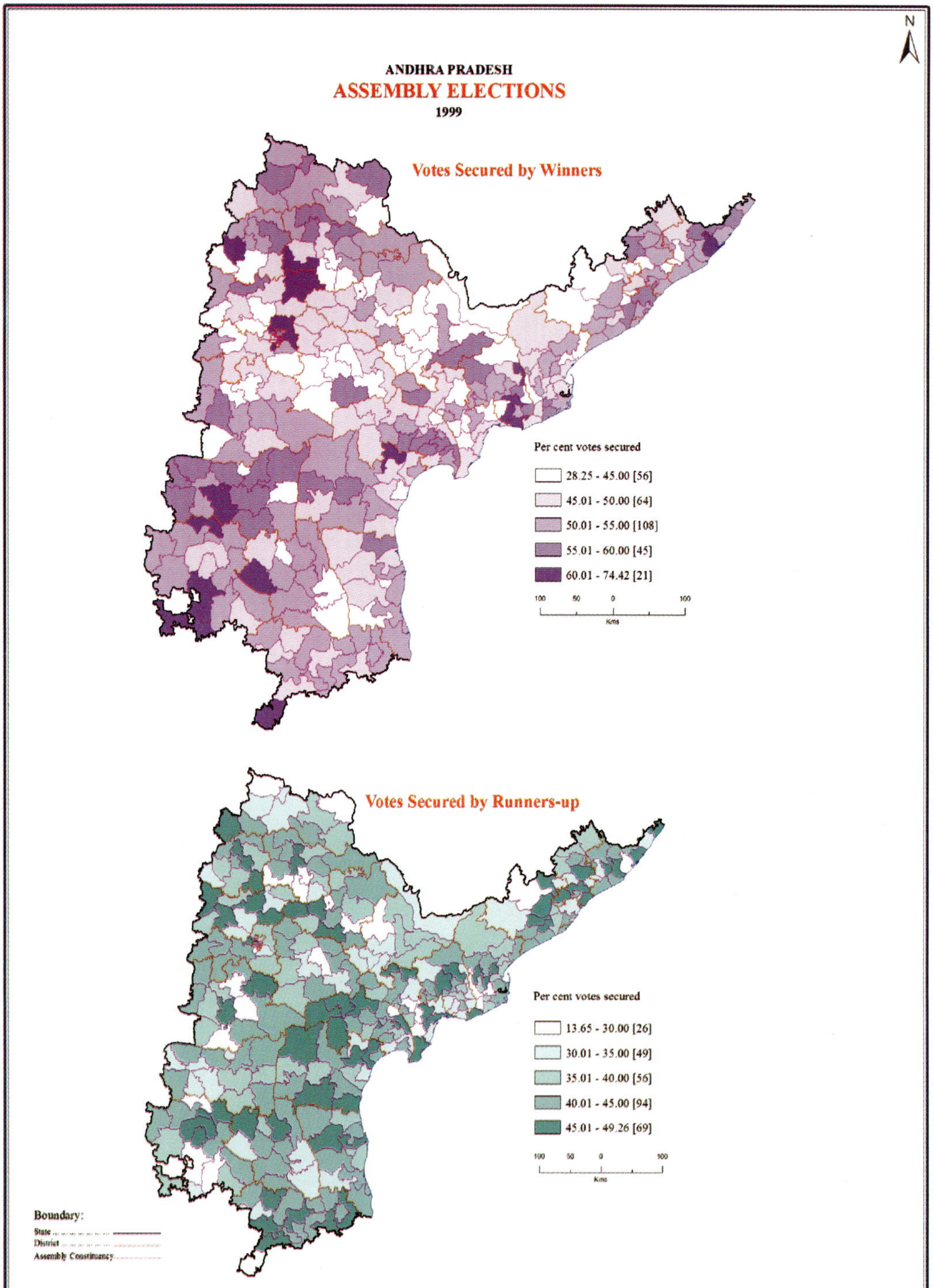

Map 3.21: Andhra Pradesh: Assembly Elections: Votes Secured by Winners and Votes Secured by Runners-up: 1999

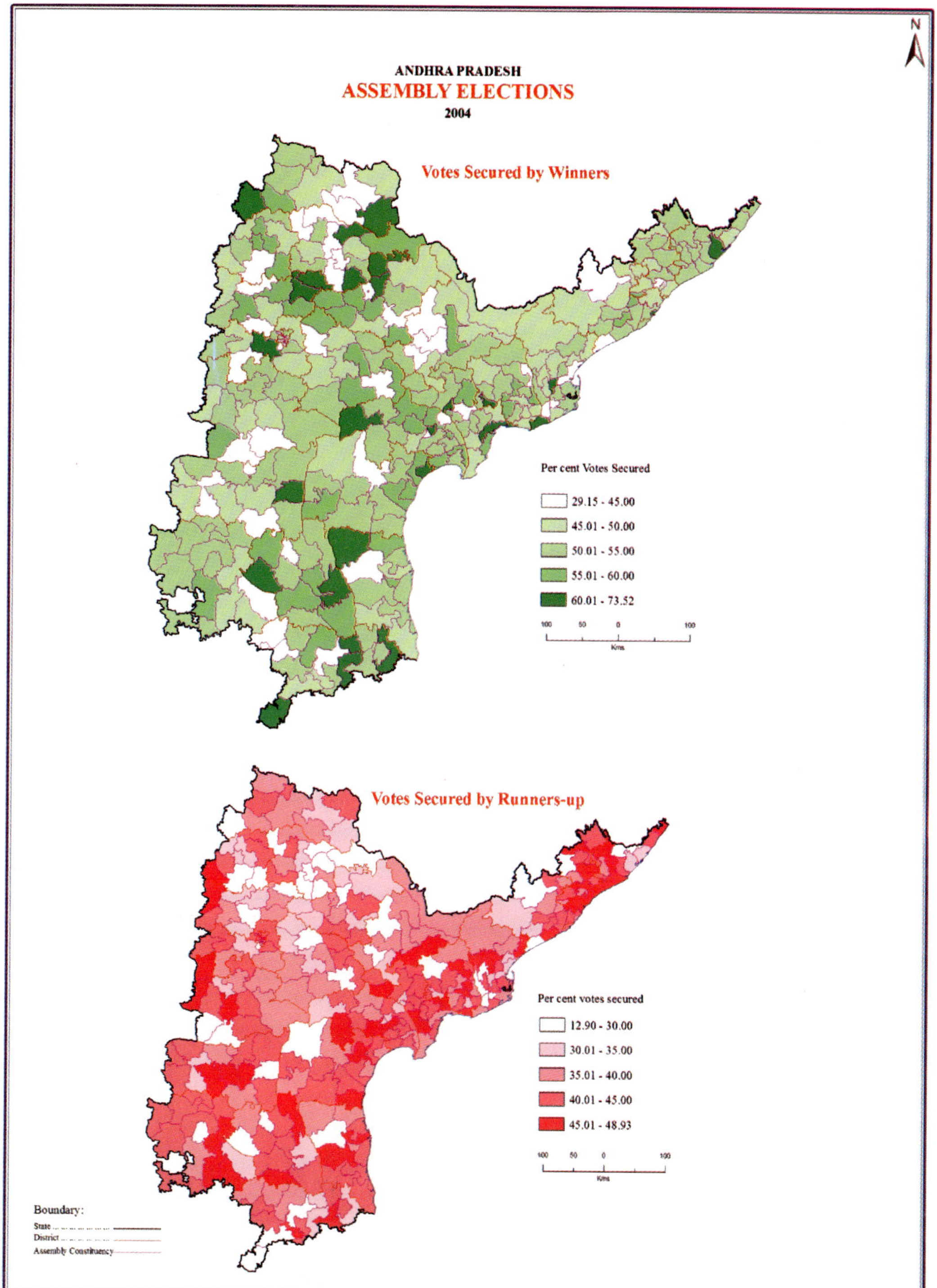

Map 3.22: Andhra Pradesh: Assembly Elections: Votes Secured by Winners and Votes Secured by Runners-up: 2004

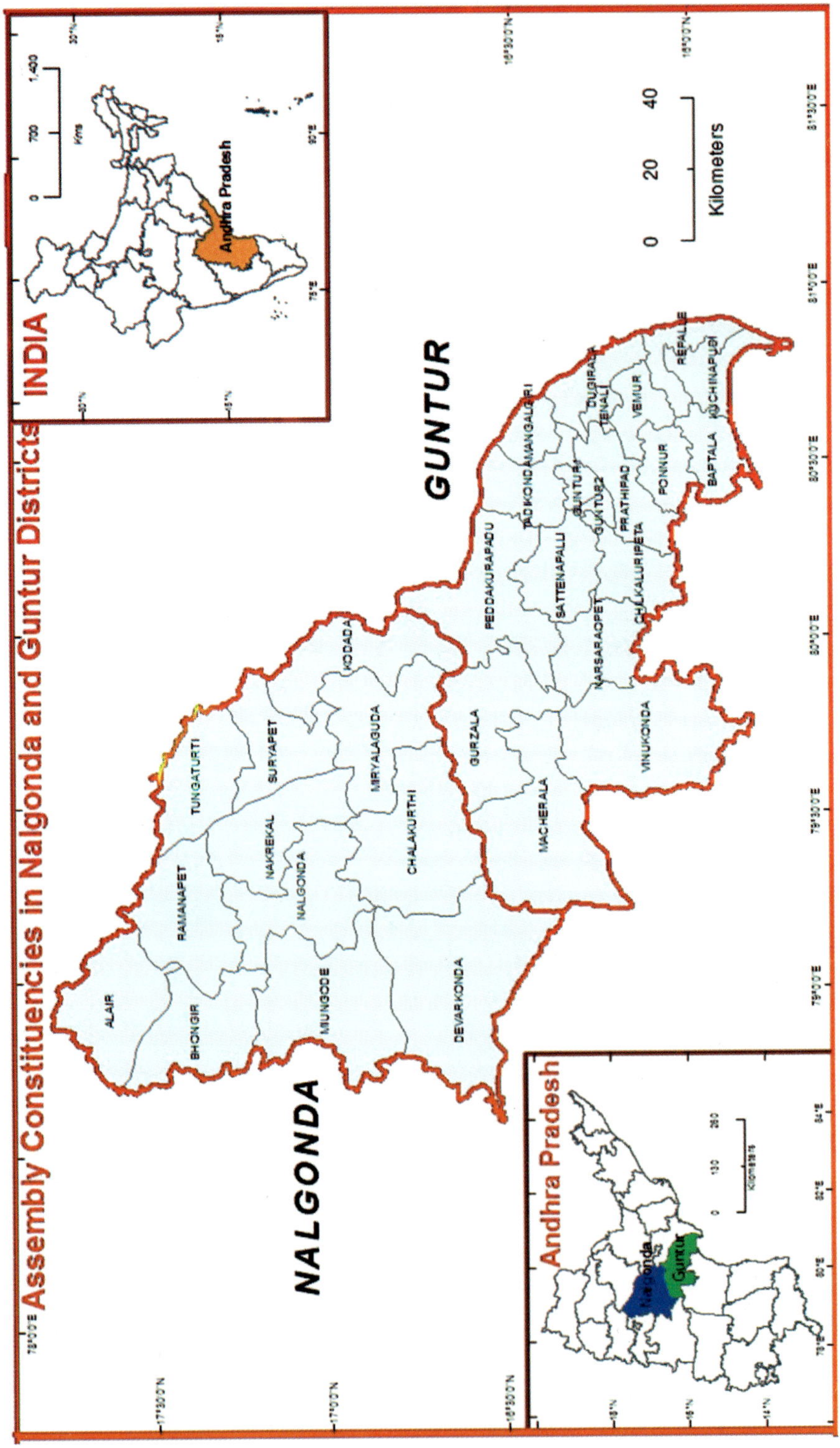

Map 4.1: Assembly Constituencies in Nalgonda and Guntur Districts

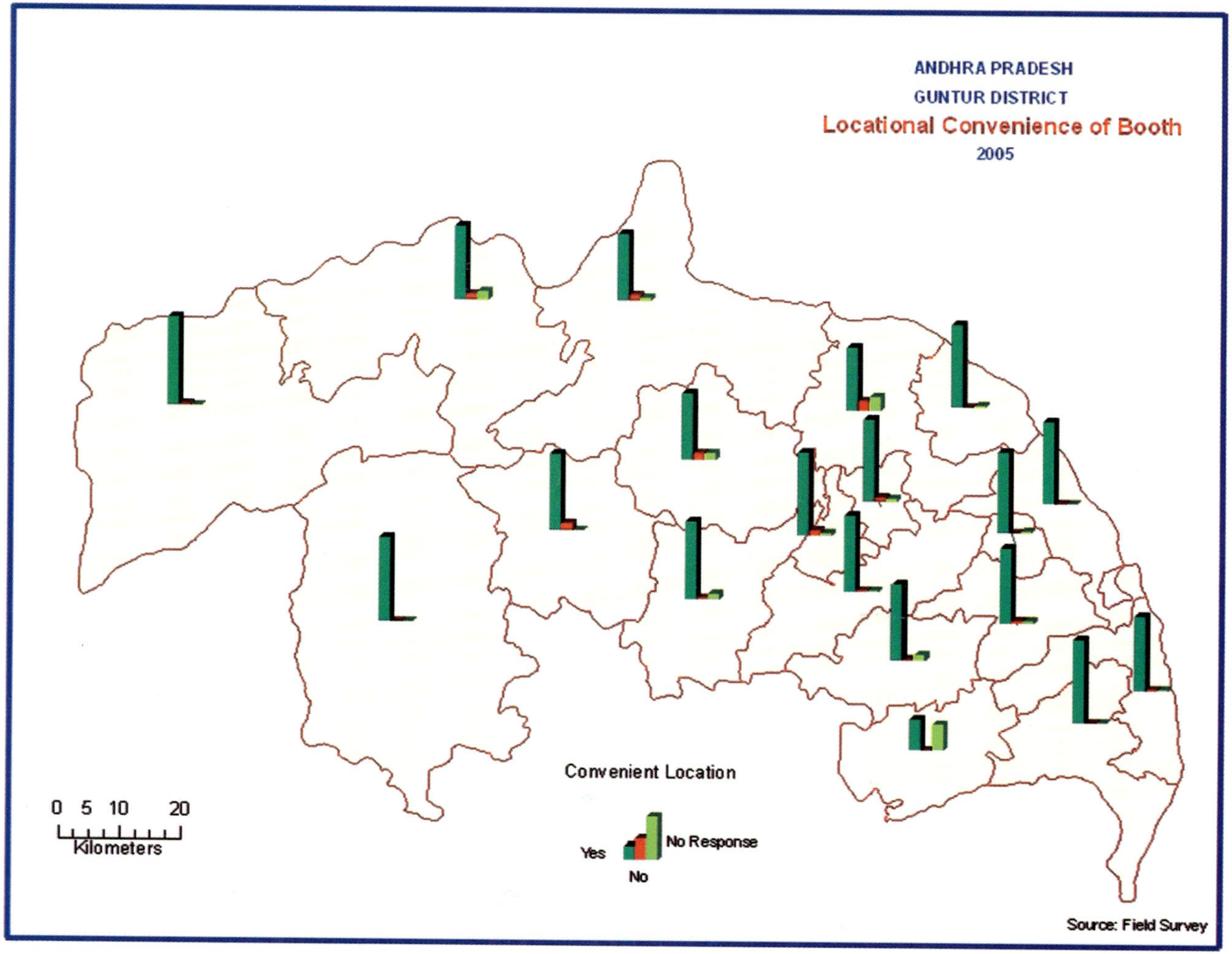

Map 4.2: Andhra Pradesh: Guntur District: Locational Convenience of Booth: 2005

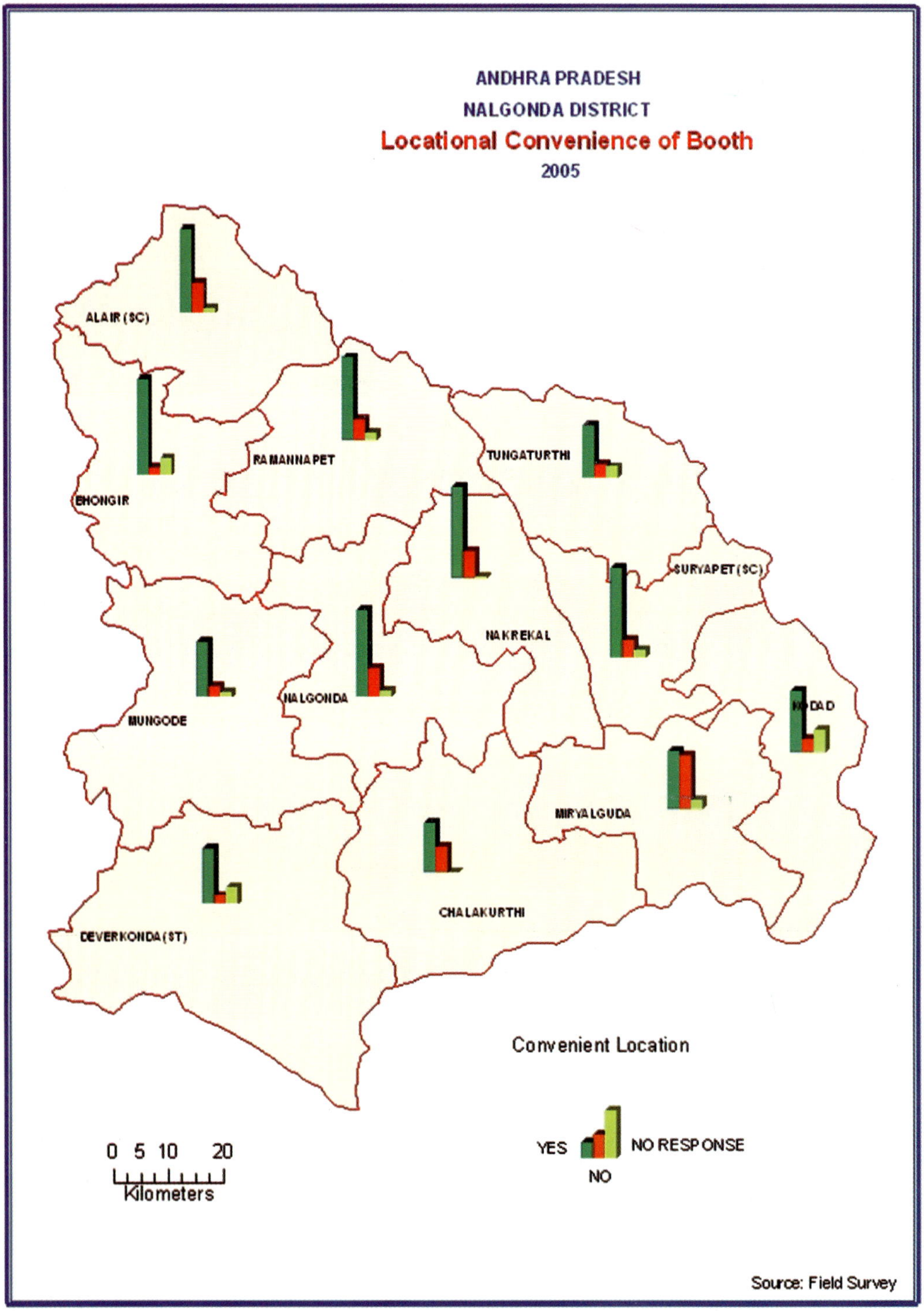

Map 4.3: Andhra Pradesh: Nalgonda District: Locational Convenience of Booth: 2005

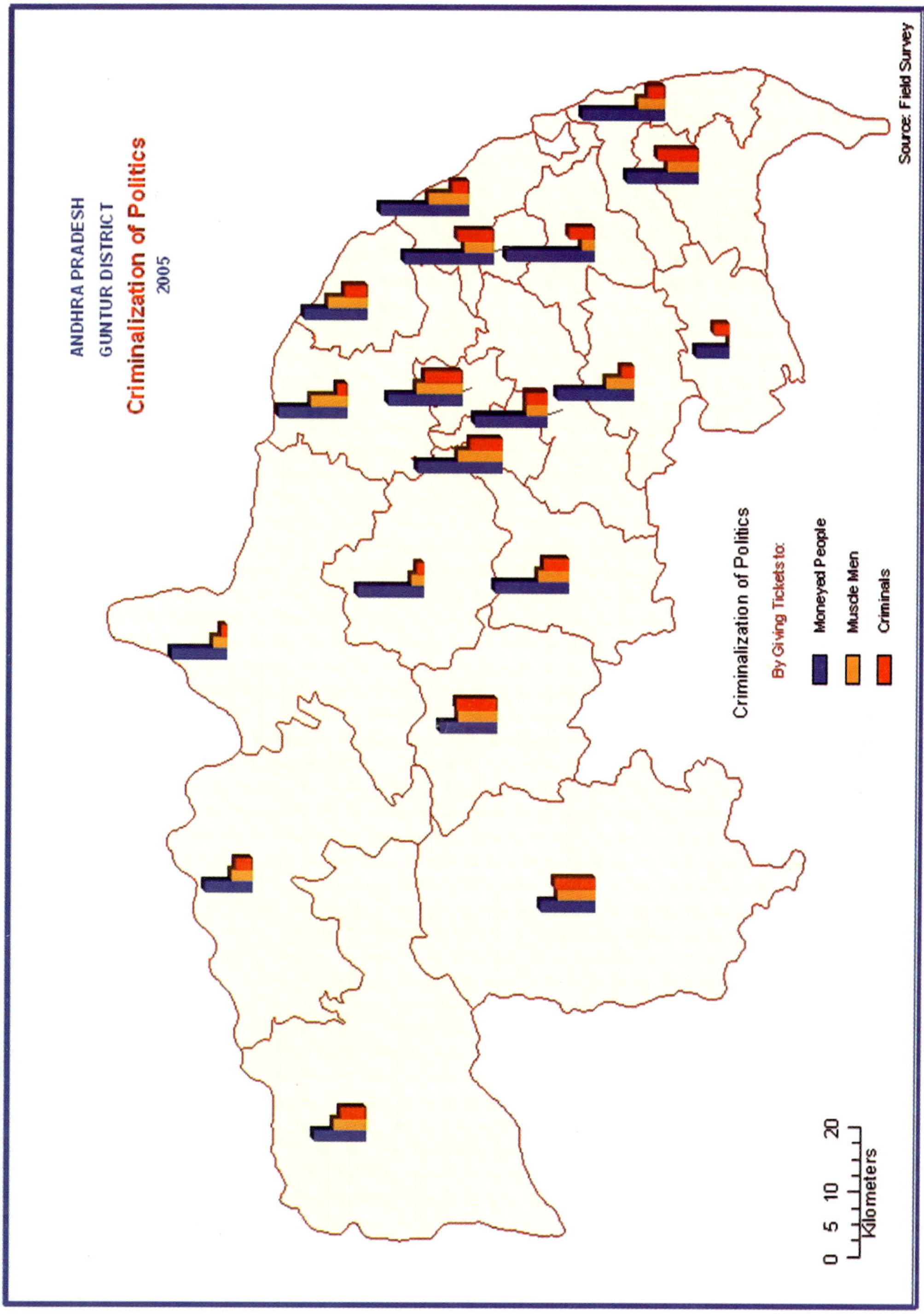

Map 4.4: Andhra Pradesh: Guntur District: Criminalization of Politics: 2005

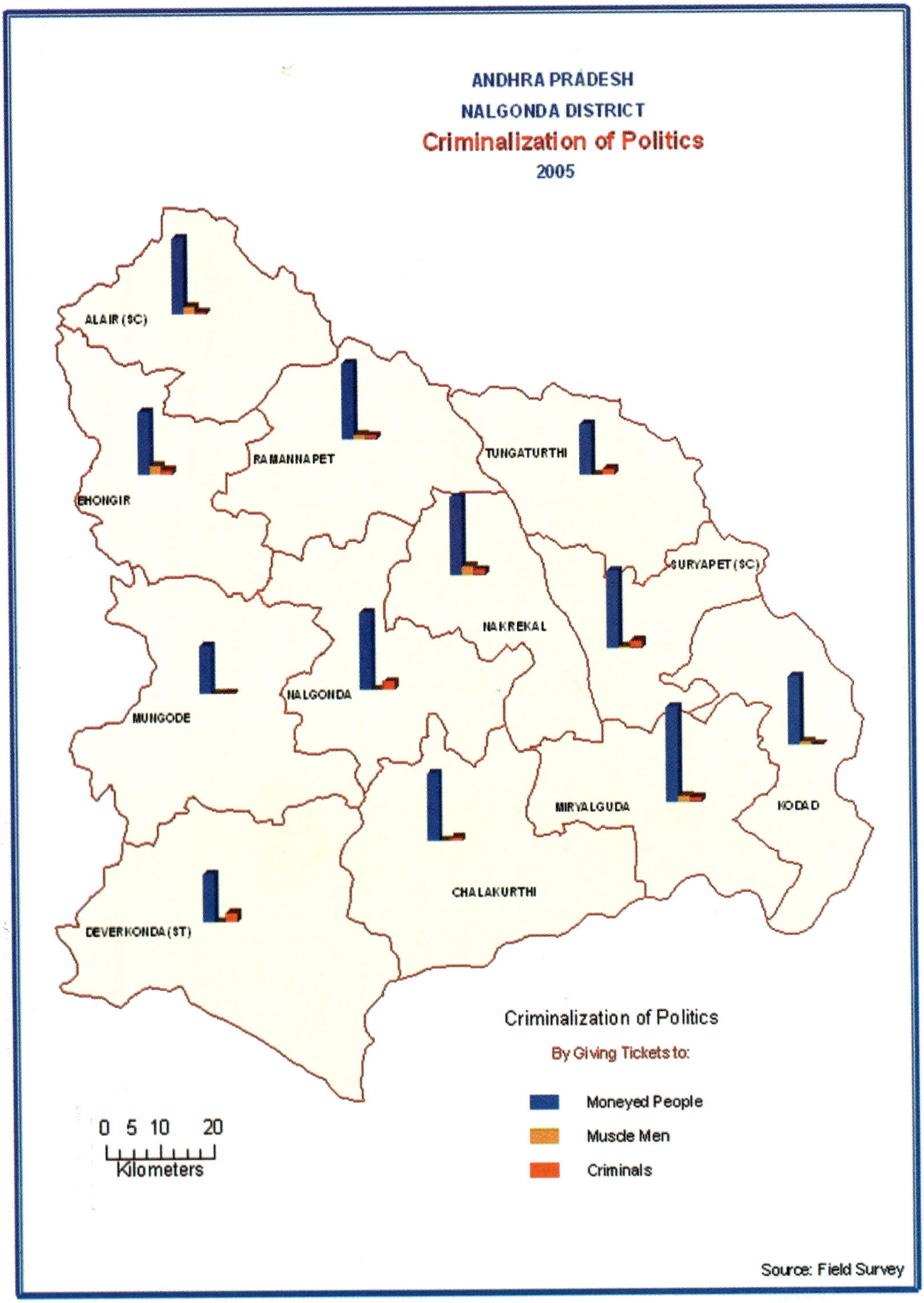

Map 4.5: Andhra Pradesh: Nalgonda District: Criminalization of Politics: 2005

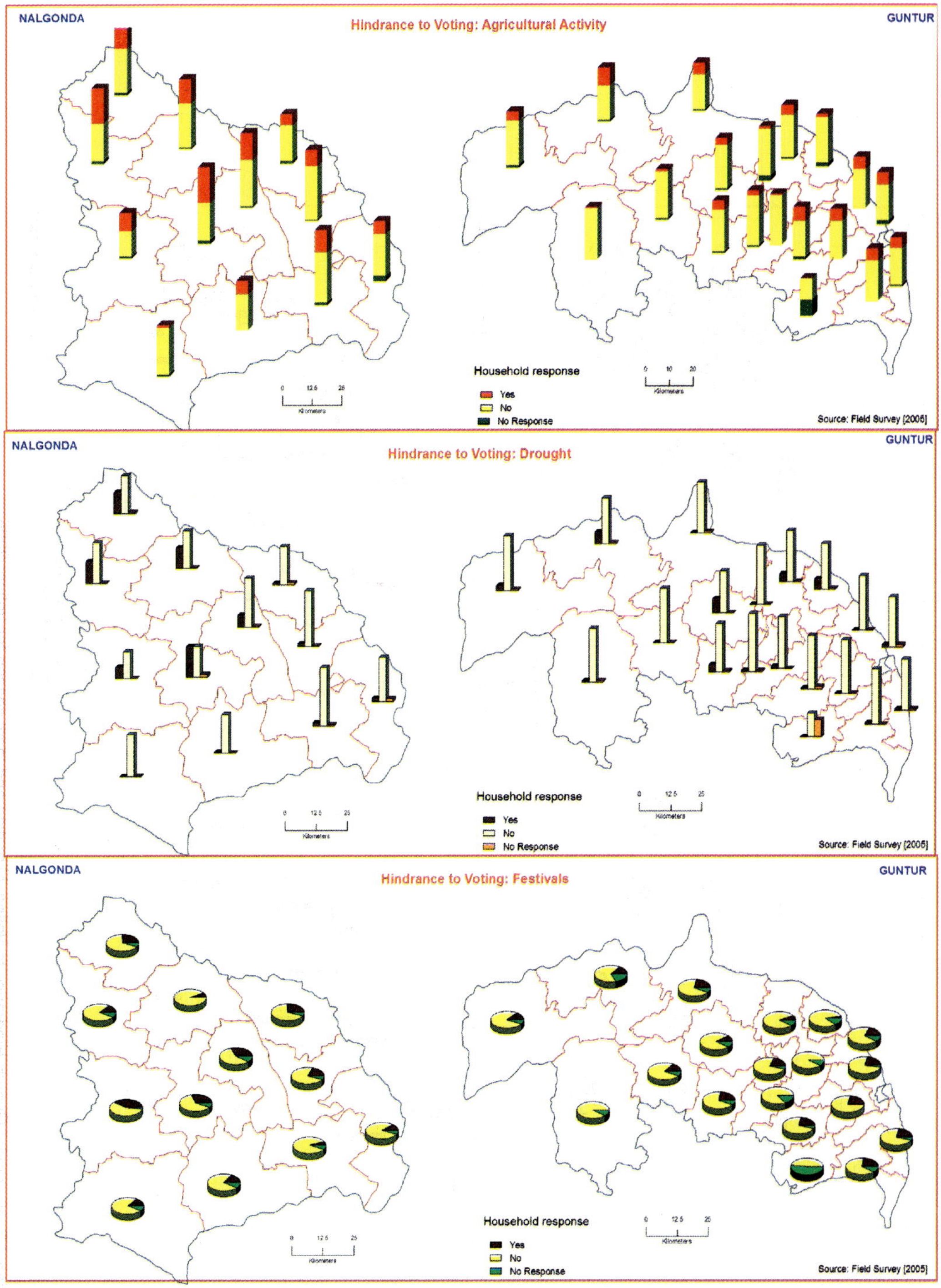

Map 4.6: Nalgonda: Guntur: Hindrance to Voting: Agricultural Activity and Drought and Festivals: 2005

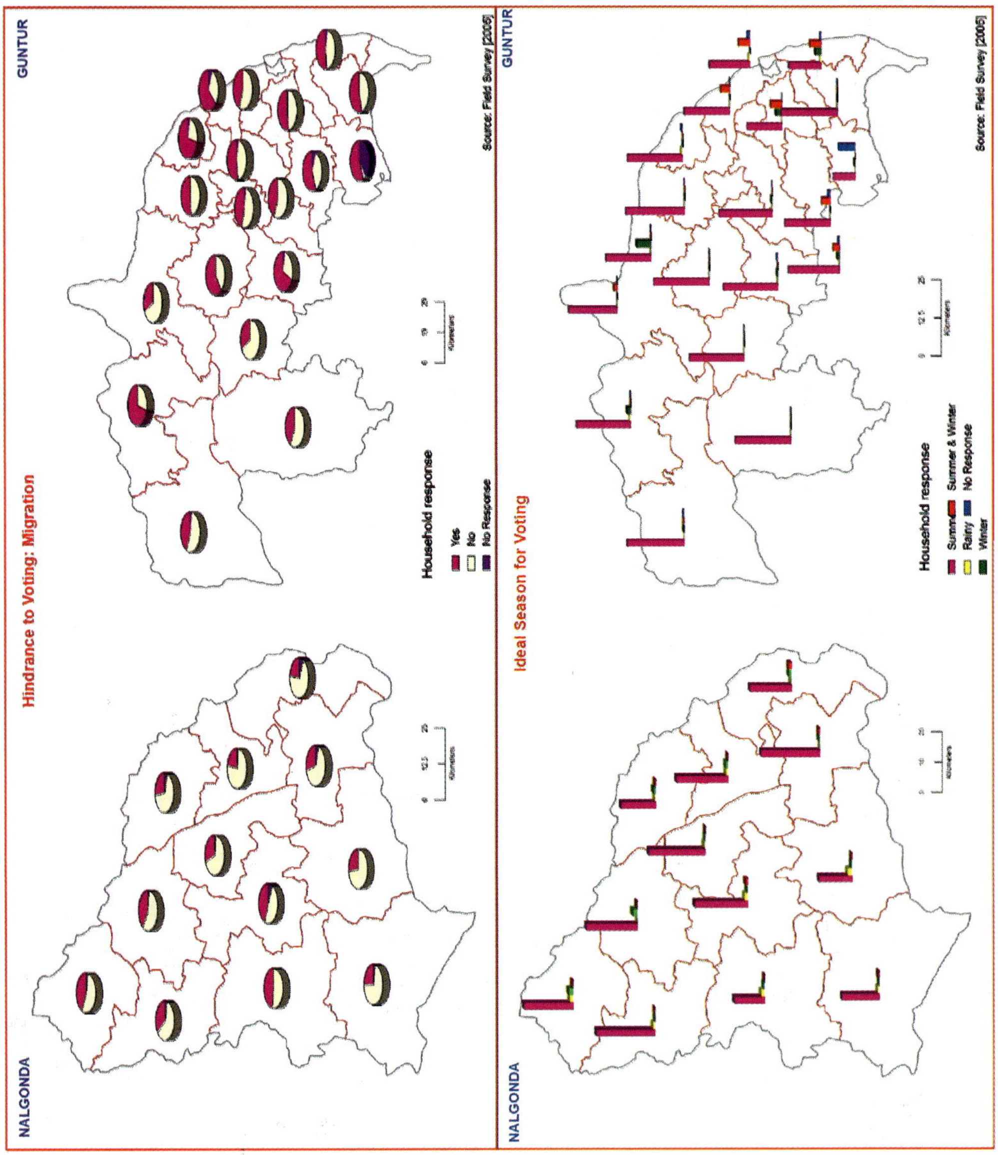

Map 4.7: Nalgonda: Guntur: Hindrance to Voting: Migration and Ideal season for Voting: 2005

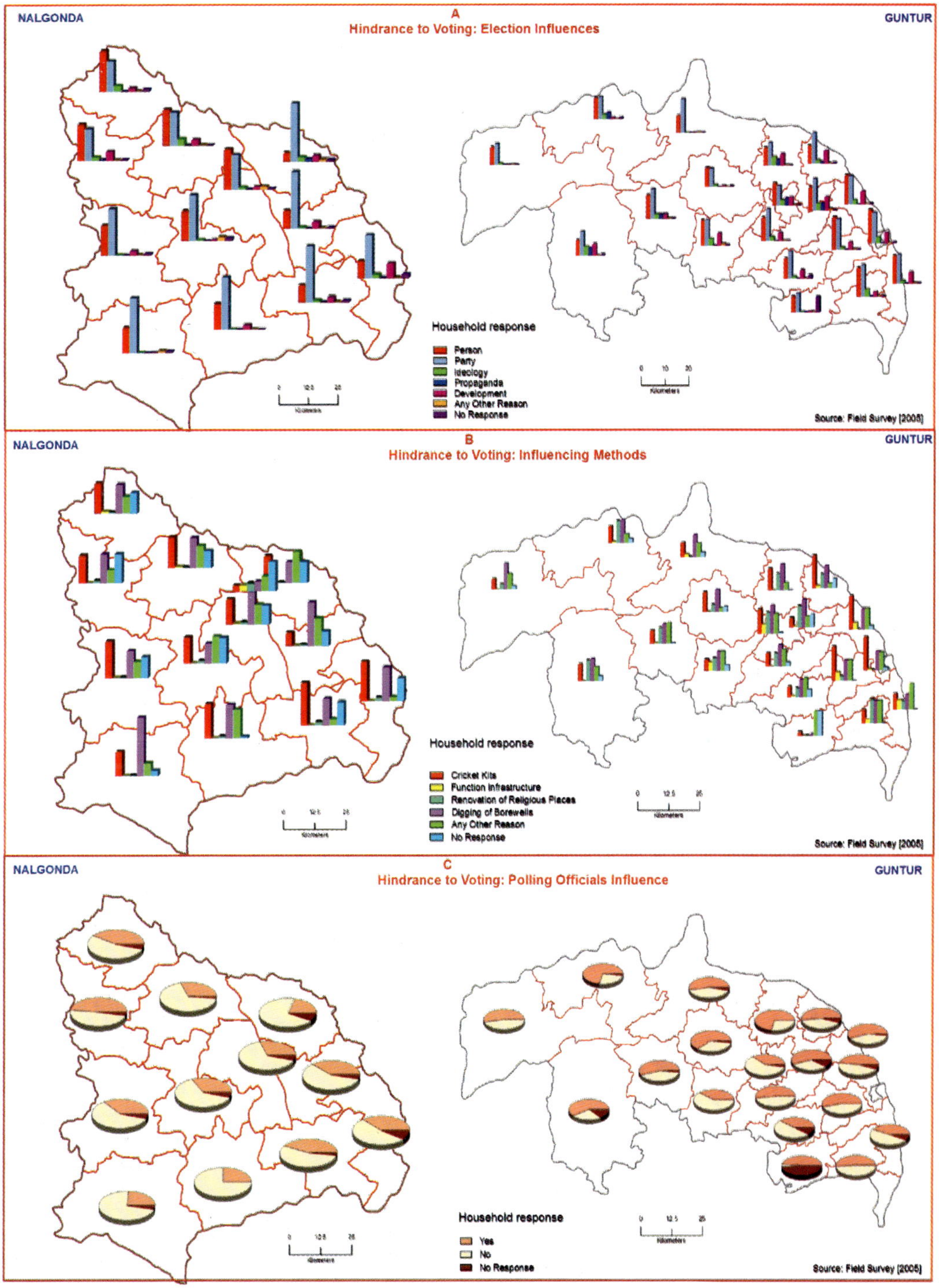

Map 4.8: Nalgonda: Guntur: Hindrance to Voting: Election influences, Influencing Methods and Polling Official's Influence: 2005

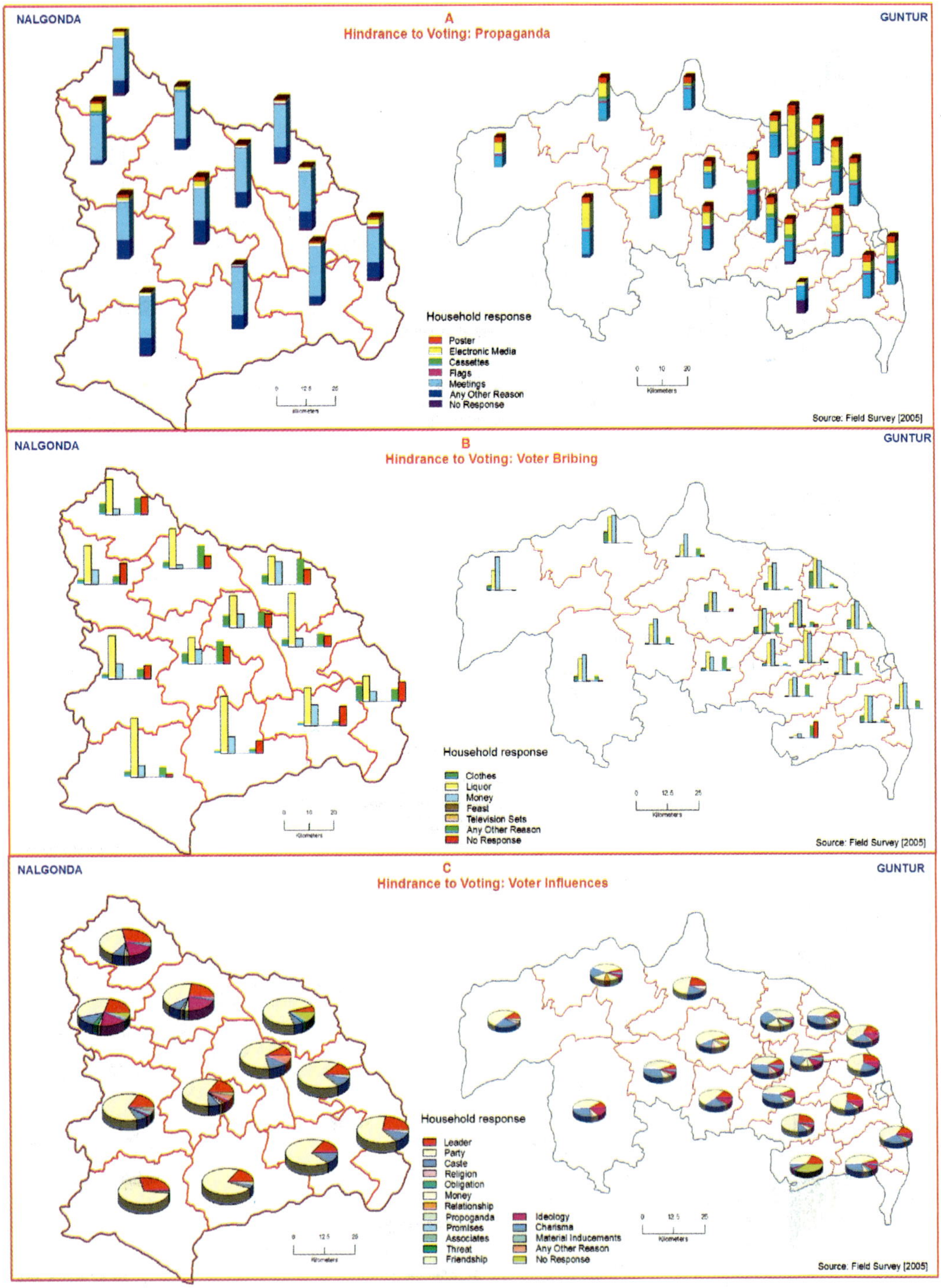

Map 4.9: Nalgonda: Guntur: Hindrance to Voting: Propaganda, Voter Bribing and Voter Influences: 2005

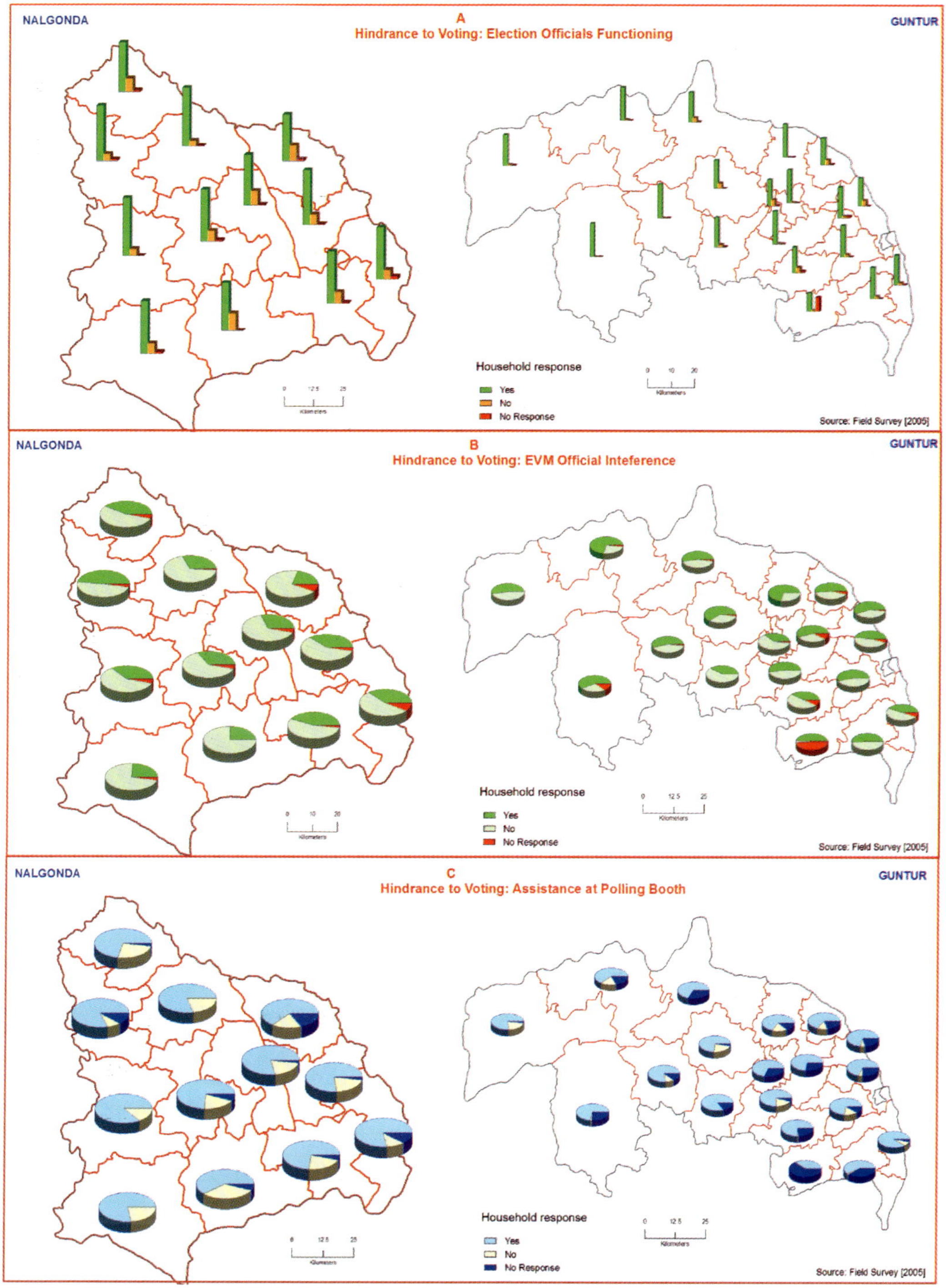

Map 4.10: Nalgonda: Guntur: Hindrance to Voting: Election Officials' Functioning, EVM Official Interference and Assistance at Polling Booth: 2005

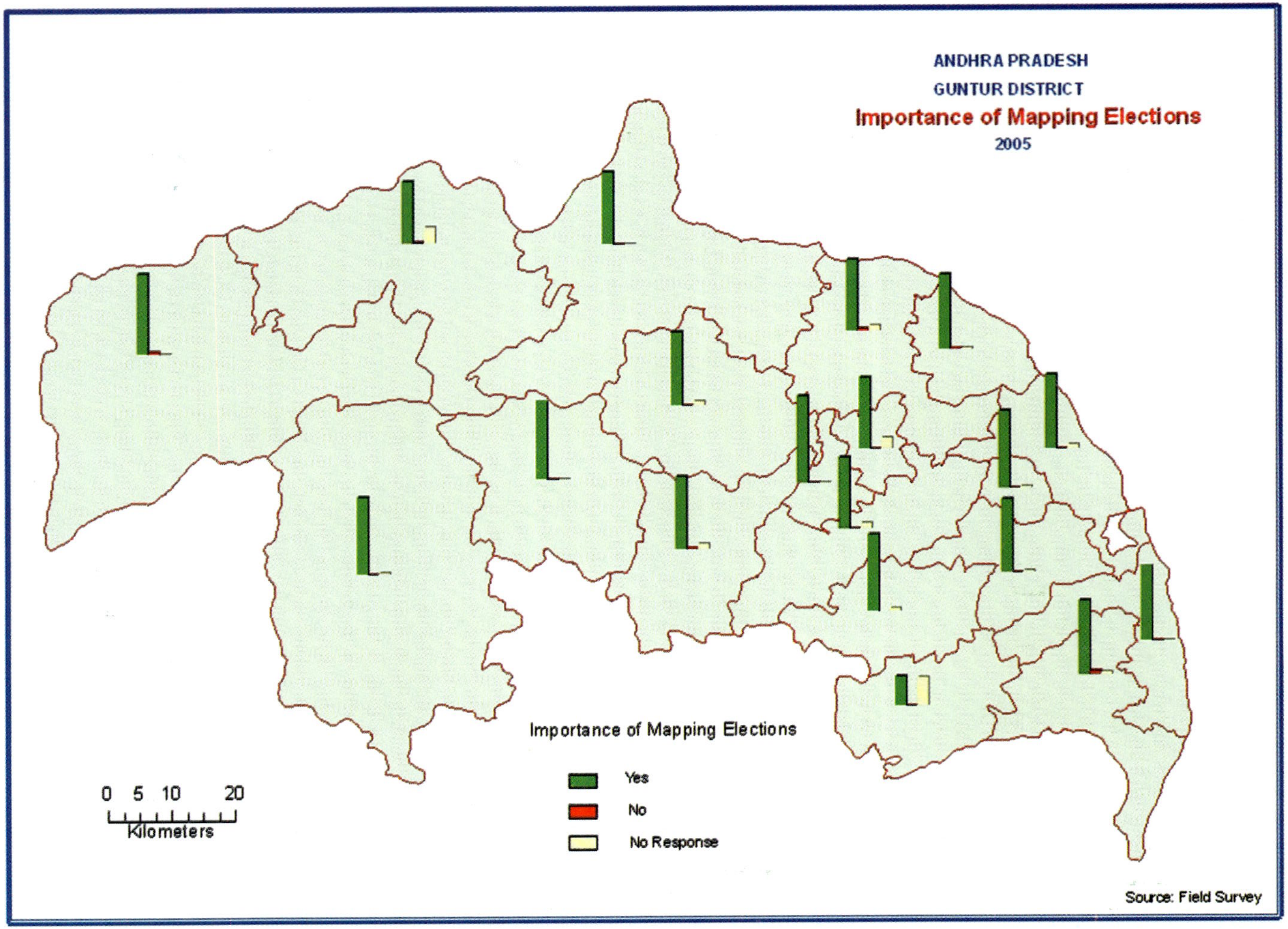

Map 4.11: Andhra Pradesh: Guntur District : Importance of Mapping Elections: 2005

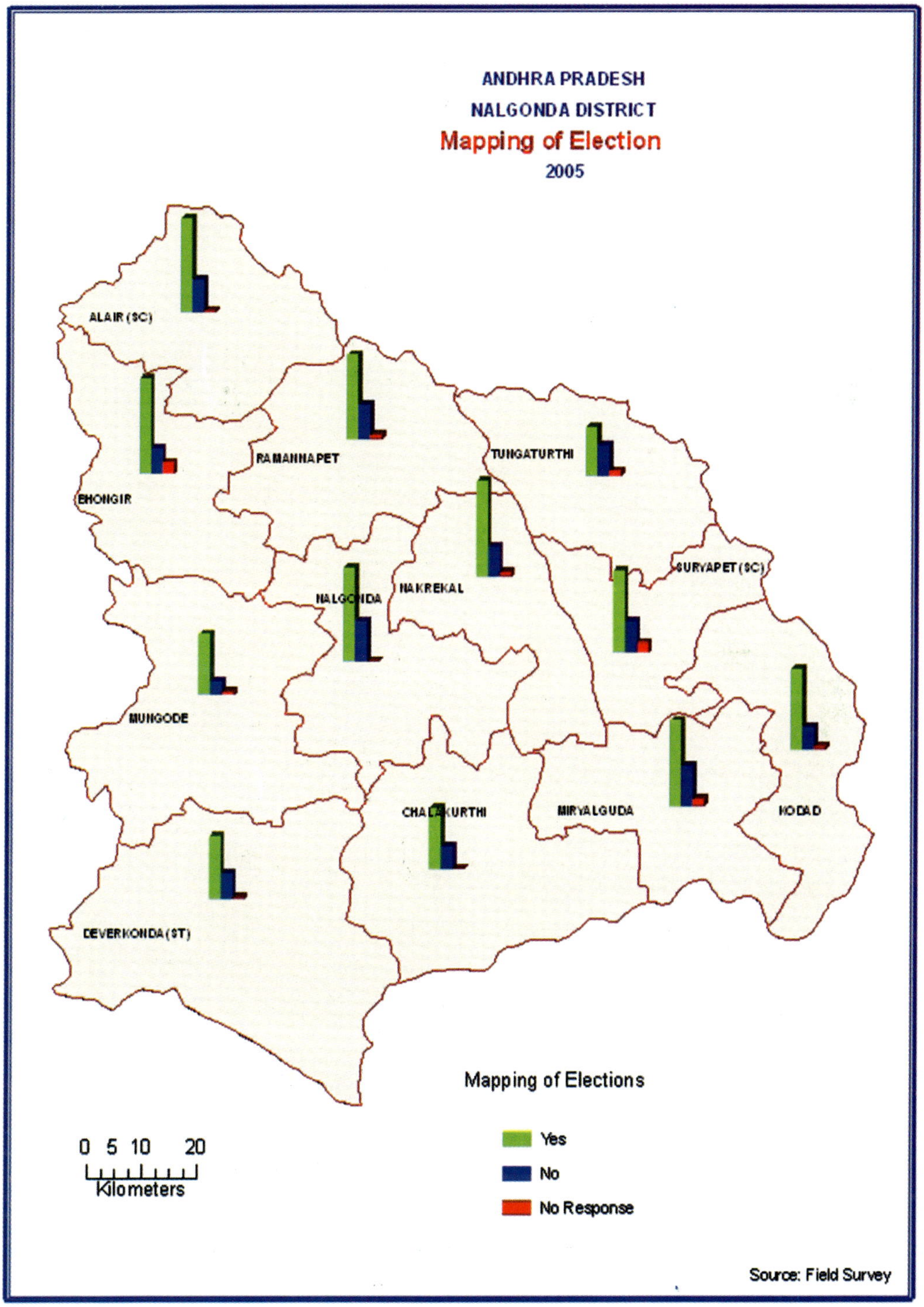

Map 4.12: Andhra Pradesh: Nalgonda District: Mapping of Elections: 2005

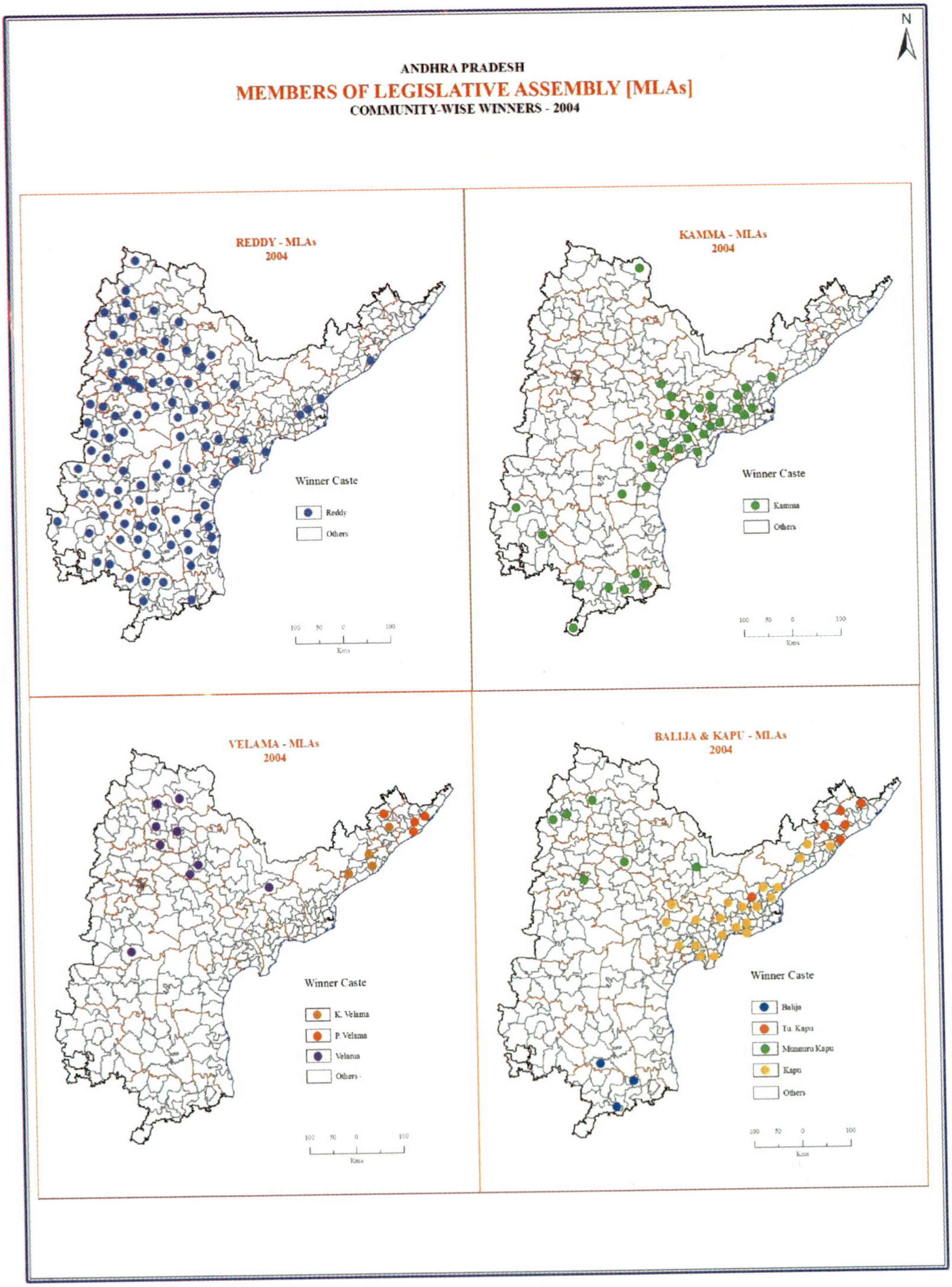

Map 5.1(a): AP. Member of Legislative Assembly: Community-Wise Winners: 2004

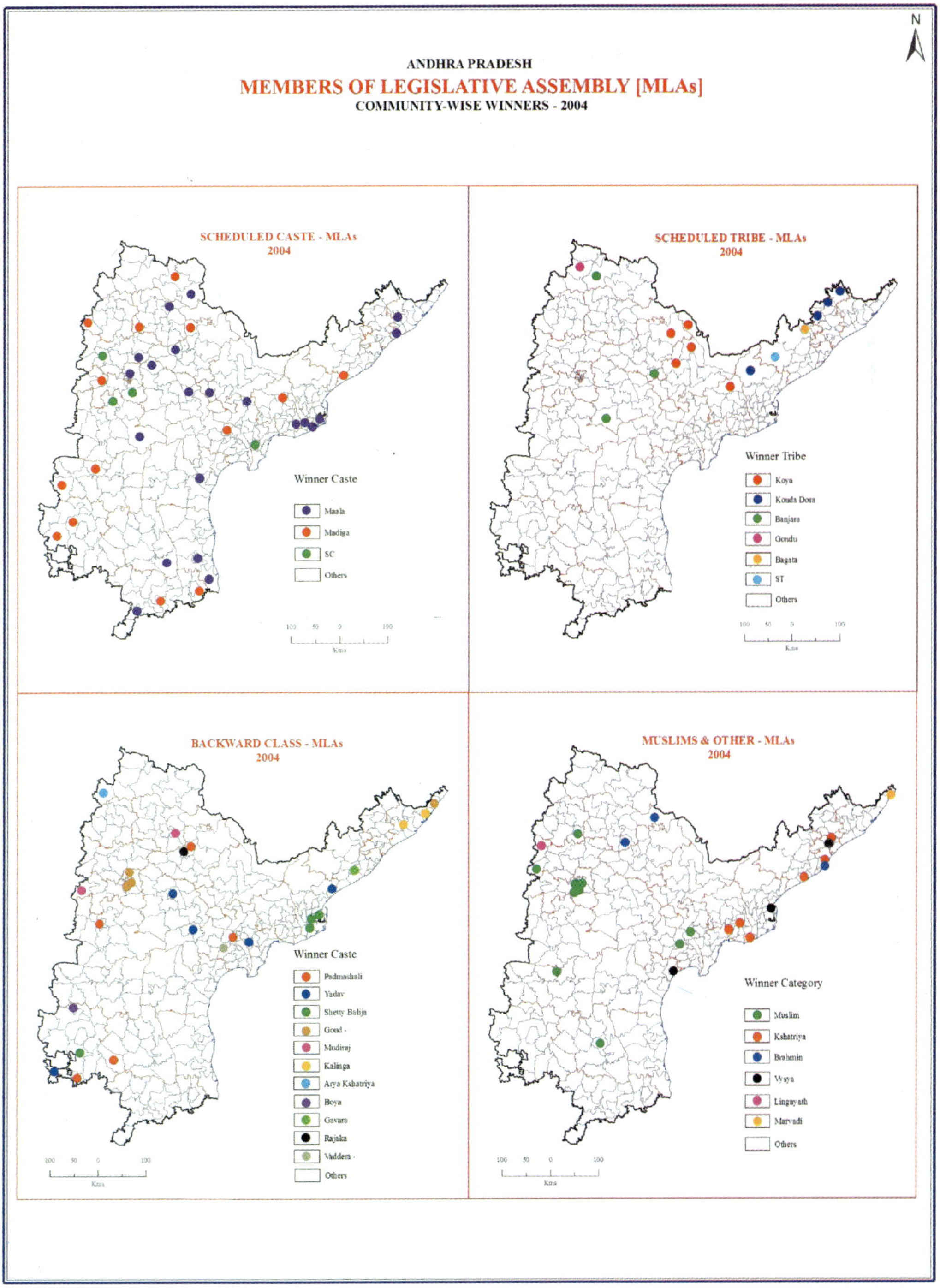

Map 5.1(b): A.P. Member of Legislative Assembly: Community-Wise Winners: 2004

ANDHRA PRADESH

MEMBERS OF LEGISLATIVE ASSEMBLY [MLAs]

COMMUNITY WISE WINNERS - 2009

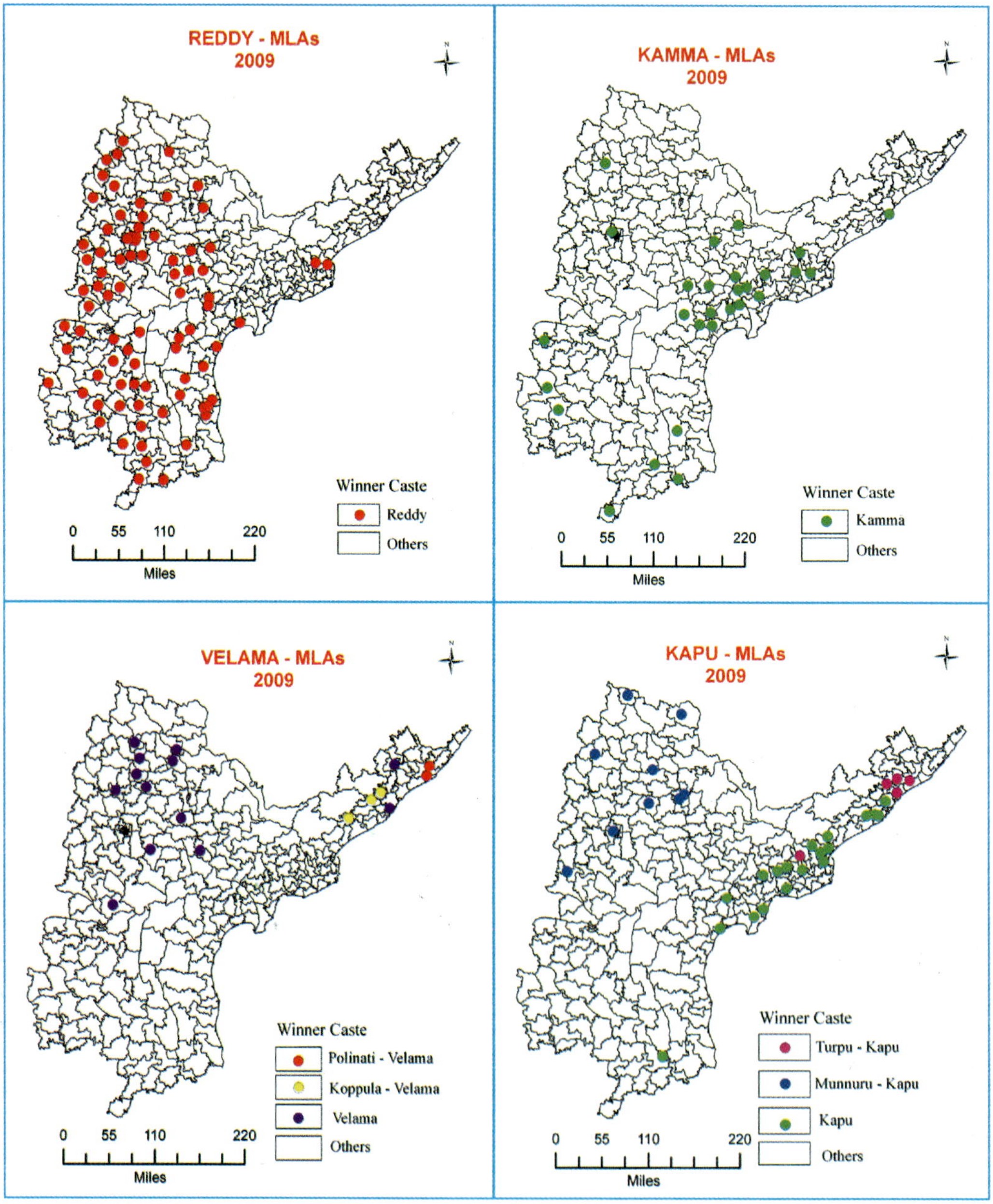

Map 5.1(c): AP. Member of Legislative Assembly: Community-Wise Winners: 2009

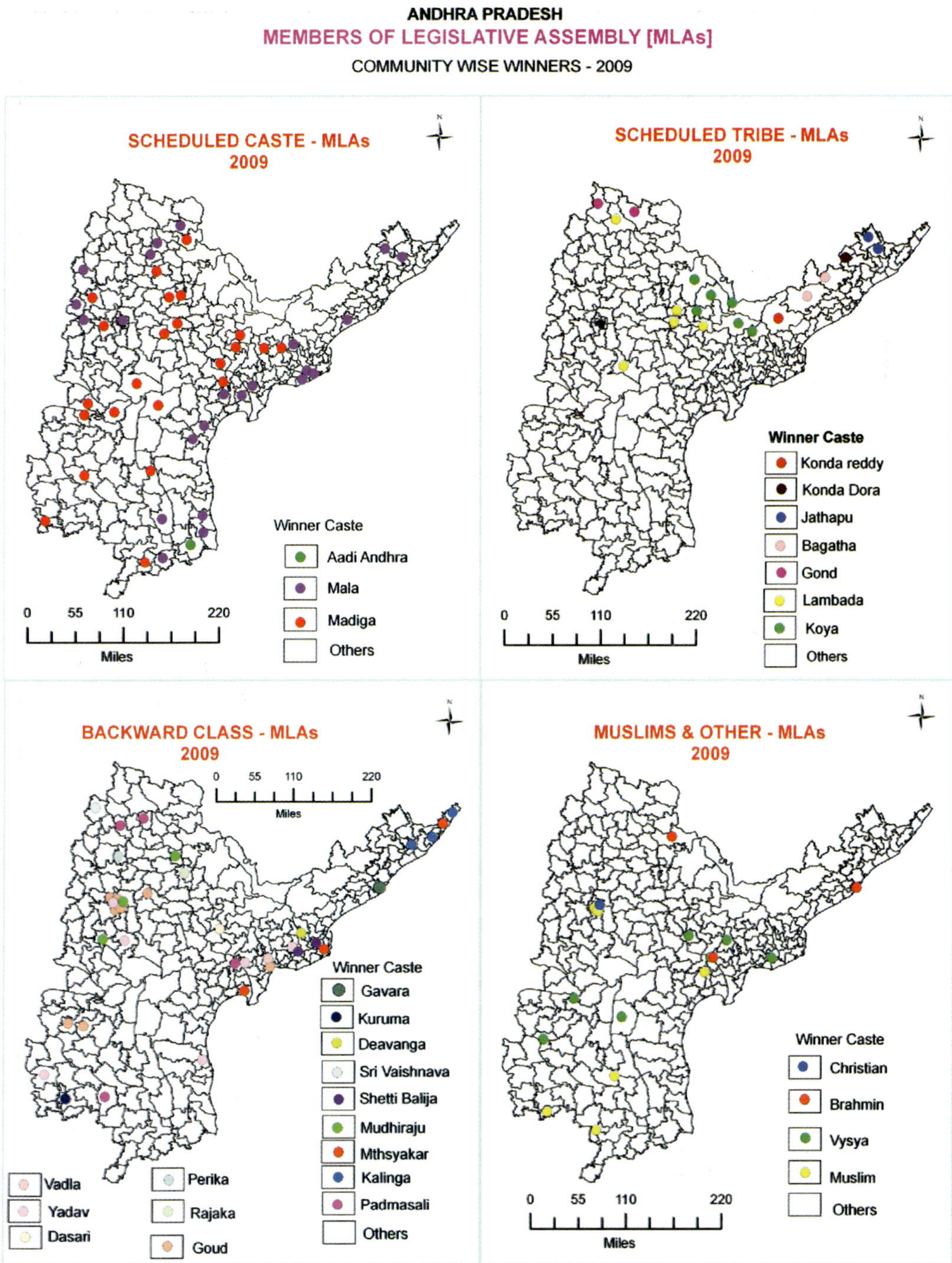

Map 5.1(d): AP. Member of Legislative Assembly: Community-Wise Winners: 2009

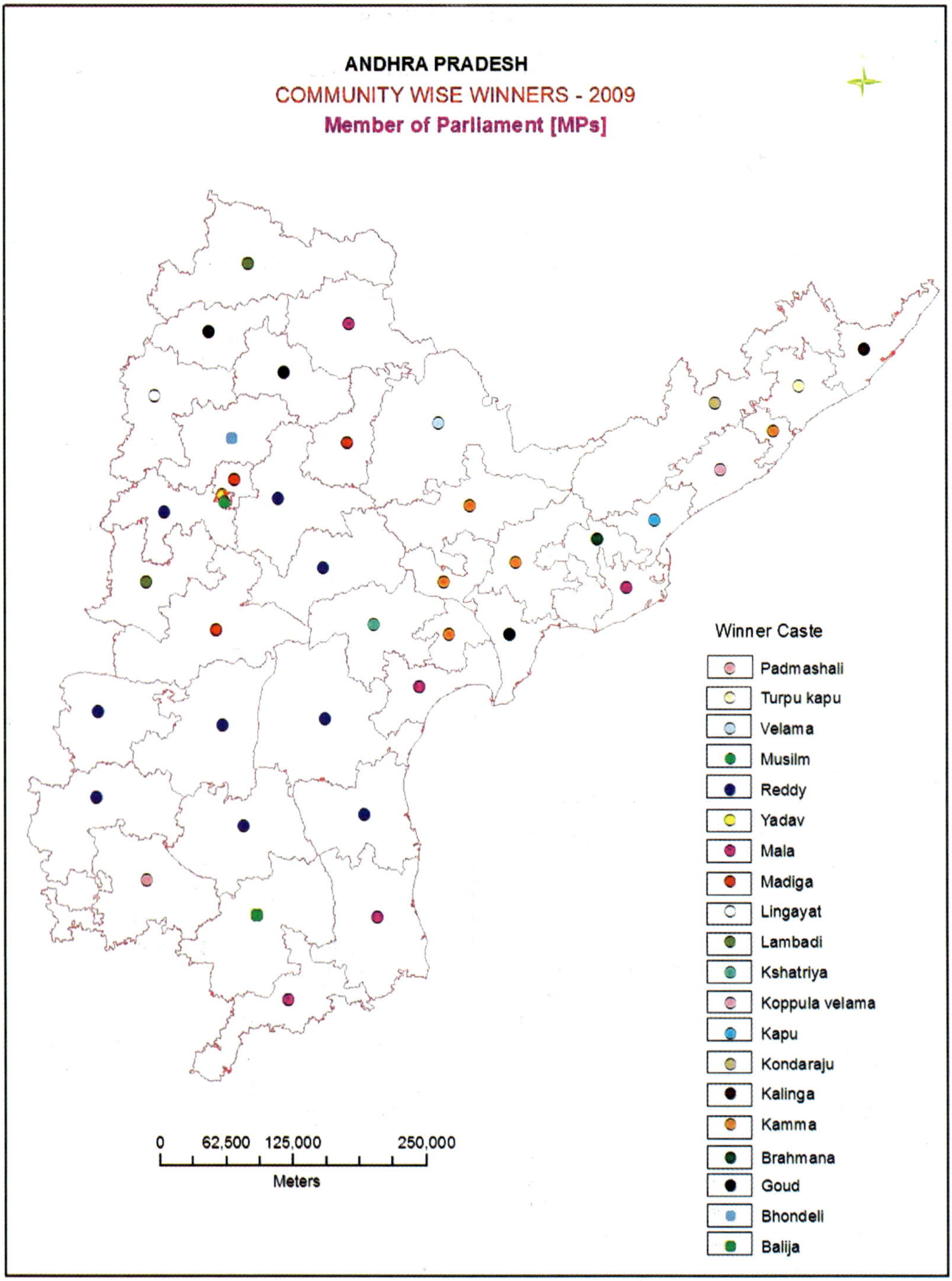

Map 5.1(e): AP. Member of Parliament Community-Wise Winners: 2009

Appendix–I

List of Constituencies (MP & MLA) and Administrative Units (Districts and Mandals)-2009

S. No.	District	Parliamentary Constituencies	Assembly Constituencies	Mandal
1	Adilabad	Adilabad (ST)	Sirpur	Kouthala, Bejjur, Kagaznagar, Sirpur (T) and Dahegaon.
2	Adilabad	Peddapalle (SC)	Chennur (SC)	Jaipur, Chennur, Kotapalli and Mandamarri.
3	Adilabad	Peddapalle (SC)	Bellampalli (SC)	Kasipet, Tandur, Bellampalli, Bhimini, Nennal and Vemanpalli
4	Adilabad	Peddapalle (SC)	Mancherial	Luxettipet, Mancherial and Dandepalli.
5	Adilabad	Adilabad (ST)	Asifabad (ST)	Kerameri, Wankdi, Sirpur (U), Asifabad, Jainoor, Narnoor, Tiryani and Rebbana.
6	Adilabad	Adilabad (ST)	Khanapur (ST)	Jannaram, Utnoor, Kaddam (Peddur), Khanapur and Indervelly.
7	Adilabad	Adilabad (ST)	Adilabad	Adilabad, Jainath and Bela.
8	Adilabad	Adilabad (ST)	Boath (ST)	Tamsi, Talamadugu, Gudihathnoor, Ichoda, Bazarhathnoor, Boath and Neradigonda.
9	Adilabad	Adilabad (ST)	Nirmal	Dilawarpur, Nirmal, Laxmanchanda, Mamda and Sarangapur.
10	Adilabad	Adilabad (ST)	Mudhole	Kuntala, Kubeer, Bhainsa, Tanoor, Mudhole and Lokeswaram.
11	Nizamabad	Nizamabad	Armur	Nandipet, Armur and Makloor.

(*Contd.*)

Appendix–I (*Contd.*)

S. No.	*District*	*Parliamentary Constituencies*	*Assembly Constituencies*	*Mandal*
12	Nizamabad	Nizamabad	Bodhan	Ranjal, Navipet, Yedpalle and Bodhan.
13	Nizamabad	Zahirabad	Jukkal (SC)	Madnoor, Jukkal, Bichkunda, Pitlam and Nizamsagar.
14	Nizamabad	Zahirabad	Banswada	Birkoor, Varni, Banswada and Kotgiri.
15	Nizamabad	Zahirabad	Yellareddy	Yellareddy, Nagareddipet, Lingampet, Tadwai, Gandhari and Sadasivanagar.
16	Nizamabad	Zahirabad	Kamareddy	Machareddy, Domakonda Kamareddy and Bhiknoor.
17	Nizamabad	Nizamabad	Nizamabad (Urban)	Nizamabad (M).
18	Nizamabad	Nizamabad	Nizamabad (Rural)	Jakranpalle and Sirkonda Nizamabad Mandal (Part) Nizamabad [Except Nizamabad (M)], Dichpalle and Dharpalle.
19	Nizamabad	Nizamabad	Balkonda	Balkonda, Mortad, Kammarpalle, Bheemgal and Velpur.
20	Karimnagar	Nizamabad	Koratla	Ibrahimpatnam, Mallapur, Koratla and Metpalle
21	Karimnagar	Nizamabad	Jagtial	Raikal, Sarangapur and Jagtial.
22	Karimnagar	Peddapalle (SC)	Dharmapuri (SC)	Dharmapuri, Dharmaram, Gollapalle, Velgatoor and Pegadapalle.
23	Karimnagar	Peddapalle (SC)	Ramagundam	Ramagundam.
24	Karimnagar	Peddapalle (SC)	Manthani	Kamanpur, Manthani, Kataram, Mahadevpur, Mutharam (Mahadevapur), Malharrao and Mutharam (Manthani).
25	Karimnagar	Peddapalle (SC)	Peddapalle	Peddapalle, Julapalle, Eligaid, Sultanabad, Odela and Srirampur.
26	Karimnagar	Karimnagar	Karimnagar	Karimnagar.
27	Karimnagar	Karimnagar	Choppadandi (SC)	Gangadhara, Ramadugu, Choppadandi, Mallial, Kodimial and Boinpalle.
28	Karimnagar	Karimnagar	Vemulawada	Vemulawada, Konaraopeta, Chandurthi, Kathlapur and Medipalle.
29	Karimnagar	Karimnagar	Sircilla	Yellareddipet, Gambhiraopet, Mustabad and Sircilla.
30	Karimnagar	Karimnagar	Manakondur (SC)	Manakondur, Ellanthakunta, Bejjanki, Timmapur (LMD Colony) and Shankarapatnam.

(*Contd.*)

Appendix–I (*Contd.*)

S. No.	*District*	*Parliamentary Constituencies*	*Assembly Constituencies*	*Mandal*
31	Karimnagar	Karimnagar	Huzurabad	Veenavanka, Jammikunta, Huzurabad and Kamalapur.
32	Karimnagar	Karimnagar	Husnabad	Chigurumamidi, Koheda, Husnabad, Saidapur, Bheemadevarpalle and Elkathurthi.
33	District: Medak	Medak	Siddipet	Siddipet, Chinnakodur and Nangnoor.
34	Medak	Medak	Medak	Medak, Papannapet, Ramayampet and Shankarampet-R.
35	Medak	Zahirabad	Narayankhed	Kangti, Manoor, Narayankhed, Kalher and Shankarampet-A.
36	Medak	Zahirabad	Andole (SC)	Tekmal, Alladurgh, Regode, Raikode, Andole, Pulkal and Munpalle.
37	Medak	Medak	Narsapur	Kowdipalle, Kulcharam, Narsapur, Hathnoora, Yeldurthy and Shivampet.
38	Medak	Zahirabad	Zahirabad (SC)	Zahirabad, Kohir, Nyalkal and Jharasangam.
39	Medak	Medak	Sangareddy	Sadasivpet, Kondapur and Sangareddy.
40	Medak	Medak	Patancheru	Jinnaram, Patancheru and Ramachandrapuram.
41	Medak	Medak	Dubbak	Mirdoddi, Doultabad, Chegunta, Dubbak and Toguta.
42	Medak	Medak	Gajwel	Tupran, Kondapak, Gajwel, Jagdevpur, Wargal and Mulug.
43	Rangareddi	Malkajgiri	Medchal	Medchal, Shamirpet, Ghatkesar and Keesara (Rural).
44	Rangareddi	Malkajgiri	Malkajgiri	Malkajgiri.
45	Rangareddi	Malkajgiri	Quthbullapur	Quthbullapur.
46	Rangareddi	Malkajgiri	Kukatpalle	Hyderabad (M Corp.) (Part) Hyderabad (M Corp.) - Ward No. 24 (Part) (Area in Balanagar) Kukatpalle (M) (Part) Kukatpalle (M) - Ward No. 5 to 16.
47	Rangareddi	Malkajgiri	Uppal	Uppal Municipality, Kapra Municipality.
48	Rangareddi	Bhongir	Ibrahimpatnam	Hayathnagar, Ibrahimpatnam, Manchal and Yacharam.

(*Contd.*)

Appendix–I *(Contd.)*

S. No.	*District*	*Parliamentary Constituencies*	*Assembly Constituencies*	*Mandal*
49	Rangareddi	Malkajgiri	Lal Bahadurnagar	Saroornagar Mandal (Part) Gaddiannaram (CT), Lal Bahadur Nagar (M+OG) (Part) Lal Bahadur Nagar (M) - Ward No. 1 to 10.
50	Rangareddi	Chevella	Maheswaram	Maheswaram and Kandukur Saroornagar Mandal (Part) Medbowli, Almasguda, Badangpet, Chintalakunta, Jalpalle, Mamidipalle, Kurmalguda and Nadargul (Rural). Hyderabad (OG) (Part) Balapur (OG) - Ward No. 36 Kothapet (OG) - Ward No. 37 Venkatapur (OG) - Ward No. 39 Mallapur (OG) - Ward No. 40 Lal Bahadur Nagar (M+OG) (Part) Lal Bahadur Nagar (M) - Ward No. 11 Nadargul (OG) (Part) - Ward No. 12 Jillalguda (OG) - Ward No. 15 Meerpet (CT).
51	Rangareddi	Chevella	Rajendranagar	Rajendranagar and Shamshabad.
52	Rangareddi	Chevella	Serilingampally	Serilingampally Mandal Balanagar Mandal (Part) Kukatpally (M) (Part) Kukatpally (M) - Ward No. 1 to 4.
53	Rangareddi	Chevella	Chevella (SC)	Nawabpet, Shankarpalle, Moinabad, Chevella and Shabad.
54	Rangareddi	Chevella	Pargi	Doma, Gandeed, Kulkacherla, Pargi and Pudur
55	Rangareddi	Chevella	Vicarabad (SC)	Marpalle, Mominpet, Vikarabad, Dharur and Bantwaram.
56	Rangareddi	Chevella	Tandur	Peddemul, Tandur, Basheerabad and Yalal.
57	Hyderabad	Secunderabad	Musheerabad	Hyderabad (M Corp.+OG) (Part) Hyderabad (M Corp.) (Part) Ward No. 1
58	Hyderabad	Hyderabad	Malakpet	Hyderabad (M Corp.+OG) (Part) Hyderabad (M Corp.) (Part) Ward No. 16 Ward No. 17 (Part)

(Contd.)

Appendix–I (*Contd.*)

S. No.	*District*	*Parliamentary Constituencies*	*Assembly Constituencies*	*Mandal*
				Block No. 8 and 9
59	Hyderabad	Secunderabad	Amberpet	Hyderabad (M Corp.+OG) (Part) Hyderabad (M Corp.) (Part) - Ward No. 2 Ward No. 3 (Part) Block No. 1 to 4
60	Hyderabad	Secunderabad	Khairatabad	Hyderabad (M Corp.+OG) (Part) Hyderabad (M Corp.) (Part) Ward No. 6 Ward No. 3 (Part) Block No. 5 and 6 Ward No. 8 (Part) Block No. 2. Ward No. 5 (Part) Block No. 10
61	Hyderabad	Secunderabad	Jubilee Hills	Hyderabad (M Corp.+OG) (Part) Hyderabad (M Corp.) (Part) Ward No. 8 (Part) Block No. 1, 3 and 4.
62	Hyderabad	Secunderabad	Sanathnagar	Hyderabad (M Corp.+OG) (Part) Hyderabad (M Corp.) (Part) Ward No. 7, 24 (Excluding The Area in Ac – 46 Kukatpalle) And 25 to 30.
63	Hyderabad	Secunderabad	Nampally	Hyderabad (M Corp.+OG) (Part) Hyderabad (M Corp.) (Part) Ward No. 10 to 12.
64	Hyderabad	Hyderabad	Karwan	Hyderabad (M Corp.+OG) (Part) Hyderabad (M Corp.) (Part) Ward No.9 Ward No. 13 (Part) Block No. 3 to 6.
65	Hyderabad	Hyderabad	Goshamahal	Hyderabad (M Corp.+OG) (Part) Hyderabad (M Corp.) (Part) Ward No. 4, 14 and 15 Ward No. 5 (Part) Block No. 1 to 9 Ward No. 13 (Part) Block No. 1 and 2.
66	Hyderabad	Hyderabad	Charminar	Hyderabad (M Corp.+OG) (Part) Hyderabad (M Corp.) (Part) Ward No. 20 to 23.
67	Hyderabad	Hyderabad	Chandrayangutta	Hyderabad (M Corp.+OG) (Part) Hyderabad (M Corp.) (Part)Ward

(*Contd.*)

Appendix–I (*Contd.*)

S. No.	*District*	*Parliamentary Constituencies*	*Assembly Constituencies*	*Mandal*
68	Hyderabad	Hyderabad	Yakutpura	No.18 (Part) Block No. 1 to 3 and 8 to 14. Hyderabad (M Corp.+OG) (Part) Hyderabad (M Corp.) (Part)- Ward No. 17 (Part) Block No. 1 to 7 Ward No. 18 (Part) Block No. 6 and 7
69	Hyderabad	Hyderabad	Bahadurpura	Hyderabad (M Corp.+OG) (Part) Hyderabad (M Corp.) (Part) Ward No. 18 (Part) Block No. 4 and 5 Ward No. 19.
70	Hyderabad	Secunderabad	Secunderabad	Hyderabad (M Corp.+OG) (Part) Hyderabad (M Corp.) (Part) Ward No. 33 (Part) Block No. 4 to 7 Ward No. 34 and 35 Osmania University Area.
71	Hyderabad	Malkajgiri	Secunderabad cantt. (SC)	Hyderabad (M Corp.+OG) (Part) Hyderabad (M Corp.) (Part) Ward No. 31 and 32 Ward No. 33 (Part) Block No.1 to 3 Secunderabad Cantonment Board.
72	Mahbubnagar	Mahbubnagar	Kodangal	Kodangal, Bomraspet, Kosgi, Doulathabad and Maddur.
73	Mahbubnagar	Mahbubnagar	Narayanpet	Koilkonda, Narayanpet, Damaragidda and Dhanwada.
74	Mahbubnagar	Mahbubnagar	Mahbubnagar	Hanwada and Mahbubnagar.
75	Mahbubnagar	Mahbubnagar	Jadcherla	Jadcherla, Nawabpet, Balanagar and Midjil.
76	Mahbubnagar	Mahbubnagar	Devarkadra	Bhoothpur, Addakal, Devarkadra, Chinna Chinta Kunta and Kothakota.
77	Mahbubnagar	Mahbubnagar	Makthal	Makthal, Maganoor, Atmakur, Narva and Utkoor.
78	Mahbubnagar	Nagarkurnool (SC)	Wanaparthy	Wanaparthy, Pebbair, Gopalpeta, Peddamandadi and Ghanpur.
79	Mahbubnagar	Nagarkurnool (SC)	Gadwal	Gadwal, Dharur, Maldakal and Ghattu.
80	Mahbubnagar	Nagarkurnool (SC)	Alampur (SC)	Ieez, Itikyal, Waddepalle, Manopad and Alampur.

(*Contd.*)

Appendix–I (*Contd.*)

S. No.	*District*	*Parliamentary Constituencies*	*Assembly Constituencies*	*Mandal*
81	Mahbubnagar	Nagarkurnool (SC)	Nagarkurnool	Nagarkurnool, Bijinapalle, Thimmajipet, Tadoor and Telkapalle.
82	Mahbubnagar	Nagarkurnool (SC)	Achampet (SC)	Balmoor, Lingal, Amrabad, Achampet, Uppununthala
83	Mahbubnagar	Nagarkurnool (SC)	Kalwakurthy	Kalwakurthy, Talakondapalle, Amangal and Madgul.
84	Mahbubnagar	Mahbubnagar	Shadnagar	Kondurg, Farooqnagar, Kothur and Keshampet.
85	Mahbubnagar	Nagarkurnool (SC)	Kollapur	Veepangandla, Kollapur, Peddakothapalle, Kodair and Pangal.
86	Nalgonda	Nalgonda	Devarakonda (ST)	Chintapalle, Gundlapalle, Chandampet, Devarakonda and Pedda Adisarlapalle.
87	Nalgonda	Nalgonda	Nagarjuna Sagar	Gurrampode, Nidamanur, Peddavoora, Anumula and Thripuraram.
88	Nalgonda	Nalgonda	Miryalaguda	Vemulapalle, Miryalaguda and Damercherla.
89	Nalgonda	Nalgonda	Huzurnagar	Neredcherla, Garidepalle, Huzurnagar, Mattampalli and Mellachervu.
90	Nalgonda	Nalgonda	Kodad	Mothey, Nadigudem, Munagala, Chilkur and Kodad.
91	Nalgonda	Nalgonda	Suryapet	Atmakur (S), Suryapet, Chivvemla and Penpahad.
92	Nalgonda	Nalgonda	Nalgonda	Thipparthi, Nalgonda and Kangal.
93	Nalgonda	Bhongir	Munugode	Munugode, Narayanapur, Marriguda, Nampalle, Chandur and Choutuppal.
94	Nalgonda	Bhongir	Bhongir	Bhongir, Bibinagar, Valigonda and Pochampalle.
95	Nalgonda	Bhongir	Nakrekal (SC)	Ramannapeta, Chityala, Kattangoor, Nakrekal, Kethepalle and Narketpalle.
96	Nalgonda	Bhongir	Thungathurthi (SC)	Thirumalagiri, Thungathurthi, Nuthankal, Jajireddigudem, Sali Gouraram and Mothkur.
97	Nalgonda	Bhongir	Alair	M.Turkapalle, Rajapet, Yadagirigutta, Alair, Gundala, Atmakur (M) and Bommalaramaram.

(Contd.)

Appendix–I (*Contd.*)

S. No.	*District*	*Parliamentary Constituencies*	*Assembly Constituencies*	*Mandal*
98	Warangal	Bhongir	Jangaon	Cherial, Maddur, Bachannapet, Narmetta and Jangaon.
99	Warangal	Warangal (SC)	Ghanpur (Station) (SC)	Ghanpur (Station), Dharmasagar, Raghunathpalle, Zaffergadh, and Lingalaghanpur.
100	Warangal	Warangal (SC)	Palakurthi	Palakurthi, Devaruppula, Kodakandla, Raiparthy and Thorrur.
101	Warangal	Mahabubabad (ST)	Dornakal (ST)	Narsimhulapet, Maripeda, Kuravi and Dornakal.
102	Warangal	Mahabubabad (ST)	Mahabubabad (ST)	Gudur, Nellikudur, Kesamudram and Mahabubabad.
103	Warangal	Mahabubabad (ST)	Narsampet	Narsampet, Khanapur, Chennaraopet, Duggondi, Nekkonda and Nallabelly.
104	Warangal	Warangal (SC)	Parkal	Parkal, Atmakur, Sangam and Geesugonda.
105	Warangal	Warangal (SC)	Warangal	Warangal Mandal (Part) Warangal (M Corp.) (Part) Warangal (M Corp.) - Ward No. 1 to 7, 15, 21 and 23 to 25
106	Warangal	Warangal (SC)	Warangal East	Warangal Mandal (Part) Warangal (M Corp.) (Part) Warangal (M Corp.) - Ward No. 8 to 14, 16 to 20 and 22.
107	Warangal	Warangal (SC)	Waradhanapet (SC)	Hasanparthy, Hanamkonda, Parvathagiri and Wardhanna Pet.
108	Warangal	Warangal (SC)	Bhupalpalle	Mogullapalle, Chityal, Bhupalpalle, Ghanpur (Mulug), Regonda and Shayampet.
109	Warangal	Mahabubabad (ST)	Mulug (ST)	Venkatapur, Eturnagaram, Mangapet, Tadvai, Kothaguda, Govindaraopet and Mulug.
110	Khammam	Mahabubabad (ST)	Pinapaka (ST)	Pinapaka, Manuguru, Gundala, Burgampahad and Aswapuram.
111	Khammam	Mahabubabad (ST)	Yellandu (ST)	Kamepalle, Yellandu, Bayyaram, Tekulapalle and Garla.
112	Khammam	Khammam	Khammam	Khammam.
113	Khammam	Khammam	Palair	Thirumalayapalem, Kusumanchi, Khammam Rural and Nelakondapalle.
114	Khammam	Khammam	Madhira (SC)	Mudigonda, Chinthakani, Bonakal, Madhira and Yerrupalem.

(*Contd.*)

Appendix–I (*Contd.*)

S. No.	*District*	*Parliamentary Constituencies*	*Assembly Constituencies*	*Mandal*
115	Khammam	Khammam	Wyra (ST)	Enkuru, Konijerla, Singareni, Julurpadu and Wyra.
116	Khammam	Khammam	Sathupalle (SC)	Sathupalle, Penuballi, Kallur, Tallada and Vemsoor.
117	Khammam	Khammam	Kothagudem	Kothagudem and Palwancha.
118	Khammam	Khammam	Aswaraopeta (ST)	Mulikalapalle, Velairpadu, Kukunoor, Chandrugonda, Aswaraopeta and Dammapeta.
119	Khammam	Mahabubabad (ST)	Bhadrachalam (ST)	Wazeed, Venkatapuram, Cherla, Dummugudem, Bhadrachalam, Kunavaram, Chintur and V.R. Puram.
120	Srikakulam	Srikakulam	Ichchapuram	Kanchili, Ichchapuram, Kaviti and Sompeta.
121	Srikakulam	Srikakulam	Palasa	Palasa, Mandasa and Vajrapukothuru.
122	Srikakulam	Srikakulam	Tekkali	Nandigam, Tekkali, Santhabommali and Kotabommali.
123	Srikakulam	Srikakulam	Pathapatnam	Pathapatnam, Meliaputti, L.N. Pet, Kothur and Hiramandalam.
124	Srikakulam	Srikakulam	Srikakulam	Gara and Srikakulam.
125	Srikakulam	Srikakulam	Amadalavalasa	Amadalavalasa, Ponduru, Sarubujjili and Burja.
126	Srikakulam	Vizianagaram	Etcherla	G. Sigadam, Laveru, Ranastalam and Etcherla.
127	Srikakulam	Srikakulam	Narasannapeta	Jalumuru, Narasannapeta, Saravakota and Polaki.
128	Srikakulam	Vizianagaram	Rajam (SC)	Vangara, Regidi Amadalavalasa, Rajam and Santhakaviti.
129	Srikakulam	Araku (ST)	Palakonda (ST)	Seethampeta, Bhamini, Palakonda and Veeraghattam.
130	Vizianagaram	Araku (ST)	Kurupam (ST)	Kurupam, Gummalakshmipuram, Jiyyammavalasa, Komarada and Garugubilli.
131	Vizianagaram	Araku (ST)	Parvathipuram (SC)	Parvathipuram, Seethanagaram and Balijipeta.
132	Vizianagaram	Araku (ST)	Salur (ST)	Salur, Pachipenta, Mentada and Makkuva.
133	Vizianagaram	Vizianagaram	Bobbili	Bobbili, Ramabhadrapuram, Badangi and Therlam.
134	Vizianagaram	Vizianagaram	Cheepurupalli	Merakamudidam, Garividi, Cheepurupalli and Gurla.
135	Vizianagaram	Vizianagaram	Gajapathinagaram	Gajapathinagaram, Bondapalli,

(*Contd.*)

Appendix–I (*Contd.*)

S. No.	*District*	*Parliamentary Constituencies*	*Assembly Constituencies*	*Mandal*
				Gantyada and Dattirajeru; and Vizinigiri, Thandrangi, Jannivalasa, Venne, Sasanapalli, Attada, Bheemasingi, Somayajulapalem, Lotlapalli, Mokhasa Kothavalasa, Kumaram and Annamrajupeta Villages of Jami.
136	Vizianagaram	Vizianagaram	Nellimarla	Nellimarla, Pusapatirega, Denkada and Bhogapuram.
137	Vizianagaram	Vizianagaram	Vizianagaram	Vizianagaram.
138	Vizianagaram	Visakhapatnam	Srungavarapukota	Srungavarapukota, Vepada, Lakkavarapukota and Kothavalasa; and Jami Mandal (Except 12 Villages I.E. Vizinigiri, Thandrangi, Jannivalasa, Venne, Sasanapalli, Attada, Bheemasingi, Somayajulapalem, Lotlapalli, Mokhasa Kothavalasa, Kumaram and Annamrajupeta)
139	Visakhapatnam	Visakhapatnam	Bhimili	Anandapuram, Padmanabham, Bheemunipatnam and Visakhapatnam Rural.
140	Visakhapatnam	Visakhapatnam	Visakhapatnam East	Visakhapatnam (Urban) (Part) Visakhapatnam (M Corp.) - Ward No.1 to 11 and 53 to 55.
141	Visakhapatnam	Visakhapatnam	Visakhapatnam South	Visakhapatnam (Urban) (Part) Visakhapatnam (M Corp.) - Ward No.12 to 34, 42 to 43 and 46 to 48.
142	Visakhapatnam	Visakhapatnam	Visakhapatnam North	Visakhapatnam (Urban) (Part) Visakhapatnam (M Corp.) - Ward No.36 to 41, 44 to 45 and 49 to 52.
143	Visakhapatnam	Visakhapatnam	Visakhapatnam West	Visakhapatnam (Urban) (Part) Visakhapatnam (M Corp.) - Ward No. 35 and 56 to 71.
144	Visakhapatnam	Visakhapatnam	Gajuwaka	Gajuwaka (Including Gajuwaka Municipality)
145	Visakhapatnam	Anakapalle	Chodavaram	Chodavaram, Butchayyapeta, Ravikamatham and Rolugunta.
146	Visakhapatnam	Anakapalle	Madugula	Madugula, Cheedikada, Devarapalle and K.Kotapadu.

(*Contd.*)

Appendix–I (*Contd.*)

S. No.	*District*	*Parliamentary Constituencies*	*Assembly Constituencies*	*Mandal*
147	Visakhapatnam	Araku (ST)	Araku Valley (ST)	Munchingiputtu, Pedabayalu, Dumbriguda, Araku Valley, Hukumpeta and Ananthagiri.
148	Visakhapatnam	Araku (ST)	Paderu (ST)	Paderu, G.Madugula, Chintapalle, Gudem Kotha Veedhi and Koyyuru.
149	Visakhapatnam	Anakapalle	Anakapalle	Kasimkota and Anakapalle.
150	Visakhapatnam	Anakapalle	Pendurthi	Pedagantyada (Excluding Areas Included in Gajuwaka Municipality), Paravada, Sabbavaram and Pendurthi
151	Visakhapatnam	Anakapalle	Yelamanchili	Rambilli, Munagapaka, Atchutapuram and Yelamanchili.
152	Visakhapatnam	Anakapalle	Payakaraopet (SC)	Kotauratla, Nakkapalle, Payakaraopeta and S.Rayavaram.
153	Visakhapatnam	Anakapalle	Narsipatnam	Nathavaram, Golugonda, Narsipatnam and Makavarapalem.
154	East Godavari	Kakinada	Tuni	Thondangi, Kotananduru and Tuni.
155	East Godavari	Kakinada	Prathipadu	Sankhavaram, Prathipadu, Yeleswaram and Rowthulapudi.
156	East Godavari	Kakinada	Pithapuram	Gollaprolu, Pithapuram and Kothapalle.
157	East Godavari	Kakinada	Kakinada Rural	Karapa and Kakinada Rural.Kakinada Urban (Part) Kakinada Urban (M) (Part) Kakinada (M) - Ward No. 66 to 70.
158	East Godavari	Kakinada	Peddapuram	Samalkota and Peddapuram.
159	East Godavari	Rajahmundry	Anaparthy	Pedapudi, Biccavolu, Rangampeta and Anaparthy.
160	East Godavari	Kakinada	Kakinada City	Kakinada Urban (Part) Kakinada Urban (M) (Part) Kakinada (M) - Ward No. 1 to 65.
161	East Godavari	Amalapuram (SC)	Ramachandrapuram	Kajuluru, Ramachandrapuram and Pamarru.
162	East Godavari	Amalapuram (SC)	Mummidivaram	Polavaram, Mummidivaram, Thallarevu and Katrenikona.
163	East Godavari	Amalapuram (SC)	Amalapuram(SC)	Uppalaguptam, Allavaram and Amalapuram.
164	East Godavari	Amalapuram (SC)	Razole (SC)	Razole, Malikipuram and Sakhinetipalle. Mamidikuduru Mandal (Part) Mamidikuduru, Geddada, Edarada, Komarada,

(*Contd.*)

Appendix–I (*Contd.*)

S. No.	*District*	*Parliamentary Constituencies*	*Assembly Constituencies*	*Mandal*
				Magatapalle and Gogannamatham Villages.
165	East Godavari	Amalapuram (SC)	Gannavaram(SC)	P.Gannavaram, Ambajipeta and Ainavilli. Mamidikuduru (Part) Pedapatnam, Appanapalle, Botlakurru Doddavaram, Pasarlapudi, Pedapatnam, Nagaram, Mogalikuduru, Makanapalem, Lutukurru, Pasarlapudilanka and Adurru Villages.
166	East Godavari	Amalapuram (SC)	Kothapeta	Ravulapalem, Kothapeta, Atreyapuram and Alamuru.
167	East Godavari	Amalapuram (SC)	Mandapeta	Mandapeta, Rayavaram and Kapileswarapuram.
168	East Godavari	Rajahmundry	Rajanagaram	Rajanagaram, Seethanagaram and Korukonda.
169	East Godavari	Rajahmundry	Rajahmundrycity	Rajahmundry Urban Mandal (Part) Rajahmundry (M Corp.) (Part) Rajahmundry (M Corp.) - Ward No. 7 to 35 and 42 to 89.
170	East Godavari	Rajahmundry	Rajahmundryrural	Kadiam and Rajahmundry Rural. Rajahmundry Urban (Part) Rajahmundry (M Corp.) (Part) Rajahmundry (M Corp.) - Ward No. 1 to 6, 36 to 41 and 90.
171	East Godavari	Kakinada	Jaggampeta	Gokavaram, Jaggampeta, Gandepalle and Kirlampudi.
172	East Godavari	Araku (ST)	Rampachodavaram (ST)	Maredumilli, Devipatnam, Y. Ramavaram, Addateegala, Gangavaram, Rampachodavaram and Rajavommangi.
173	West Godavari	Rajahmundry	Kovvur (SC)	Kovvur, Chagallu and Tallapudi.
174	West Godavari	Rajahmundry	Nidadavole	Nidadavole, Undrajavaram and Peravali.
175	West Godavari	Narsapuram	Achanta	Penugonda, Achanta and Penumantra. Poduru (Part) Kavitam, Jagannadhapuram, Pandithavilluru, Miniminchilipadu, Poduru, Pemmarajupolavaram and Gummaluru Villages.

(*Contd.*)

Appendix–I (*Contd.*)

S. No.	*District*	*Parliamentary Constituencies*	*Assembly Constituencies*	*Mandal*
176	West Godavari	Narsapuram	Palacole	Palacole and Yelamanchili. Poduru (Part) Kommuchikkala, Vedangi, Jinnuru, Mattaparru, Penumadam, Ravipadu and Vaddiparru Villages.
177	West Godavari	Narsapuram	Narasapuram	Mogalthur and Narasapuram.
178	West Godavari	Narsapuram	Bhimavaram	Veeravasaram and Bhimavaram. Bhimavaram (M+OG) Bhimavaram (M) - Ward No. 1 to 27 China-Amiram (OG) (Part) - Ward No. 28 Rayalam (R) (OG) (Part) - Ward No. 29.
179	West Godavari	Narsapuram	Undi	Kalla, Palacoderu, Undi and Akividu.
180	West Godavari	Narsapuram	Tanuku	Tanuku, Attili and Iragavaram.
181	West Godavari	Narsapuram	Tadepalligudem	Tadepalligudem and Pentapadu.
182	West Godavari	Eluru	Unguturu	Unguturu, Bhimadole, Nidamarru and Ganapavaram.
183	West Godavari	Eluru	Denduluru	Pedavegi, Pedapadu and Denduluru Eluru (Part) Malkapuram, Chataparru, Jalipudi, Katlampudi, Madepalli, Manuru, Sreeparru, Kalakurru, Komatilanka, Gudivakalanka, Kokkirailanka, Pydichintapadu and Prathikolla Lanka Villages.
184	West Godavari	Eluru	Eluru	Eluru Mandal (Part) Eluru (M) (Part) Eluru (M) - Ward No. 1 to 28 Eluru Mandal (Part) Eluru Mandal (OG) (Part) Satrampadu (OG) - Ward No.29 Gavaravaram (OG) - Ward No.30 Tangellamudi (R) (OG) - Ward No. 31 Komadavolu (OG) (Part) - Ward No. 32 Eluru (R) (OG) (Part) - Ward No. 33 Eluru (Part) Chodimella, Sanivarapupeta, Eluru (Rural), Komadavole (Rural) and Ponangi Villages.

(*Contd.*)

Appendix–I (*Contd.*)

S. No.	*District*	*Parliamentary Constituencies*	*Assembly Constituencies*	*Mandal*
185	West Godavari	Rajahmundry	Gopalapuram (SC)	Dwaraka Tirumala, Nallajerla, Devarapalli and Gopalapuram.
186	West Godavari	Eluru	Polavaram (ST)	Polavaram, Buttayagudem, Jeelugumilli, Koyyalagudem and T. Narasapuram.
187	West Godavari	Eluru	Chintalapudi (SC)	Chintalapudi, Lingapalem, Kamavarapukota and Jangareddigudem.
188	Krishna	Vijayawada	Tiruvuru (SC)	Vissannapet, Gampalagudem, Tiruvuru and A.Konduru.
189	Krishna	Eluru	Nuzvid	Agiripalli, Chatrai, Musunuru and Nuzvid.
190	Krishna	Machilipatnam	Gannavaram	Bapulapadu, Gannavaram and Unguturu Vijayawada (Rural) Mandal (Part) Ambapuram, Phiryadi Nainavaram, Pathapadu, Nunna, Enikepadu, Nidamanuru, Done Atkuru, Gudavalli, Prasadampadu and Ramavarappadu Villages.
191	Krishna	Machilipatnam	Gudivada	Gudlavalleru, Gudivada and Nandivada.
192	Krishna	Eluru	Kaikalur	Mandavalli, Kaikalur, Kalidindi and Mudinepalle.
193	Krishna	Machilipatnam	Pedana	Gudur, Pedana, Bantumilli and Kruthivennu.
194	Krishna	Machilipatnam	Machilipatnam	Machilipatnam Mandal.
195	Krishna	Machilipatnam	Avanigadda	Challapalli, Mopidevi, Avanigadda, Nagayalanka, Koduru and Ghantasala.
196	Krishna	Machilipatnam	Pamarru (SC)	Pamarru, Thotlavalluru, Pamidimukkala, Movva and Pedaparupudi.
197	Krishna	Machilipatnam	Penamaluru	Kankipadu, Vuyyuru and Penamaluru.
198	Krishna	Vijayawada	Vijayawada West	Vijayawada Urban (Part) Vijayawada Urban (M.Corp) (Part) Vijayawada (M Corp.) - Ward No.1 to 13, 15 to 19, 75 and 76.
199	Krishna	Vijayawada	Vijayawadacentral	Vijayawada Urban (Part) Vijayawada Urban (M.Corp) (Part)

(*Contd.*)

Appendix–I (*Contd.*)

S. No.	*District*	*Parliamentary Constituencies*	*Assembly Constituencies*	*Mandal*
200	Krishna	Vijayawada	Vijayawada East	Vijayawada (M Corp.) - Ward No.14, 20 to 31, 33 to 35, 42 to 44, 49, 77 and 78. Vijayawada Urban (Part) Vijayawada Urban (M.Corp) (Part) Vijayawada (M Corp.) - Ward No. 32, 36 to 41, 45 to 48 and 50 to 74.
201	Krishna	Vijayawada	Mylavaram	Ibrahimpatnam, G.Konduru, Mylavaram and Reddigudem. Vijayawada (Rural) (Part) Kotturu, Tadepalle, Vemavaram, Shabada, Paidurupadu, Rayanapadu, Gollapudi and Jakkampudi Villages.
202	Krishna	Vijayawada	Nandigama (SC)	Kanchikacherla, Chandarlapadu and Veerullapadu Nandigama (Part) Pedavaram, Thakkellapadu, Munagacherla, Latchapalem, Lingalapadu, Adiviravulapadu, Chandapuram, Kethaveeruni Padu, Kanchela, Ithavaram, Ambarupeta, Nandigama, Satyavaram, Pallagiri and Raghavapuram Villages.
203	Krishna	Vijayawada	Jaggayyapeta	Vatsavai, Jaggayyapeta and Penuganchiprolu Nandigama Mandal (Part) Magallu, Konduru, Ramireddipalle, Jonnalagadda, Konathamatmakuru, Torragudipadu, Damuluru, Somavaram, Rudravaram and Gollamudi Villages.
204	Guntur	Narasaraopet	Pedakurapadu	Bellamkonda, Atchampet, Krosuru, Amaravathi and Pedakurapadu.
205	Guntur	Guntur	Tadikonda (SC)	Tulluru, Tadikonda, Phirangipuram and Medikonduru.
206	Guntur	Guntur	Mangalagiri	Tadepalli, Mangalagiri and Duggirala.

(*Contd.*)

Appendix–I (*Contd.*)

S. No.	*District*	*Parliamentary Constituencies*	*Assembly Constituencies*	*Mandal*
207	Guntur	Guntur	Ponnuru	Ponnuru, Chebrolu and Pedakakani.
208	Guntur	Bapatla (SC)	Vemuru (SC)	Vemuru, Kolluru, Tsunduru, Bhattiprolu and Amarthaluru.
209	Guntur	Bapatla (SC)	Repalle	Nizampatnam, Nagaram, Cherukupalli and Repalle.
210	Guntur	Guntur	Tenali	Kollipara and Tenali.
211	Guntur	Bapatla (SC)	Bapatla	Bapatla, Pittalavanipalem and Karlapalem.
212	Guntur	Guntur	Prathipadu (SC)	Guntur Mandal (Except M.Corp.) Vatticherukuru, Prathipadu, Pedanandipadu and Kakumanu.
213	Guntur	Guntur	Guntur West	Guntur Mandal (Part) Guntur (M. Corp) (Part) Guntur (M Corp.) - Ward No.1 to 6 and 24 to 28.
214	Guntur	Guntur	Guntur East	Guntur Mandal (Part) Guntur (M. Corp) (Part) Guntur (M Corp.) - Ward No. 7 to 23.
215	Guntur	Narasaraopet	Chilakaluripet	Nadendla, Chilakaluripet and Edlapadu.
216	Guntur	Narasaraopet	Narasaraopet	Rompicherla and Narasaraopet.
217	Guntur	Narasaraopet	Sattenapalle	Sattenapalli, Rajupalem, Nekarikallu and Muppalla.
218	Guntur	Narasaraopet	Vinukonda	Bollapalli, Vinukonda, Nuzendla, Savalyapuram and Ipur.
219	Guntur	Narasaraopet	Gurajala	Gurajala, Dachepalli, Piduguralla and Machavaram.
220	Guntur	Narasaraopet	Macherla	Macherla, Veldurthi, Durgi, Rentachintala and Karempudi.
221	Prakasam	Ongole	Yerragondapalem (SC)	Yarragondapalem and Pedda Araveedu, Pullalacheruvu, Tripuranthakam, Dornala and Peda Araveedu.
222	Prakasam	Ongole	Darsi	Donakonda, Kurichedu, Mundlamuru, Darsi and Thallur.
223	Prakasam	Bapatla (SC)	Parchur	Yeddanapudi, Parchur, Karamchedu, Inkollu, Chinaganjam and Martur.
224	Prakasam	Bapatla (SC)	Addanki	J. Panguluru, Addanki, Santhamaguluru, Ballikurava and Korisapadu.

(*Contd.*)

Appendix–I (*Contd.*)

S. No.	*District*	*Parliamentary Constituencies*	*Assembly Constituencies*	*Mandal*
225	Prakasam	Bapatla (SC)	Chirala	Chirala and Vetapalem.
226	Prakasam	Bapatla (SC)	Santhanuthalapadu (SC)	Naguluppalapadu, Maddipadu, Chimakurthi and Santhanuthalapadu.
227	Prakasam	Ongole	Ongole	Ongole and Kothapatnam.
228	Prakasam	Nellore	Kandukur	Kandukur, Lingasamudram, Gudluru, Ulavapadu and Volivetivaripalem.
229	Prakasam	Ongole	Kondapi (SC)	Singarayakonda, Kondapi, Tangutur, Jarugumalli, Ponnaluru and Marripudi.
230	Prakasam	Ongole	Markapuram	Konakanamitla, Podili, Markapur and Tarlupadu.
231	Prakasam	Ongole	Giddalur	Bestavaripeta, Racherla, Giddalur, Komarolu, Cumbum and Ardhaveedu.
232	Prakasam	Ongole	Kanigiri	Hanumanthunipadu, Chandrasekharapuram, Pamur, Veligandla, Pedacherlopalle and Kanigiri.
233	Nellore	Nellore	Kavali	Kavali, Bogole, Allur and Dagadarthi.
234	Nellore	Nellore	Atmakur	Chejerla, Atmakur, Anumasamudrampeta, Marripadu, Sangam and Ananthasagaram.
235	Nellore	Nellore	Kovur	Vidavalur, Kodavalur, Kovur, Buchireddipalem and Indukurpet.
236	Nellore	Nellore	Nellore City	Nellore Mandal (Part) Nellore Mandal (M+OG) (Part) Nellore (M) - Ward No.1 to 15, 27, 28 and 31 to 44.
237	Nellore	Nellore	Nellore Rural	Nellore Mandal (Part) Golla Kandukur, Sajjapuram, Vellanti, Kandamur, Upputur, South Mopur, Mogallapalem, Mattempadu, Amancherla, Mannavarappadu, Mulumudi, Devarapalem, Pottepalem, Akkacheruvupadu, Ogurupadu, Ambapuram, Donthali, Buja Buja Nellore (Rural), Kallurpalle (Rural), Kanuparthipadu, Allipuram (Rural), Gudipallipadu,

(*Contd.*)

Appendix–I (*Contd.*)

S. No.	*District*	*Parliamentary Constituencies*	*Assembly Constituencies*	*Mandal*
				Pedda, Cherukur, Chintareddipalem, Visavaviletipadu, Gundlapalem, Kakupalle-I, Kakupalle-II (Madaraja Gudur) and Penubarthi Villages. Nellore Mandal (M+OG) (Part) Nellore (M) - Ward No. 16 to 26, 29 and 30 Allipuram (OG) (Part) - Ward No. 45 Kallurpalle (OG) (Part) - Ward No. 46 Buja Buja Nellore (OG) (Part) - Ward No. 47 Nellore (Bit.1) (OG) - Ward No. 48.Mogallapalem, Mattempadu, Amancherla,
238	Nellore	Tirupati (SC)	Sarvepalli	Podalakur, Thotapalligudur, Muthukur, Venkatachalam and Manubolu.
239	Nellore	Tirupati (SC)	Gudur (SC)	Gudur, Chillakur, Kota, Vakadu and Chittamur.
240	Nellore	Tirupati (SC)	Sullurpeta (SC)	Ojili, Naidupet, Pellakur, Doravarisatram, Sullurpeta and Tada.
241	Nellore	Tirupati (SC)	Venkatagiri	Kaluvoya, Rapur, Sydapuram, Dakkili, Venkatagiri and Balayapalle.
242	Nellore	Nellore	Udayagiri	Jaladanki, Seetharamapuram, Udayagiri, Varikuntapadu, Vinjamur, Duttalur, Kaligiri and Kondapuram.
243	Kadapa	Kadapa	Badvel (SC)	Kalasapadu, B.Kodur, Sri Avadhutha Kasinayana, Porumamilla, Badvel, Gopavaram and Atlur.
244	Kadapa	41-Rajampet	Rajampet	Sidhout, Vontimitta, Nandalur, Rajampet, Veeraballe and T Sundupalle.
245	Kadapa	38-Kadapa	Kadapa	Kadapa.
246	Kadapa	Rajampet	Kodur (SC)	Penagalur, Chitvel, Pullampeta, Obulavaripalle and Kodur.

(*Contd.*)

Appendix–I (*Contd.*)

S. No.	*District*	*Parliamentary Constituencies*	*Assembly Constituencies*	*Mandal*
247	Kadapa	Rajampet	Rayachoti	Sambepalle, Chinnamandem, Rayachoti, Galiveedu, Lakkireddipalli and Ramapuram.
248	Kadapa	Kadapa	Pulivendla	Simhadripuram, Lingala, Thondur, Pulivendla, Vemula, Vempalle and Chakrayapet.
249	Kadapa	Kadapa	Kamalapuram	Pendlimarri, Chinthakommadinne, Kamalapuram, Vallur, Veerapunayunipalle and Chennur.
250	Kadapa	Kadapa	Jammalamadugu	Peddamudium, Mylavaram, Kondapuram, Jammalamadugu, Muddanur and Yerraguntla.
251	Kadapa	Kadapa	Proddatur	Rajupalem and Proddatur.
252	Kadapa	Kadapa	Mydukur	Duvvur, S. Mydukur, Khajipet, Brahmamgarimattam and Chapad.
253	Kurnool	Nandyal	Allagadda	Sirvel, Allagadda, Dornipadu, Uyyalawada, Chagalamarri and Rudravaram.
254	Kurnool	Nandyal	Srisailam	Srisailam, Atmakur, Velgode, Bandi Atmakur and Mahanandi.
255	Kurnool	Nandyal	Nandikotkur (SC)	Nandikotkur, Pagidyala, J. Bungalow, Kothapalle, Pamulapadu and Midthur.
256	Kurnool	Kurnool	Kurnool	Kurnool Mandal (Part) Kurnool (M Corp.) (Part) Kurnool (M Corp.) - Ward No. 1 to 69.
257	Kurnool	Nandyal	Panyam	Kallur, Orvakal, Panyam and Gadivemula.
258	Kurnool	Nandyal	Nandyal	Nandyal and Gospadu.
259	Kurnool	Nandyal	Banaganapalle	Banaganapalle, Owk, Koilkuntla, Sanjamala and Kolimigundla.
260	Kurnool	Nandyal	Dhone	Bethamcherla, Dhone and Peapally.
261	Kurnool	Kurnool	Pattikonda	Krishnagiri, Veldurthi, Pattikonda, Maddikera and Tuggali.
262	Kurnool	Kurnool	Kodumur (SC)	C.Belagal, Gudur and Kodumur. Kurnool Mandal (Part) R.Kanthalapadu, Sunkesula, Remata, Ulchala, Basavapuram, Edurur, G.Singavaram, Nidzur, Munagalapadu, Mamidalapadu, Panchalingala, E. Thandrapadu,

(*Contd.*)

Appendix–I *(Contd.)*

S. No.	*District*	*Parliamentary Constituencies*	*Assembly Constituencies*	*Mandal*
				Gondiparla, Dinnedevarapadu, B. Thandrapadu, Pasupula, Rudravaram, Noothanapalle, Devamada, Pudur, Gargeyapuram and Diguvapadu Villages.
263	Kurnool	Kurnool	Yemmiganur	Nandavaram, Yemmiganur and Gonegandla.
264	Kurnool	Kurnool	Mantralayam	Peda Kadubur, Maṇtralayam, Kosigi and Kowthalam.
265	Kurnool	Kurnool	Adoni	Adoni.
266	Kurnool	Kurnool	Alur	Devanakonda, Holagunda, Halaharvi, Alur, Aspari and Chippagiri.
267	Anantapur	Anantapur	Rayadurg	D.Hirehal, Rayadurg, Kanekal, Bommanahal and Gummagatta.
268	Anantapur	Anantapur	Uravakonda	Vidapanakal, Vajrakarur, Uravakonda, Beluguppa and Kudair.
269	Anantapur	Anantapur	Guntakal	Guntakal, Gooty and Pamidi.
270	Anantapur	Anantapur	Tadpatri	Peddavadugur, Yadiki, Tadpatri and Peddapappur.
271	Anantapur	Anantapur	Singanamala (SC)	Garladinne, Singanamala, Putlur, Yellanur, Narpala and B. K. Samudram.
272	Anantapur	Anantapur	Anantapur Urban	Anantapur Mandal (Part) Anantapur (M+OG) (Part) Anantapur (M) - Ward No.1 to 28 Narayanapuram (OG) - Ward No. 29 Kakkalapalle (R) (OG) (Part) - Ward No. 30 Anantapur (R) (OG) - Ward No. 31.
273	Anantapur	Anantapur	Kalyandurg	Brahmasamudram, Kalyandurg, Settur, Kundurpi and Kambadur.
274	Anantapur	Hindupur	Raptadu	Atmakur, Raptadu, Kanaganapalli, C. K. Palli and Ramagiri Mandals, Anantapur Mandal (Part) Kodimi, Thaticherla, Somanadoddi, Rachanapalle, Sajjalakalva, Kurugunta, Gollapalle, Kamarupalle, Alamuru, Katiganikalva, Kakkalapalle (Rural), Upparapalle, Itikalapalle,

(Contd.)

Appendix–I (*Contd.*)

S. No.	*District*	*Parliamentary Constituencies*	*Assembly Constituencies*	*Mandal*
				Jangalapalle, Kandakur, Chiyyedu, Mannila and Papampet (CT) Villages.
275	Anantapur	Hindupur	Madakasira (SC)	Madakasira, Amarapuram, Gudibanda, Rolla and Agali.
276	Anantapur	Hindupur	Hindupur	Hindupur, Lepakshi and Chilamathur.
277	Anantapur	Hindupur	Penukonda	Parigi, Penukonda, Gorantla, Somandepalle and Roddam.
278	Anantapur	Hindupur	Puttaparthi	Nallamada, Bukkapatnam, Kothacheruvu, Puttaparthi, O. D. Cheruvu and Amadagur.
279	Anantapur	Hindupur	Dharmavaram	Dharmavaram, Bathalapalle, Tadimarri and Mudigubba.
280	Anantapur	Hindupur	Kadiri	Talupula, Nambulipulikunta, Gandlapenta, Kadiri, Nallacheruvu and Tanakal.
281	Chittoor	Rajampet	Thamballapalle	Mulakalacheruvu, Thamballapalle, Peddamandyam, Kurabalakota, Peddathippasamudram and B. Kothakota.
282	Chittoor	Rajampet	Pileru	Gurramkonda, Kalakada, K. V. Palle, Pileru, Kalikiri and Valmikipuram.
283	Chittoor	Rajampet	Madanapalle	Madanapalle, Nimmanapalle and Ramasamudram.
284	Chittoor	Rajampet	Punganur	Sodam, Somala, Chowdepalle, Punganur, Pulicherla and Rompicherla.
285	Chittoor	Chittoor (SC)	Chandragiri	Tirupati (Rural), Chandragiri, Pakala, Ramachandrapuram, Chinnagottigallu and Yerravaripalem. Tirupati (Urban) (Part) Konkachennaiahgunta, Mangalam and Chennayyagunta Villages.
286	Chittoor	Tirupati (SC)	Tirupati	Tirupati (Urban) (Part) Tirumala (CT) Tirupati (NMA) (CT) Akkarampalle (CT)

(*Contd.*)

Appendix–I (*Contd.*)

S. No.	District	Parliamentary Constituencies	Assembly Constituencies	Mandal
				Tirupati (M+OG) (Part).
287	Chittoor	Tirupati (SC)	Srikalahasti	Renigunta, Yerpedu, Srikalahasti and Thottambedu.
288	Chittoor	Tirupati (SC)	Satyavedu (SC)	Narayanavanam, B. N. Kandriga, Varadaiahpalem, K.V.B.Puram, Pitchatur, Satyavedu and Nagalapuram.
289	Chittoor	Chittoor (SC)	Nagari	Nindra, Vijayapuram, Nagari, Puttur and Vadamalapeta.
290	Chittoor	Chittoor (SC)	Gangadhara Nellore (SC)	Vedurukuppam, Karvetinagar, Penumuru, S. R. Puram, G. D. Nellore and Palasamudram.
291	Chittoor	Chittoor (SC)	Chittoor	Chittoor and Gudipala.
292	Chittoor	Chittoor (SC)	Puthalapattu (SC)	Puthalapattu, Irala, Thavanampalle, Bangarupalem and Yadamari.
293	Chittoor	Chittoor (SC)	Palamaner	Gangavaram, Palamaner, Baireddipalle, V. Kota and Peddapanjani.
294	Chittoor	Chittoor (SC)	Kuppam	Santipuram, Gudupalle, Kuppam and Ramakuppam.

(*Contd.*)

Appendix–II

Lok Sabha and Assembly Constituencies in AP (1976-2004)

S. No.	*District*	*Parliamentary Constituencies*	*Assembly Constituencies*
1.	Srikakukam	Srikakulam	Ichapuram
2.	Srikakukam	Srikakulam	Sompeta
3.	Srikakukam	Srikakulam	Tekkali
4.	Srikakukam	Srikakulam	Harishchandrapuram
5.	Srikakukam	Srikakulam	Narasannapeta
6.	Srikakukam	Parvathipuram (ST)	Patapatnam
7.	Srikakukam	Parvathipuram (ST)	Kothuru (ST)
8.	Vizianagaram	Parvathipuram (ST)	Naguru (ST)
9.	Vizianagaram	Parvathipuram (ST)	Parvathipuram
10.	Vizianagaram	Parvathipuram (ST)	Salur (ST)
11.	Vizianagaram	Bobbili	Bobbili
12.	Vizianagaram	Bobbili	Therlam
13.	Srikakukam	Parvathipuram (ST)	Vunukuru
14.	Srikakukam	Parvathipuram (ST)	Palakonda (SC)
15.	Srikakukam	Srikakulam	Amadalavalasa
16.	Srikakukam	Srikakulam	Srikakulam
17.	Srikakukam	Bobbili	Etcherla (SC)
18.	Vizianagaram	Bobbili	Cheepurapalli
19.	Vizianagaram	Bobbili	Gajapathinagaram
20.	Vizianagaram	Bobbili	Vizianagaram
21.	Vizianagaram	Bobbili	Sathivada
22.	Vizianagaram	Visakhapatnam	Bhogapuram
23.	Visakhapatnam	Visakhapatnam	Bheemunipatnam
24.	Visakhapatnam	Visakhapatnam	Visakhapatnam - I
25.	Visakhapatnam	Visakhapatnam	Visakhapatnam - II
26.	Visakhapatnam	Visakhapatnam	Pendurthi
27.	Vizianagaram	Visakhapatnam	Uttarapalli
28.	Vizianagaram	Visakhapatnam	Srugavarapukota (ST)

(*Contd.*)

Appendix–II (*Contd.*)

S. No.	*District*	*Parliamentary Constituencies*	*Assembly Constituencies*
29.	Visakhapatnam	Bhadrachalam	Paderu (ST)
30.	Visakhapatnam	Anakapalli	Madugula
31.	Visakhapatnam	Anakapalli	Chodavaram
32.	Visakhapatnam	Anakapalli	Anakapalli
33.	Visakhapatnam	Anakapalli	Paravada
34.	Visakhapatnam	Anakapalli	Elamanchili
35.	Visakhapatnam	Anakapalli	Payakaraopeta (SC)
36.	Visakhapatnam	Anakapalli	Narsipatnam
37.	Visakhapatnam	Bhadrachalam (ST)	Chintapalli (ST)
38.	East Godavari	Bhadrachalam	Yellavaram (ST)
39.	East Godavari	Rajahmundry	Burugupudi
40.	East Godavari	Rajahmundry	Rajahmundry
41.	East Godavari	Rajahmundry	Kadiam
42.	East Godavari	Kakinada	Jaggampeta
43.	East Godavari	Kakinada	Peddapuram
44.	East Godavari	Kakinada	Prathipadu
45.	East Godavari	Kakinada	Tuni
46.	East Godavari	Kakinada	Pithapuram
47.	East Godavari	Kakinada	Sampara
48.	East Godavari	Kakinada (Urban)	Kakinada (Urban)
49.	East Godavari	Amalapuram	Tallarevu
50.	East Godavari	Rajahmundry	Anaparthi
51.	East Godavari	Rajahmundry	Ramachandrapuram
52.	East Godavari	Rajahmundry	Alamuru
53.	East Godavari	Amalapuram	Mummidivaram (SC)
54.	East Godavari	Amalapuram	Allavaram (SC)
55.	East Godavari	Amalapuram	Amalapuram
56.	East Godavari	Amalapuram	Kothapeta
57.	East Godavari	Amalapuram	Nagaram (SC)
58.	East Godavari	Amalapuram	Razole
59.	West Godavari	Narsapur	Narsapur
60.	West Godavari	Narsapur	Palacole
61.	West Godavari	Narsapur	Achanta (SC)
62.	West Godavari	Narsapur	Bhimavaram
63.	West Godavari	Narsapur	Undi
64.	West Godavari	Narsapur	Penugonda
65.	West Godavari	Eluru	Tanuku
66.	West Godavari	Narsapur	Attili
67.	West Godavari	Eluru	Tadepalligudem
68.	West Godavari	Eluru	Ungutur
69.	West Godavari	Eluru	Dendulur
70.	West Godavari	Eluru	Eluru
71.	West Godavari	Bhadrachalam	Gopalapuram (SC)

(*Contd.*)

Appendix–II (*Contd.*)

S. No.	*District*	*Parliamentary Constituencies*	*Assembly Constituencies*
72.	West Godavari	Rajahmundry	Kovvuru
73.	West Godavari	Bhadrachala (ST)	Polavaram (ST)
74.	West Godavari	Eluru	Chintalapudu
75.	Krishna	Vijayawada	Jaggayyapet
76.	Krishna	Vijayawada	Nandigama
77.	Krishna	Vijayawada	Vijayawada East
78.	Krishna	Vijayawada	Vijayawada (East)
79.	Krishna	Vijayawada	Kankipadu
80.	Krishna	Vijayawada	Mylavaram
81.	Krishna	Vijayawada	Tiruvuru (SC)
82.	Krishna	Machilipatnam	Nuzvid
83.	Krishna	Machilipatnam	Gannavaram
84.	Krishna	Machilipatnam	Vuyyur
85.	Krishna	Machilipatnam	Gudivada
86.	Krishna	Machilipatnam	Mudinepalli
87.	Krishna	Eluru	Kaikalur
88.	Krishna	Machilipatnam	Malleswaram
89.	Krishna	Machilipatnam	Bandar
90.	Krishna	Tenali	Nidumolu (SC)
91.	Krishna	Tenali	Avanigadda
92.	Guntur	Bapatla	Kuchinapudi
93.	Guntur	Tenali	Repalle
94.	Guntur	Tenali	Vemur
95.	Guntur	Tenali	Duggirala
96.	Guntur	Tenali	Tenali
97.	Guntur	Bapatla	Ponnur
98.	Guntur	Bapatla	Bapatla
99.	Guntur	Guntur	Prathipadu
100.	Krishna	Guntur	Guntur
101.	Krishna	Guntur	Guntur-I
102.	Guntur	Tenali	Mangalagiri
103.	Guntur	Guntur	Tadikonda (SC)
104.	Guntur	Guntur	Sattenapalli
105.	Guntur	Guntur	Peddakurapadu
106.	Guntur	Narasaraopet	Gurzala
107.	Guntur	Narasaraopet	Macherla
108.	Guntur	Narasaraopet	Vinukonda
109.	Guntur	Narasaraopet	Narasaraopet
110.	Guntur	Guntur	Chilakaluripet
111.	Prakasham	Bapatla	Chirala
112.	Prakasham	Bapatla	Parchur
113.	Prakasham	Bapatla	Martur
114.	Prakasham	Bapatla	Addanki

(*Contd.*)

Appendix–II (*Contd.*)

S. No.	*District*	*Parliamentary Constituencies*	*Assembly Constituencies*
115.	Prakasham	Ongole	Ongole
116.	Prakasham	Ongole	Santhanuthalapadu (SC)
117.	Prakasham	Ongole	Kandkur
118.	Prakasham	Ongole	Kanigiri
119.	Prakasham	Ongole	Kondapi
120.	Prakasham	Narasaraopet	Cumbum
121.	Prakasham	Narasaraopet	Darsi
122.	Prakasham	Narasaraopet	Markapur
123.	Prakasham	Anantapur	Giddalur
124.	Nellore	Ongole	Udayagiri
125.	Nellore	Ongole	Kavali
126.	Nellore	Nellore	Allur
127.	Nellore	Nellore	Kovvur
128.	Nellore	Nellore	Atmakur
129.	Nellore	Nellore	Rapur
130.	Nellore	Nellore	Nellore
131.	Nellore	Nellore	Sarvepalli
132.	Nellore	Nellore	Gudur (SC)
133.	Nellore	Tirupathi	Sullurpet (SC)
134.	Nellore	Tirupathi	Venkatagiri
135.	Chittoor	Tirupathi	Srikalahasti
136.	Chittoor	Tirupathi	Satyavedu (SC)
137.	Chittoor	Tirupathi	Nagari
138.	Chittoor	Tirupathi	Puttur
139.	Chittoor	Chittioor	Vepenjeri (SC)
140.	Chittoor	Chittioor	Chittor
141.	Chittoor	Chittioor	Palamaner (SC)
142.	Chittoor	Chittioor	Kuppam
143.	Chittoor	Chittioor	Punganur
144.	Chittoor	Rajampet	Madanapalle
145.	Chittoor	Rajampet	Thamballapalli
146.	Chittoor	Rajampet	Vayalpad
147.	Chittoor	Chittioor	Pileru
148.	Chittoor	Chittioor	Chandragiri
149.	Chittoor	Tirupathi	Tirupathi
150.	Cuddapah	Rajampet	Kodur (SC)
151.	Cuddapah	Rajampet	Rajampet
152.	Cuddapah	Rajampet	Rayachoti
153.	Cuddapah	Rajampet	Lakkireddipally
154.	Cuddapah	Cuddapah	Cuddapah
155.	Cuddapah	Cuddapah	Badvel
156.	Cuddapah	Cuddapah	Mydukur
157.	Cuddapah	Cuddapah	Proddutur

(*Contd.*)

Appendix–II (*Contd.*)

S. No.	*District*	*Parliamentary Constituencies*	*Assembly Constituencies*
158.	Cuddapah	Cuddapah	Jammalamadugu
159.	Cuddapah	Cuddapah	Kamalapuram
160.	Cuddapah	Cuddapah	Pulivendula
161.	Anantapur	Hindupur	Kadiri
162.	Anantapur	Hindupur	Nallamada
163.	Anantapur	Hindupur	Gorantla
164.	Anantapur	Hindupur	Hindupur
165.	Anantapur	Hindupur	Madakasira
166.	Anantapur	Hindupur	Penukonda
167.	Anantapur	Anantapur	Kalyandurg (SC)
168.	Anantapur	Anantapur	Rayadurg
169.	Anantapur	Anantapur	Uravakonda
170.	Anantapur	Anantapur	Gooty
171.	Anantapur	Anantapur	Singanamala (SC)
172.	Anantapur	Anantapur	Anantapur
173.	Anantapur	Hindupur	Dharmavaram
174.	Anantapur	Anantapur	Tadipatri
175.	Kurnool	Kurnool	Alur (SC)
176.	Kurnool	Kurnool	Adoni
177.	Kurnool	Kurnool	Yemmiganur
178.	Kurnool	Kurnool	Kodumur (SC)
179.	Kurnool	Kurnool	Kurnool
180.	Kurnool	Kurnool	Pattikonda
181.	Kurnool	Kurnool	Dhone
182.	Kurnool	Nandyal	Kolikuntla
183.	Kurnool	Nandyal	Allagadda
184.	Kurnool	Nandyal	Panyam
185.	Kurnool	Nandyal	Nandikotkur
186.	Kurnool	Nandyal	Nandyal
187.	Kurnool	Nandyal	Atmakur
188.	Mahbubnagar	Nagarkurnool	Achampet (SC)
189.	Mahbubnagar	Nagarkurnool	Nagarkurnool
190.	Mahbubnagar	Nagarkurnool	Kalwakurthi
191.	Mahbubnagar	Nagarkurnool	Shadnagar (SC)
192.	Mahbubnagar	Nagarkurnool	Jadcherla
193.	Mahbubnagar	Mahbubnagar	Mahabubnagar
194.	Mahbubnagar	Mahbubnagar	Wanaparthy
195.	Mahbubnagar	Nagarkurnool	Kollapur
196.	Mahbubnagar	Mahbubnagar	Alampur
197.	Mahbubnagar	Mahbubnagar	Gadwal
198.	Mahbubnagar	Mahbubnagar	Amarchinta
199.	Mahbubnagar	Mahbubnagar	Makthal
200.	Mahbubnagar	Mahbubnagar	Kodangal

(*Contd.*)

Appendix–II (*Contd.*)

S. No.	*District*	*Parliamentary Constituencies*	*Assembly Constituencies*
201.	Ranga Reddy	Hyderabad	Tandur
202.	Ranga Reddy	Hyderabad	Vikarabad (SC)
203.	Ranga Reddy	Nagarkurnool	Pargi
204.	Ranga Reddy	Hyderabad	Chevella
205.	Ranga Reddy	Nalgonda	Ibrahimpatnam (SC)
206.	Hyderabad (M.C.H.)	Secunderabad	Musheerabad
207.	Hyderabad (M.C.H.)	Secunderabad	Himayatnagar
208.	Hyderabad (M.C.H.)	Secunderabad	Sanathnagar
209.	Hyderabad (M.C.H.)	Secunderabad	Secunderabad
210.	Hyderabad (M.C.H.)	Secunderabad	Khairatabad
211.	Hyderabad (M.C.H.)	Siddipet	Secunderabad Cantonment (SC)
212.	Hyderabad (M.C.H.)	Nalgonda	Malakpet
213.	Hyderabad (M.C.H.)	Secunderabad	Asafnagar
214.	Hyderabad (M.C.H.)	Secunderabad	Maharajgunj
215.	Hyderabad (M.C.H.)	Hyderabad	Karwan
216.	Hyderabad (M.C.H.)	Hyderabad	Yakutpura
217.	Hyderabad (M.C.H.)	Hyderabad	Chandrayan-Gutta
218.	Hyderabad (M.C.H.)	Hyderabad	Charminar
219.	Ranga Reddy	Siddipet	Medchal
220.	Medak	Siddipet	Siddipet
221.	Medak	Siddipet	Dommat
222.	Medak	Siddipet	Gajwel (SC)
223.	Medak	Siddipet	Narsapur
224.	Medak	Medak	Sangareddy
225.	Medak	Medak	Zahirabad
226.	Medak	Medak	Naryannkhed
227.	Medak	Medak	Medak
228.	Medak	Siddipet	Ramayampet
229.	Medak	Medak	Andole (SC)
230.	Nizamabad	Nizamabad	Balkonda
231.	Nizamabad	Nizamabad	Armoor
232.	Nizamabad	Medak	Kamareddy
233.	Nizamabad	Medak	Yellareddy
234.	Nizamabad	Nizamabad	Jukkal (SC)
235.	Nizamabad	Nizamabad	Banswada
236.	Nizamabad	Nizamabad	Bodhan
237.	Nizamabad	Nizamabad	Nizamabad
238.	Nizamabad	Nizamabad	Dichpalli
239.	Adilabad	Adilabad	Mudhole
240.	Adilabad	Adilabad	Nirmal
241.	Adilabad	Adilabad	Boath (ST)
242.	Adilabad	Adilabad	Adilabad
243.	Adilabad	Adilabad	Khanapur (ST)

(*Contd.*)

Appendix–II (*Contd.*)

S. No.	*District*	*Parliamentary Constituencies*	*Assembly Constituencies*
244.	Adilabad	Adilabad	Asifabad (SC)
245.	Adilabad	Peddapalli	Luxettipet
246.	Adilabad	Adilabad	Sirpur
247.	Adilabad	Peddapalli	Chinnur (SC)
248.	Karimnagar	Peddapalli	Manthani
249.	Karimnagar	Peddapalli	Peddapalli
250.	Karimnagar	Peddapalli	Mydaram (SC)
251.	Karimnagar	Peddapalli	Huzurabad
252.	Karimnagar	Hanamkonda	Kamalapur
253.	Karimnagar	Peddapalli	Indurthi
254.	Karimnagar	Karimnagar	Karimnagar
255.	Karimnagar	Karimnagar	Choppadandi
256.	Karimnagar	Karimnagar	Jagtial
257.	Karimnagar	Karimnagar	Buggaram
258.	Karimnagar	Karimnagar	Metpalli
259.	Karimnagar	Karimnagar	Siricilla
260.	Karimnagar	Karimnagar	Narella (SC)
261.	Warangal	Hanamkonda	Cheriyal
262.	Warangal	Hanamkonda	Jangaon
263.	Warangal	Warangal	Chennur
264.	Warangal	Warangal	Dornakal
265.	Warangal	Warangal	Mahbubabad
266.	Warangal	Warangal	Narsampet
267.	Warangal	Warangal	Wardhannapet
268.	Warangal	Hanamkonda	Ghanpur (SC)
269.	Warangal	Warangal	Warangal
270.	Warangal	Hanamkonda	Hanamakonda
271.	Warangal	Hanamkonda	Shyampet
272.	Warangal	Hanamkonda	Parkal (SC)
273.	Warangal	Warangal	Mulug (ST)
274.	Khammam	Bhadrachalam	Bhadrachalam (ST)
275.	Khammam	Bhadrachalam	Burgamphad (ST)
276.	Khammam	Khammam	Kothagudem
277.	Khammam	Khammam	Sathupalli
278.	Khammam	Khammam	Madhira
279.	Khammam	Khammam	Palair (SC)
280.	Khammam	Khammam	Khammam
281.	Khammam	Khammam	Sujathanagar
282.	Khammam	Khammam	Yellandu (ST)
283.	Nalgonda	Miryalguda	Tungaturthi
284.	Nalgonda	Miryalguda	Suryapet (SC)
285.	Nalgonda	Miryalguda	Kodad
286.	Nalgonda	Miryalguda	Miryalguda

(*Contd.*)

Appendix–II (*Contd.*)

S. No.	*District*	*Parliamentary Constituencies*	*Assembly Constituencies*
287.	Nalgonda	Miryalguda	Chalakurthi
288.	Nalgonda	Miryalguda	Nakrekal
289.	Nalgonda	Nalgonda	Nalgonda
290.	Nalgonda	Miryalguda	Ramannapet
291.	Nalgonda	Nalgonda	Alair (SC)
292.	Nalgonda	Nalgonda	Bhongir
293.	Nalgonda	Nalgonda	Mungode
294.	Nalgonda	Nalgonda	Deverkonda (ST)

Index